IMPACT OF
ON-LINE RETRIEVAL SERVICES:
A Survey of Users, 1974-75

IMPACT OF
ON-LINE RETRIEVAL SERVICES:
A Survey of Users, 1974-75

Judith Wanger

Carlos A. Cuadra

Mary Fishburn

SYSTEM DEVELOPMENT CORPORATION

Santa Monica, California

Z699
W21

This study was conducted with the support of the National Science Foundation
(Grant Number SI74-03465 A01).

ISBN: 0-916368-01-7

TABLE OF CONTENTS

List of Figures

1. INTRODUCTION AND METHODOLOGY

2. RESPONDENT BACKGROUND

3. INTRODUCTION OF ON-LINE SERVICES

4. SELECTION AND TRAINING OF STAFF

5. LEVELS OF ON-LINE USE

6.   SELECTION, ACCESS, AND USE OF ON-LINE SYSTEMS

7. SELECTION AND USE OF ON-LINE DATA BASES

9.   PROBLEMS IN USING ON-LINE SERVICES

10. SPECIAL CHALLENGES

11. MAJOR AREAS OF IMPACT

PREFACE

All of us who are involved in providing on-line services have been caught up in the excitement of creating a new and important type of information tool. We sense that our services are generating intense interest within the library and information science community--particularly among those who have become on-line system users--and growing recognition within the broader scientific, technical, and business communities.

Working on this study of the impact of on-line systems has been particularly rewarding, because it has given us an opportunity to describe an important happening in our profession, to systematize and document some baseline data for both historical and future-study value, and to help focus and shape some of the likely research, development, and practices in the years to come. On-line services will continue to develop, both in the technology that supports them and in the ways that users and suppliers relate to each other. We hope that this study will make a significant contribution to this next stage of development.

Several individuals at System Development Corporation (SDC) made important contributions to this study. We would particularly like to thank Donald V. Black, Cynthia C. Hull, Dr. Robert V. Katter, and Ann W. Luke (now at RAND Corporation). We are also extremely grateful for the assistance of Gloria N. Cuadra in finalizing this manuscript.

The on-line suppliers whose users we surveyed also gave very generously of their time at several stages in the course of the study. We would like to express our appreciation to all of our key contacts in these organizations: Energy Research and Development Administration; Battelle Memorial Institute; Canadian Institute for Scientific and Technical Information; Defense Documentation Center; European Space Agency; Lockheed Missiles and Space Company; National Aeronautics and Space Administration; National Library of Medicine; and State University of New York.

Finally, we want to acknowledge the main contributors to this study: the over 1250 on-line users we surveyed who gave a great deal of their time in responding to the many and sometimes difficult questionnaire items and who were so willing to give even more of their time for the on-site interviews. Their responses were detailed and thoughtful, and we believe that they conveyed a tremendous personal interest both in having this kind of study performed and in sharing their experiences and views about the on-line services.

Responsibility for the contents of this report is solely that of the authors. The conclusions, opinions, and recommendations do not necessarily reflect the views or position of the National Science Foundation, nor of the other participating on-line suppliers.

J.W. and C.A.C.
SDC, Santa Monica, California
January, 1976

1. INTRODUCTION AND METHODOLOGY

The 1970's have seen tremendous growth in the use of on-line technology for access to bibliographic-type information, i.e., citations or citations and abstracts of published literature, reports, and research in progress. The application of on-line technology to these particular kinds of data bases is not an innovation of the 1970's, for some limited on-line service has been available since the middle 1960's. However, the widespread acceptance and use of on-line bibliographic services is a recent phenomenon, and one that has provided the impetus for this particular study.

As one of the suppliers of on-line services, System Development Corporation (SDC) became more and more aware, through seminars and workshops, site visits, user training sessions, and trouble calls, of the kinds of impact that on-line services were having on the library and information service community. We were also aware that opinions were developing and questions were being raised within this community that could not be addressed with any degree of confidence in the broad-based reliability of the responses. Furthermore, we did not believe that these issues could be addressed on the basis of data formed on a single set of on-line users. If we were to capture and describe the impact of this initial stage of formal adoption, we would need to conduct a broadly based study--broad in terms of user participation and broad in terms of the scope of questions to be posed; hence this study. We believe that, with the gracious cooperation of nine other major on-line bibliographic suppliers and 1273 study participants, we have been able to obtain the broadly based data necessary to describe the state of on-line services today. In the remainder of this chapter, we will describe our methodology and outline the rationale and purpose of the study report.

DESCRIPTION OF STUDY OBJECTIVES AND METHODOLOGY

The On-Line Impact Study was conducted by SDC, under a grant from the U.S. National Science Foundation. The primary purpose of this study was to describe and assess the impact of the introduction and use of on-line bibliographic information retrieval systems, focusing particularly on three major areas: 1) the impact of on-line retrieval usage on the on-line searcher; 2) the impact of on-line literature-searching services on the using organizations; and 3) the impact, as perceived by the information intermediary organization, of on-line literature-searching services on the information-seeking and -use habits of the information consumer. The overall focus of the study was to be on the using community in general, and on the actual users of the systems, and the emphasis was to be on their use of the on-line technology represented by the several systems and services. The objective of this study was not to evaluate each of the different on-line systems and services, nor to compare the various retrieval systems in use today. Although we recognize that there are differences among the systems and services, and that variations in impact can result from these differences, particularly in the area of costs, we believed at the time, and still believe, that many of the basic questions, problems, and issues related to on-line systems and services transcend these differences.

To achieve these study objectives, several tasks needed to be accomplished:

- Development of genuine cooperation from, and involvement by, all major participants, vendors and users

- Development of the survey instruments

- Conduct of the questionnaire survey and follow-up interviews

- Preparation and analysis of the data

These four tasks are described further in the sections that follow.

Eliciting On-Line Supplier and User Cooperation

The On-Line Suppliers

The definition of an on-line supplier of bibliographic information was formed through a process of discussion with other suppliers, including some suppliers who elected not to be included in our study. Two major requirements evolved from these preliminary discussions. The first requirement was that the on-line service must be available to organizations and individuals external to the supplier's own organization. Therefore, some of the data base developers and organizations in business and industry that have developed and maintained an on-line system for internal use on their reports and documents would not be considered suppliers, for purposes of this study.

The second requirement was that the bibliographic data bases were being used for literature-searching services. Therefore, a major on-line supplier such as the Ohio College Library Center (OCLC), which at the time was primarily providing a cataloging/acquisition support service, was not invited to participate in our study. We recognize that any of the on-line services--and the data bases that they make available--can be used for these technical-support functions, or the quick-reference function, but we attempted to focus only on the literature-searching aspect, to keep the scope of the study within manageable bounds.

In discussions with representatives from Mead Data Corporation, a supplier of on-line services primarily in the legal area, and with the New York Times Information Bank, a relative newcomer at the time of the discussions in 1974, we learned that both of these companies were targeting their services toward individuals in organizational units other than the library community. Both of these suppliers felt that their users would not be able to answer the questionnaires comfortably, since most of their users were not information intermediaries and their data bases were not very comparable to the bibliographic data bases offered by other suppliers. Therefore, they finally elected not to participate.

Two other on-line suppliers of bibliographic data bases also elected not to participate in the study. We believe that the remaining group represented at the time of the study--and still does represent--the world's major suppliers of on-line literature-searching services. These ten suppliers are listed in Exhibit 1, along with the names of their retrieval systems. As the reader can see from this list, the on-line supplier group, like its counterparts in other areas of information services, is very diverse and includes all sectors: private/not-for-profit, private/for-profit, federal, and intergovernmental. In addition, it is world-wide.

The differences among on-line suppliers in clientele and charging policies that stem from their placement in the economic sector probably account for many of the differences among the user groups discussed in the following chapters: commercial, government, and educational. For example, we believe that about 50% to 60% of the educational institution units in our study population are health-science-related libraries that are primarily users of the National Library of Medicine service, but may also be using one or two of the commercial services. About 20% are main reference libraries, which tend to use the commercially available services. The remainder are a combination of other specialized libraries and departments in higher education and elementary/secondary education units, which also use the commercially available services. Therefore, the data from educational institutions reflect two kinds of experience: the experience of MEDLINE users, who have had a history since 1970-71 of paying only nominal fees for these services, and the experience of other users, whose use of on-line services began only in 1973-74 and has most likely been with the commercial, non-subsidized services.

The commercial organizations, at the time the data were collected, were primarily using the commercially available on-line services; as we will see from the data, they are the least experienced of the three major organizational-type users. The government agencies represent a mix of users, some of whom have been using the federally subsidized services in their areas for up to six years, and others of whom are using only, or additionally, one or more of the commercially available services.

Each of the participating suppliers was asked to help in several areas of our study: 1) to provide us with their user list, or to mail our questionnaires directly to their users; 2) to review our questionnaires and assist in revising items developed by SDC or adding items where coverage was needed; 3) to review the preliminary data and the draft final report. The suppliers were most cooperative in all areas and contributed many hours of their time in all of these areas. We believe that our first feedback conference with suppliers to review the preliminary study data marked the first time that representatives from all of the suppliers had sat around the same table to discuss the on-line services.

ON-LINE SUPPLIER	CURRENT SYSTEM (RETRIEVAL PROGRAM) NAME
Battelle Memorial Institute	BASIS
European Space Research Organization (ESRO), now the European Space Agency (ESA)	RECON
Lockheed Missiles and Space Company	DIALOG
National Science Library of Canada, now the Canadian Institute for Scientific and Technical Information (CISTI)	CAN/OLE
State University of New York (SUNY)	STAIRS
System Development Corporation (SDC)	ORBIT
U.S. Atomic Energy Commission (now ERDA)	AEC/RECON
U.S. Defense Documentation Center (DDC)	RDT&E On-Line System
U.S. National Aeronautics & Space Administration (NASA)	NASA/RECON
U.S. National Library of Medicine (NLM)	ELHILL III

Exhibit 1. List of 10 Participating On-Line Suppliers

Identification of the Study Population

Six of the on-line suppliers agreed to provide their user lists to SDC. The other three organizations (Lockheed, CISTI, and ESA) mailed the questionnaires that we provided, under their own cover letters.

The same mailing procedure was used by all suppliers: each supplier conducted a two-phase mailing, with a follow-up in each phase. We first sent a letter to each of the using organizations, addressed to the key contact who had been identified by each supplier. This letter, which is shown as Exhibit 2, described the study and asked these persons whether they would be willing to participate. The letter further explained that we were asking for the participation of two different groups: managers or other individuals who were in the best position to assess the overall impact of introducing on-line services into their organization; and their on-line system searchers.

A Response Form, shown in Exhibit 3, was enclosed with the letter of invitation. Through the Response Form, we asked that recipients verify the name of the individual in the organization who was their key contact person and confirm that he or she should be the recipient of the Manager questionnaire. We also requested that they identify any additional managers who operated a separate unit within their organization. Finally, the managers were asked to specify the number of Searcher questionnaires (up to a maximum of 3) that should be enclosed with the Manager questionnaire.

To the extent possible, we eliminated duplicate names among the six mailing lists used in the SDC mailouts. To help eliminate the remaining duplications that were possible, SDC and the three suppliers who mailed questionnaires directly to their users asked organizations that received more than one letter of invitation and Response Form to respond formally to only one supplier, but to return other copies to the respective suppliers, indicating that they were returning their formal reply to another supplier.

Development of the Survey Instruments

SDC developed two survey questionnaires, the Manager questionnaire (see Appendix A) and the Searcher questionnaire (see Appendix B), to address questions relative to the three major areas of concern in this study. The questionnaire technique was chosen as the most cost-effective method of surveying the on-line user community and obtaining comprehensive and broadly based data. Drafts of both questionnaires were reviewed extensively by representatives of the on-line suppliers who participated in the study and by about 10 selected on-line users in several different environments.

**System
Development
Corporation**

2500 COLORADO AVENUE · SANTA MONICA, CALIFORNIA 90406
TELEPHONE (213) 393-9411

July 12, 1974

Dear On-Line System User:

Under a grant from the National Science Foundation and with the cooperation
of ten major suppliers of on-line bibliographic services, System Development
Corporation is conducting a study of the impact of on-line literature-searching systems. Your on-line supplier(s) and the SDC project team invite your
organization to participate in this study. The project includes a questionnaire survey and a selected number of field interviews with system users at
their facility or location. We intend to share the results of the study
with all participants and on-line suppliers.

We would first appreciate your completing the enclosed Response Form and
returning it in the prepaid return envelope. This will indicate your
willingness to participate in the questionnaire-survey portion of the
study.

After we receive the Response Form we will send you the following questionnaires: (1) one copy of a questionnaire addressed to the manager, director,
or individual in the best position to assess the overall impact of introducing on-line services in your organization; and (2) one to three copies of
a questionnaire addressed to the on-line system searcher. According to our
pretests, each of the two questionnaires takes approximately 45 minutes to
complete. Most questions require only a check-mark response; others ask
for a brief description. All responses will be kept in strict confidence,
and no answers will be associated with specific organizations without their
express approval.

We realize that you may have some questions about the study, and we invite
you to read the summary description that is enclosed with this letter.
Since the mailings are being accomplished either by SDC--from lists provided
by suppliers--or by the other participating suppliers directly to their
system users, you _may_ receive more than one of these initial packages. If
so, please complete only one Response Form--preferably the one for the
system you used first--and _return_ any others you receive to the sender
marked "RESPONSE ALREADY SUBMITTED." We would greatly appreciate receiving
your responses no later than Monday, July 29.

Exhibit 2. Letter of Invitation to On-Line Users Identified
by each On-Line Supplier (page 1 of 2)

SYSTEM DEVELOPMENT CORPORATION - Page 2 July 12, 1974

This study will be the first systematic attempt at gathering user-based data on several on-line systems. We believe that you will find the results very valuable for your own planning, and we know that your contribution will be very important in helping us to create a factual and timely picture of on-line system usage.

Thank you for your cooperation.

Sincerely,

Judy Wanger

Judith Wanger, Project Director

Carlos A Cuadra

Carlos A. Cuadra, Principal Investigator

Exhibit 2. Letter of Invitation to On-Line Users Identified by each On-Line Supplier (page 2 of 2)

RESPONSE FORM

ON-LINE IMPACT STUDY

Sponsored by the National Science Foundation

We are pleased to invite your organization's participation in a forthcoming questionnaire survey of users of on-line bibliographic services. To help us in our preparation for mailing, we would appreciate your answering the two questions on the reverse side and returning the Response Form in the enclosed prepaid envelope.

We will be mailing two types of questionnaires, one for each of the two audiences of interest to this study:

- MANAGER QUESTIONNAIRE

  This questionnaire should be completed by an individual in the organization who can respond to questions regarding: (1) promotion of on-line services; (2) problems in integrating on-line literature searching into an organizational setting; (3) staffing of on-line services; (4) budgeting and accounting; and (5) overall assessment of the impact--positive and negative--of the services on both the organization and the "end users." You may specify more than one manager, if you have more than one organizational unit using on-line services.

- SEARCHER QUESTIONNAIRE

  This questionnaire is to be completed by individuals who actually perform on-line searches. The questions cover the following areas: (1) training and learning; (2) problems and preferences in areas of system features and services; (3) experiences with multiple-system and multiple-data-base usage. We would like to have this questionnaire filled out by up to three searches for each organizational unit.

Thank you for your cooperation.

NSF-Sponsored On-Line Impact Study
System Development Corporation
2500 Colorado Avenue
Santa Monica, California 90406

Exhibit 3. Response Form Used in Phase I Mailing (page 1 of 2)

To help us in identifying the one or more managers to whom we should send questionnaires, and to know how many searcher questionnaires should be enclosed in the mailing, we would appreciate your answering the following two questions.

1. Are the name and address below the correct "manager" contact for the questionnaire mailing?

    ☐ YES   ☐ NO

    If NO, please provide the correct name and address here:

    ☐ No. SQ's

    If YES, please provide the names of any additional managers (e.g., from different groups or divisions within your organization) who you think should complete a separate questionnaire:

    ☐ No. SQ's

    _____   _____
    Name   Title

    _____
    Address

    ☐ No. SQ's

    _____   _____
    Name   Title

    _____
    Address

    (If more space is needed, please attach a separate sheet of paper.)

2. For each manager identified above, please indicate in the small box labeled "No. SQ's" the number (up to 3) of SEARCHER QUESTIONNAIRES (SQ's) that should be enclosed with the MANAGER QUESTIONNAIRE.

Exhibit 3. Response Form Used in Phase I Mailing (page 2 of 2

The first part of each questionnaire was used to gather background information on the respondents: the type of parent organization (e.g., commercial organization or government agency) and the specific organizational unit in which they work. The Manager questionnaire posed additional background questions about the number of on-line systems to which the organization had access; the length of time that these system(s) had been used; the clientele for whom literature searching services were provided; the number and positions of the searchers who performed literature searches. The Searcher questionnaire asked respondents to describe their positions and experience levels with on-line searching, as well as the number of systems and data bases which they were using at the time.

The Manager questionnaire was designed for the manager, director, or individual in the best position to assess the overall impact of introducing on-line services into the organization. The questionnaire items addressed the following areas of interest:

- goals and objectives of on-line service

- budgeting and accounting

- staffing of on-line services

- equipment and facilities needed for on-line service

- promotion of on-line services

- the impact of on-line searching on the information consumer

- problems in integrating on-line literature searching into an organizational setting

The Searcher questionnaire was designed for the individual or individuals in the organization who actually perform on-line searches. The following areas were addressed in this questionnaire:

- training and learning

- importance and level of use of selected system features

- the use of on- and off-line printing

- scheduling approaches and access time requirements for on-line searching

- availability and level of use of communications with the on-line suppliers

- problem areas with systems and system use

- general attitudes toward on-line searching

- experiences with the use of multiple data bases and multiple systems

Conduct of the Questionnaire Survey

SDC mailed questionnaire packets, which included one Manager questionnaire, from one to three Searcher questionnaires, and a cover letter to 419 organizations during the months of August and September of 1974. One follow-up mailing was conducted to encourage the return of these fairly lengthy and detailed questionnaires. The cutoff date for acceptance of returns was extended several times--for SDC mailouts through January 1975, and for one supplier group, through March 1975--so that the continuing returns could be included in the analysis of the data.

Responses and Response Rates

It is somewhat difficult to characterize the study population in terms of the universe of on-line users. We realized at the time we proposed the study that the choice had to be made between having the full participation of suppliers and having the full range of demographic and other data that a rigorous study would require. We elected to seek the full participation, accepting some limitations in our ability to describe the study population. In any event, the presentation of mailout and return data is somewhat complicated, for two reasons. First, there are two groups--managers and searchers--represented in the study, but they are from basically the same population base. Each of these two groups was treated separately in the data analysis.

A second complexity in the data is that we are dealing with organizational units rather than unique "parent" organizations. Although our initial contact with users was at the organizational level, we encouraged these contacts to identify other specific units within their organizations, because we did not believe that the experiences of one group would necessarily be fully represented in a single Manager questionnaire return. The danger in limiting the number of questionnaires to one per organization was that the responses might either show a best-foot-forward bias or else might move toward a middle, "typical" position that did not adequately reflect the various differences that could exist within the organization. For example, the experiences of a health-science library that began as a MEDLINE center in 1971 would be considerably different from the experiences of a main reference library on that same campus, that started with one or more of the commercially available services in 1973 or 1974; and both of their experiences would probably differ from those of the faculty and students in one of the academic departments that had begun to use one or more of the commercially available services.

We have summarized the mailout and return data for both phases of mailings in Exhibit 4, to characterize what we consider to be the major relationships in our study population that we can account for. The total study population numbers that will occur throughout the data are: 472 managers and 801 searchers. These 1273 respondents represent a total of 546 organizational units, which, in turn, represent 469 unique parent organizations. Assuming an equal response rate from the other three mailings, there were probably about 800 organizations using the services of the participating suppliers at the time of the data collection. We believe, therefore, that our study population represents more than 65% of the entire population of on-line users.

SDC Mailings (7 Suppliers)

Phase I (Invitation Stage)

	Units	Mailed	Returned
Parent Organizations Willing to Participate		665	419
Duplicates of Other Organizations			+ 92
			511 (76.8%)
(Nonrespondents **or** respondents for other suppliers)			154 (23.2%)

Phase II (Questionnaire Stage)

Units		Mailed	Usable Returns
Organizational Units representing Parent (unique) Organizations		524	327 (62.4%)
Parent (unique) Organizations		419	334 (79.7%)

Questionnaires		Mailed	Usable Returns
Manager Questionnaires		524	327 (62.4%)
Searcher Questionnaires		969	542 (55.9%)

ALL MAILINGS (10 Suppliers)

Units		Mailed	Usable Returns
Organizational Units representing Parent (unique) Organizations		419	469

Questionnaires		Mailed	Usable Returns
Manager Questionnaires Only			41 (7.5%)
Manager + 1 Searcher Questionnaire			234 (42.9%)
Manager + 2 Searcher Questionnaires			125 (22.9%)
Manager + 3 Searcher Questionnaires			72 (13.2%)
Searcher Questionnaires Only			74 (13.6%)
Total		546	546

Exhibit 4. Mailout/Return Report for Phase I and Phase II Mailings

Geographical Representation

In Exhibit 5, we have displayed the geographical locations of the organizational units to which SDC mailed questionnaires and the locations of those units that are included in the study population.

A total of six states were not represented in the SDC mailouts and an additional two states are not included because we did not receive completed questionnaires from any users in those states. Thus, a total of eight states--Arkansas, Louisiana, Maine, Mississippi, North Dakota, South Dakota, Utah, and Wyoming--are not represented in the returns from seven U.S.-based suppliers. (We do not have geographical representation data from Lockheed.)

Data Preparation and Analysis

The SDC project team examined each returned questionnaire to determine its suitability for analysis. A total of 51 questionnaires (25 Manager questionnaires and 26 Searchers questionnaires) were not included in the analysis because of incomplete data or late return. During the screening process, we prepared each questionnaire for keyboarding. This involved performing internal checks for consistency of response and coding the responses. In addition, open-ended responses that were not suitable for computer analysis were tabulated manually. Standard statistical programs were used to generate frequencies, means, and cross-tabulations and otherwise analyze the questionnaire data.

Field Interviews

To supplement the data derived from the questionnaire sample, and to provide additional information on various aspects of on-line retrieval system use and impact, we conducted on-site interviews with 25 organizations and some 50 individuals. Interviewees were selected from among the questionnaire respondents who indicated in their returned questionnaires that they would be willing to participate in one of the planned interviews.

Candidates for these interviews were selected along the following dimensions: geographical location within the United States; organization type (Government, Commercial, Educational, and Other organizations); unit type (library and non-library units); experience (less than one year, one year or more); number of systems (single-system and multiple-system users); number of data bases (single-data-base and multiple-data-base users); fee-for-service policy (charge and no-charge policies).

GEOGRAPHICAL AREAS IN 9 SUPPLIER MAILOUT/RETURNS					
STATE	MAILED	RETURNED	STATE	MAILED	RETURNED
Alabama	4	2	Nevada	2	2
Alaska	1	1	New Hampshire	3	3
Arizona	2	2	New Jersey	35	26
Arkansas	1	0	New Mexico	6	6
California	61	46	New York	40	29
Colorado	7	5	North Carolina	7	7
Connecticut	10	7	North Dakota	0	0
Delaware	3	2	Ohio	26	19
District of Columbia	38	24	Oklahoma	2	2
Florida	9	6	Oregon	5	5
Georgia	8	6	Pennsylvania	27	20
Hawaii	2	2	Rhode Island	4	1
Idaho	2	1	South Carolina	1	1
Illinois	29	25	South Dakota	0	0
Indiana	5	4	Tennessee	10	8
Iowa	1	1	Texas	16	10
Kansas	1	1	Utah	0	0
Kentucky	6	4	Vermont	1	1
Louisiana	1	0	Virginia	12	8
Maine	0	0	Washington (St.)	13	6
Maryland	44	29	West Virginia	3	2
Massachusetts	16	9	Wisconsin	5	4
Michigan	20	11	Wyoming	0	0
Minnesota	15	10			
Mississippi	0	0	Non-U.S. Locations		
Missouri	8	8	Canada	–	24
Montana	8	8	Other	–	16
Nebraska	3	2			

Exhibit 5. Geographical Representation of Study
Participants from the SDC Mailouts

We first categorized all of the organizational units willing to be interviewed by the above dimensions. For example, one group was created of organizational units comprising government libraries that were multiple-system and multiple-data-base users with more than one year of experience and that did not charge end-users for on-line searches. The questionnaires of the organizational units in each grouping were then read to see if any contained descriptions of exemplary activities or particularly difficult problems. For example, there were very few organizations that reported the goals and benefits that they had hoped would accrue from their on-line service were not realized, so we selected several of these organizations for our sample. In addition, we selected several non-library units in the study.

A structured interview guide that covered the following areas and topics was developed and pretested:

- <u>Training and learning to use on-line systems</u>. Topics included: learning methods used for the on-line systems; searcher specialization by system or data bases; intra-staff communications; consultation needed for system problems.

- <u>Operations</u>. Topics included: the number of data bases used for the average search; the frequency with which duplicate citations are encountered; how the decision is made to print the search results off-line; final packaging of the printed products that correspond to the on-line data bases accessed; problem areas.

- <u>End-Users</u>. Topics included: plans to increase the number of on-line service users; differences among end-users; preferred ways of interacting with end-users when performing searches; the possibility that end-users will do their own searches in the future.

- <u>Budget</u>. Topics included: initial budget allocation; adequacy of this allocation; the issue of charging clients for on-line searches.

- <u>Impact of On-Line Services</u>. Topics included: extra staff needed because of extra work from the on-line service; change in staff productivity because of the introduction of on-line searching.

- <u>The Future</u>. Topics included: time periods that on-line files should cover; need for communication among on-line system users in different organizations; changes that should be made in the systems and data bases.

ORGANIZATION OF STUDY DATA

The main body of this report is organized into 10 chapters, each of which presents data from the two questionnaires and follow-up interviews, as they relate to a major topic or impact area. In a final chapter, we highlight the major findings of the study issues that we believe require further study or action by users or suppliers, or both. We have elected to target our report primarily to the current and potential users of on-line services, along with the suppliers of these services. Thus, our focus has been on problems, practices, issues, and baseline data relating to the use of on-line services, rather than on methodological or future-research questions.

Definitions and Terminology

In dealing with a relatively new technology and a varied group of suppliers and users, we can expect to encounter some difficulties in terminology. We succeeded in reducing some of the ambiguities in our new language, but certainly not all of them. Perhaps this study can help to promote further work in the definition of terms related to the on-line environment.

A few of the major definitions used in the questionnaires and in our study report are identified and discussed below.

- Users and Searchers. On-line suppliers tend to look upon both the individuals and the organizations who use their systems as "users." When these same users are information intermediaries or information units, they tend to view the patrons or clients of their services as "users," as well. We have attempted to maintain a distinction between these two common usages. We have referred to the persons who operate the terminals variously as searchers, as on-line users or, sometimes, just as users. However, when we refer to the information consumer, or clients of these users, we call them "end-users."

- Systems. The word system is used to refer to the on-line systems and generally includes the retrieval programs and all of the other components of the computer hardware and software configuration. When it has been important, in the text of the questionnaire items or in the study report, to distinguish between the retrieval program and the computer system or one of its components, we have done so. One difficult problem for the NLM users in adjusting to this definition is that MEDLINE and TOXLINE--both of which are data bases--are frequently described as systems, i.e., "the MEDLINE system." This difficulty became acute for these users when they were responding to the question about the number of systems (and data bases) that they used.

- Data Bases. Counting data bases or files, two terms that are often used interchangeably, also presented users with a definition problem. As we describe in further detail in a later chapter, there are at least two kinds of data base definitions represented in the field today: 1) similar data bases that belong to a family, e.g., the MEDLARS (or MEDLINE) data bases, including MEDLINE, SERLINE, and SDILINE, or the INSPEC data base family of the Institute of Electrical Engineers, and 2) unique data bases, such as ERIC, COMPENDEX, and Chemical Abstracts Condensates, which are produced by different suppliers and have different coverage, different record formats and elements, and different vocabulary structures and vocabularies. We made no distinction between these two definitions in our questionnaires, but have referred to this definition problem in interpreting some of the study data.

We believe that in all future studies it will be particularly important to define these terms carefully.

Presentation of the Analyzed Data

The frequency data for all items in the Manager questionnaire and the Searcher questionnaire are provided in Appendix A and Appendix B, respectively. Much of these data are also presented within the text of the report, usually in summarized form. Although interorganizational differences were not always great, we have also presented breakdowns of the data for many questionnaire items by each of the four major user groups that we identified in the study population: Government agency users, Commercial organization users, Educational institution users (primarily universities), and Other users. The composition of these groups is discussed further in Chapter 2.

2. RESPONDENT BACKGROUND

This chapter describes the respondents and their organizations. The descriptive data will be presented in four parts, dealing, respectively, with:

- characteristics of the participating organizations

- experience of the participating organizations with on-line searching

- characteristics of the on-line searcher

- the clientele or end-users of the information retrieved through the on-line systems

The data are based on questions asked in each of the two questionnaires. In both the Manager and the Searcher questionnaires, we asked the respondents to characterize their parent organization and the organizational unit in which they work. Each group of respondents was also asked about the number of on-line systems used and the extent of experience with on-line systems. The responses to these questions characterize system use and experience, both for the organization as a whole and for the individual who performs the on-line searches. In the Manager questionnaire only, we asked the respondents to describe their organization's clientele and the number and positions of staff members who perform on-line searches. In the Searcher questionnaire only, respondents were asked to describe their current position in the organization.

As indicated in Chapter 1, the sampling plan permitted up to three searchers from each organization or organizational unit to participate in the study. The ratio of searchers to managers in our population study is less than three to one, however, because some organizations have only one searcher, and for those with more than one searcher, the managers may have designated only one or two searchers to participate in the study.

CHARACTERISTICS OF THE PARTICIPATING ORGANIZATIONS

Types of Organizations

We asked both the managers and searchers to characterize the organizations in which they work. Exhibits 6 and 7 present the results.

Both sets of questionnaire data show that organizations from most sectors of our economy--but primarily the commercial, university, and federal government sectors--are users of on-line services. Approximately 80% of the managers and searchers who participated in the study identified themselves as working in one of these three sectors. The not-for-profit and other categories account for the next largest group of respondents. The five remaining categories of organization types account for only about 5% of the organizations represented in the

study. No public libraries*, and only a sprinkling of junior colleges, participated in the study.

The on-line system users who chose the Other response most often characterized
their parent organizations as a hospital or some variant of a community health
services center or a multi-funded (e.g., government and university) not-for-
profit organization.

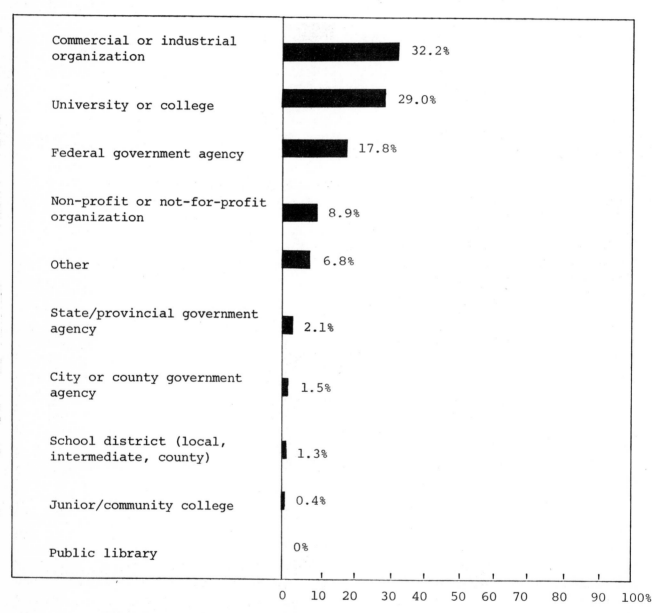

Exhibit 6. Parent Organizations of the Managers (N=472)

*By 1975 a few public libraries were beginning to use on-line services, with
 impetus from an NSF grant providing for initial subsidization of on-line
 service in selected public libraries.

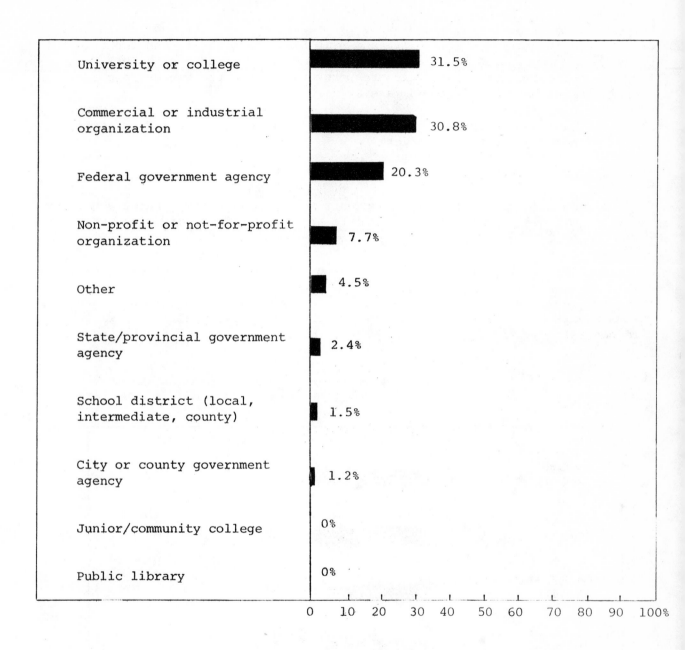

Exhibit 7.   Parent Organizations of the Searchers (N=801)

Because of the wide range of both commercial and other on-line suppliers who participated in the study, we are confident that the users of these on-line suppliers who responded to the questionnaires also represent quite accurately the types of organizations that were--and were not--using on-line bibliographic retrieval systems at the time that the data were collected.

For ease of data analysis, given the very small number of respondents in some of the organization-type categories shown in Exhibits 6 and 7, the ten original organization categories have been collapsed into four broad user groups. The four broader categories, into which respondents to both the Manager and Searcher questionnaires have been grouped, are as follows:

- Government users (all respondents to the Federal, State/Provincial, and City/County categories)

- Commercial users

- Educational users (all respondents to the university, junior/community colleges, and local, intermediate and county school district categories)

- Other users (all respondents to the non-profit and other categories)

Exhibits 8 and 9 show the results of this new grouping of Manager and Searcher questionnaire respondents. These four groups of organizational users will be used consistently throughout this report to discuss the response data.

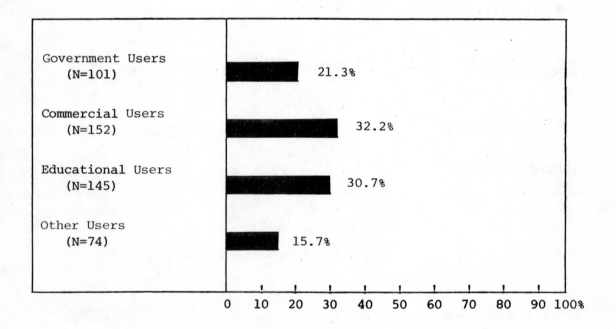

Exhibit 8. Collapsed Organization-Type User Groups, for Managers (N=472)

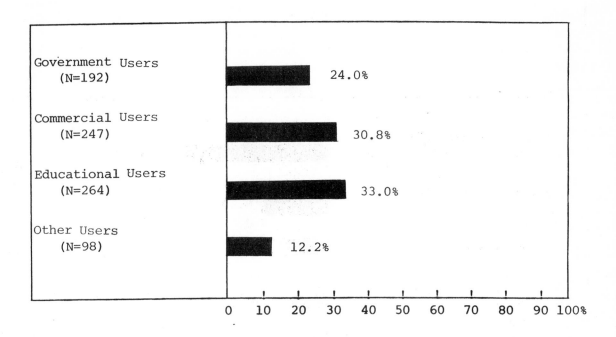

Exhibit 9. Collapsed Organization-Type User Groups, for Searchers (N=801)

Types of Intra-Organizational Units

The majority of the respondents to the questionnaires were working in libraries
and traditional information service units. This can be seen in Exhibits 10 and
11, which show the responses of the managers and searchers, respectively, to
questions asking them to identify the organizational units in which they worked
and in which the on-line systems were actually being used. More than 80% of
both the managers and searchers were working in libraries and traditional information service units, whereas only about 15% of them were working in non-library
units.

As the data in Exhibits 10 and 11 show, the predominant work setting is the
special library or its university equivalent, the department or subject-area
library. Nearly 70% of the searchers and nearly 62% of the managers were
working in those settings.

The Other responses reported by the managers and searchers merit some mention.
These responses represent a mixture of library and non-library units, and no
one type of organizational unit dominates the results. Managers placed themselves in such diverse unit types as a media center, an interlibrary loan office,
an industrial hygiene service group, and an indexing and abstracting unit.
Searcher responses included such unit types as an educational resource center,
a scientific editing group, and an administrative support unit.

It is also interesting that on-line use for important organizational functions
such as marketing is still minimal. This may reflect the fact that relatively
few business-type data bases were available on-line at the time that the survey
data were being collected. This situation is changing rapidly.

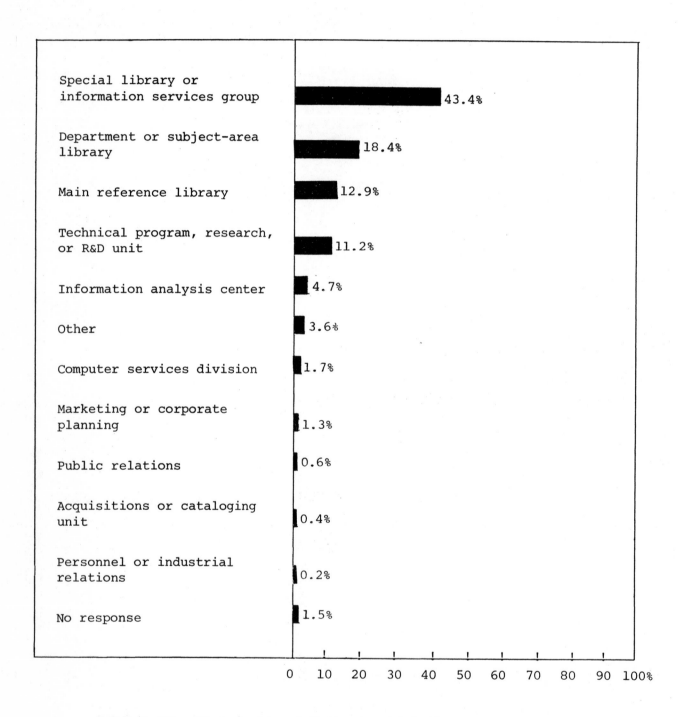

Exhibit 10. Organizational Units in which the Managers Work
and the On-line Systems are Used (N=472)

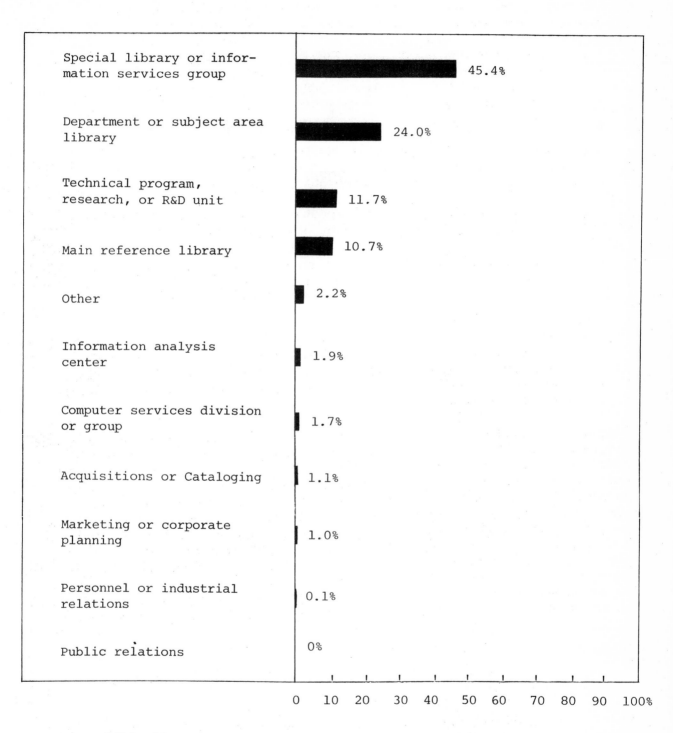

Exhibit 11. Organizational Units in which the Searchers Work
and the On-line Systems are Used (N=801)

The following patterns emerged when the organizational-unit data reported by both managers and searchers were analyzed by organization type:

- Government users work predominantly in special libraries or information service groups. Nearly 58% of the managers and 69% of the searchers work in such units. About 14% of the managers and 13% of the searchers work in a non-library setting, e.g., a technical program or research unit.

- A majority of the Commercial users of on-line systems--63% of the managers and 70% of the searchers--work in special libraries. Nearly 16% of each group work in a technical program or research unit.

- Nearly 50% of the managers and 65% of the searchers in Educational organizations work in department or subject-area libraries. Another 20% of the managers and 9% of the searchers characterized their work unit as a special library, and they should probably be added to the department or subject-area library percentages above. Approximately 17% of each group work in main reference libraries.

- Most of the on-line system users whose organizations were placed in the Other category work in special libraries. Some 52% of the managers and 60% of the searchers fall into this category. About 10% of the managers and nearly 20% of the Other searchers work in technical programs or research units.

Although it would have been instructive to do so, we did not perform a comparative analysis of Library/Information Center users (i.e., information intermediaries) and Non-Library/Information users (i.e., end-users). The reason for this is that the possibility of some ambiguity in role definitions was revealed from an analysis of the results of several questions in which we asked only end-users or only information intermediaries to respond. Some of the end-users (classified as such by their responses to the background questions) answered items intended for information intermediaries only. This cross-over response from about 20% of the end-users may mean that some of them are serving as information intermediaries on particular projects or within research/department units. Without some better understanding of the end-users in our study, we believe that any comparisons would be inconclusive and/or misleading.

EXPERIENCE OF USERS WITH ON-LINE SEARCHING

We asked the managers to indicate, for the (up to) four most frequently used systems, the period of time that each of those systems had been available in their organization. The managers were asked not to identify by name any of the systems used in their organization, but instead to use the numbers (i.e., System 1, System 2, etc.) consistently throughout the questionnaire to represent the systems in the order in which they began using them. If more than four systems were used in their organization, they were asked to confine their responses to the four systems that were most often used.

The responses shown in Exhibit 12 confirm that the use of multiple systems was just beginning at the time that the survey data were collected. As the reader can see, the number of respondents in each category drops markedly as the number of systems increases. Thus, while the organizations of 472 respondents were using at least one on-line system, only 53 (11%) were using as many as four systems. The experience on each system also drops as the number of systems increases. While almost 55% of the respondents indicated that their organization had had more than one year of experience with System 1, of those organizations that used a second and third system, only 27% and 18%, respectively, had had more than one year of experience with those systems.

Systems	Experience Level		No Response
	1 Year or Less	More than 1 Year	
System 1 (N=472)	43.8%	54.7%	1.5%
System 2 (N=239)	72.0%	27.2%	.8%
System 3 (N=120)	80.0%	18.3%	1.7%
System 4 (N=53)	47.1%	18.9%	34.0%

Exhibit 12. Experience Levels for Each System Reported by Managers

The system experience data reported by the managers were analyzed by organization type. Consistent with the historical development of on-line services and their target user communities, Government agency users were found to have the most on-line experience, with 46% having from one to three years' experience, and 22% having over three years' experience. Educational organizations were also highly experienced on-line users, with 57% having from one to three years' experience and 13% having over three years' experience. Some 42% of the organizations in the Other category had had less than one year of experience, while the majority had used on-line systems for more than one year. Commercial organizations appear to have been the newest entrants to the on-line user community at the time our survey was conducted; the majority, nearly 70%, had had less than one year of on-line experience.

The experience data were also examined in relation to the number of systems available in the organization to see whether any differences existed between single- and multiple-system (2 or more) users. As we might expect, multiple-system users had more years of on-line experience than did single-system users. About 62% of the multiple-system users--compared to about 50% of the single-system users--had more than one year of experience.

CHARACTERISTICS OF ON-LINE SEARCHERS

We can look at the on-line searcher population both through the report by managers on their searchers as a group and by looking at the specific searcher population in this study.

In each of the three following sections, on the number of searchers in an organization, their job positions, and levels of on-line experience, we will first present data provided by the managers for their organizations or units and then relate the characteristics of our searcher population to that picture.

Numbers of Searchers

The managers were first asked to estimate the number of regular and infrequent searchers in their units or organizations. A regular searcher was defined in the questionnaire as someone who uses the system at least once or twice a week, while an infrequent searcher was one who uses the system about once a month or less. Exhibit 13 shows that the number of regular searchers ranged from 1 searcher in 26% of the organizations to 50 searchers in fewer than 1% of the organizations. The mean number of regular searchers was 3.43; the mode was 1. Thus the typical on-line operation seems to involve only a small number of regular searchers.

NUMBER OF SEARCHERS			
Regular Searchers	Percentage (N=425)	Infrequent Searchers	Percentage (N=276)
1	26.4%	1	20.1%
2	24.1%	2	15.6%
3	16.1%	3	6.1%
4	5.7%	4	4.0%
5-50	19.5%	5-200	12.5%
No response	9.9%	No response	41.5%
Mean = 3.43		Mean = 5.92	
Median = 2.27		Median = 2.08	
Mode = 1.00		Mode = 1.00	

Exhibit 13. Managers' Report on Number of Regular and Infrequent Searchers in their Organizations

Approximately 40% of the managers did not answer the section dealing with infrequent searchers. For those who did respond, the number of infrequent searchers in the unit or organization ranged from 1 searcher in 20% of the organizations to 200 searchers in fewer than 1% of the organizations. The mean number of infrequent searchers across all responding organizations was 5.92, and the mode was 1. (The mean is inflated because of the extremely high number of infrequent searchers reported by only 11 of the managers.) Given the fact that there were only a small number of infrequent on-line searchers in most organizations and that 40% of the responding organizations did not report having infrequent searchers at all, the total of on-line systems by infrequent searchers seems minimal. However, as we will discuss in Chapter 3, a frequent user of one system may still be an infrequent user of another system.

An analysis of the regular searcher data by organizational user group is shown in Exhibit 14. Commercial organizations tend to have relatively few regular searchers: 56.6% of them have only one or two searchers. Government agencies differed appreciably from the overall averages: almost 27% of the managers in Government agencies, as compared to under 7% of the managers in Commercial and Educational organizations, reported having between 6 and 50 regular searchers.

	NUMBER OF SEARCHERS				
	1	2	3-5	6-50	No Response
Government Users (N=101)	22.8%	23.8%	22.8%	26.7%	3.9%
Commercial Users (N=152)	29.6%	27.0%	23.7%	6.6%	13.1%
Educational Users (N=145)	22.1%	24.1%	37.9%	6.9%	9.0%
Other Users (N=74)	33.8%	18.9%	18.9%	13.5%	14.9%

Exhibit 14. Number of Regular On-Line Searchers Reported by Managers, by Organization Type

This same exhibit helps to explain the composition of the searcher population in our study. The 801 searchers in our study are associated with 503 unique organizational units, which represents a ratio of 1.6 searchers to each unique organizational unit. Although there are slightly more Commercial users represented in the study (152 Commercial organizations as compared to 145 Educational and 101 Government), the total number of searchers in these Commercial organizations (247 searchers) is fewer than the total in Educational institutions (264 searchers).

Job Positions of On-Line Searchers

Managers' Report

Managers were asked to identify the positions of the searchers, both regular and infrequent. The data in Exhibit 15 indicate that on-line searching is viewed primarily as a professional function and that librarians or information specialists with specific subject expertise or general reference experience predominate among the regular searchers. Other professional or technical personnel, such as educators, scientists, program specialists, and researchers, constitute the largest group of infrequent users.

A small group--less than 20%--of on-line searchers is made up of clerical personnel or paraprofessionals. Of interest here is the actual role of the clerical/paraprofessional in formulating and carrying out the on-line search. Do such personnel formulate on-line search strategies or do they simply key in a search prepared by a professional librarian/information specialist or otherwise act as an aide to the librarian/information specialist? From our in-depth field interviews, it seems that the latter situation is the more typical case. We suspect that one role of the clerical/paraprofessional worker is to perform on-line checking of bibliographic records of publications being ordered or cataloged.

Only a very small number of managers reported that graduate or undergraduate students comprise any part of their on-line searcher staffs. When they were included, however, graduate or undergraduate students were cited as infrequent searchers about twice as often as they were cited as regular searchers. One possible explanation might be that students in some educational institutions are allowed to perform occasional on-line searches for their own research. Or again, as in the case of the clerical/paraprofessional workers, students working in the library/information center may be assisting in literature searches or checking bibliographic citations as a part of part-time student-clerk work.

When the data on the positions of the regular and infrequent searchers were analyzed by organization type, Government and Commercial organizations emerged as those most likely to have non-library professional or technical personnel as regular searchers, while Educational organizations were the least likely. Some 36% of the Government managers and 28% of the Commercial managers characterized some of their regular searchers as being non-library professional or technical personnel, as compared to only 11% of the Educational managers. This same disparity exists for infrequent searchers who are professional or technical personnel.

	"Regular" Searchers (N=425)	"Infrequent" Searchers (N=276)
Librarians or information specialists with specific subject expertise	63.2%	33.3%
Librarians with general reference experience	38.3%	25.0%
Other professional/technical personnel (e.g., educators, scientists, etc.)	25.8%	41.6%
Clerical/paraprofessionals	12.4%	17.3%
Graduate students	3.2%	8.3%
Other	1.8%	3.9%
Undergraduate students	0.4%	3.6%

Exhibit 15. Managers' Report on Positions Held by Regular and Infrequent Searchers

Another difference, and an understandable one, is that Commercial organizations had fewer library personnel with general reference experience than did the other types of organizations. Only 23% of the Commercial managers, as compared to 40% of the Government managers and 44% of the Educational managers, characterized some of their regular searchers in this way. Finally, Commercial organizations least often have clerical workers as either regular or infrequent searchers. Only 7% of the Commercial managers reported that at least some of their regular searchers are clerical workers, as compared to 13% of the Educational managers and 16% of the Government managers. The same pattern holds for infrequent searchers.

Searcher Population in Our Study

Respondents to the Searcher questionnaire were asked to define their current staff position by choosing one of nine categories. Exhibit 16 shows their responses by category, and it appears that the population of searchers in our study is representative of the picture reported by the managers. As the reader can see, most of the respondents are Librarian/Information Specialists; other Professional or Technical Personnel constitute the second largest group. Although, as mentioned earlier there is some ambiguity in the relation between searchers' job positions and the units in which they work, we believe that this second group is primarily an end-user group who perform their own on-line searches or who are specially assigned as information specialists within their technical unit. There were very few respondents in the Other category, and their self-characterizations for the most part were ambiguous. Some of the respondents described their background and experience rather than their position.

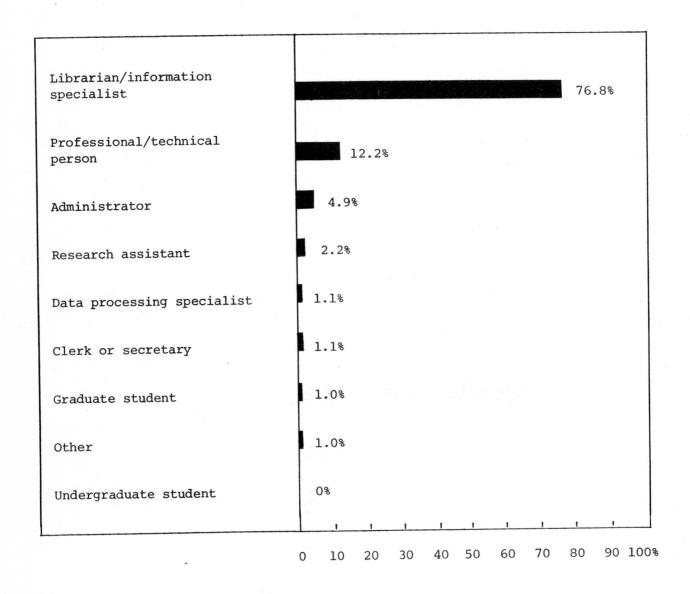

Exhibit 16. Searchers' Report on their Current Job Positions (N=801)

An analysis of searcher positions by organization type revealed that searchers in Educational organizations are more likely to be Librarian/Information Specialists and less likely to be Professional or Technical Personnel than searchers in the other organizations. Approximately 89% of the searchers in Educational organizations are Librarians, as compared to 70% of the searchers in Government, Commercial, and Other organizations. Only 4% of the searchers in Educational organizations are Professional or Technical Personnel, as compared to 20% of the searchers in Commercial organizations, 14% in Government organizations, and 10% of the Other organizations.

Searchers' Experience with On-Line Systems

The searchers were asked to indicate the length of time that they had been performing on-line literature searches. The seven response choices are shown in Exhibit 17 along with the searchers' responses to this question.

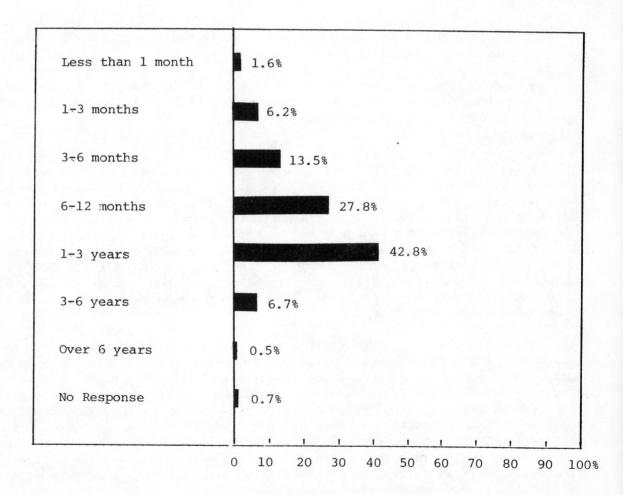

Exhibit 17. Levels of Experience with On-Line Searching Reported by Searchers (N=801)

One immediate observation that can be made is that the searcher population as a whole is relatively experienced with on-line searching, even more so than the organizations as a whole, as reported by managers. Over one-half of the group had had more than one year's experience. Approximately 43% of the searchers--the largest group--had had from 1 to 3 years of on-line experience. Only 21% of the population had had 6 months or less of experience at the time of the survey.

The reason that our searcher population is weighted even more toward experienced users, particularly in the 1- to 3-year category, is because of the Educational institution user group. As we noted earlier, there are more searchers in Educational institutions than in Commercial organizations. When these data were analyzed by organization type, the patterns seen earlier with organizations as a whole are also seen for the searchers: Government and Educational searchers emerged as the most experienced group, while the Commercial searchers were the least experienced.

- Nearly 11% of the Government and Educational searchers had had over three years of on-line experience, while the comparable figure of Commercial searchers was less the 1%.

- 57% of the Government searchers and 63% of the Educational searchers had had one year or more of experience, while only 32% of the commercial searchers had had that much experience.

The experience data were analyzed in relation to the number of on-line systems and data bases used by the searchers. It appears that the number of systems used was related to experience, while the number of data bases used was not. Nearly 65% of the searchers with six months or less of experience had used only one on-line system. The number using more than one system begins to climb with experience; 53% of the searchers with from 1 to 3 years of experience reported using two or more systems. On the other hand, the use of multiple data bases appears to be common across all experience levels. Even for searchers with less than six months of experience, 79% of them were using two or more data bases at the time of the study.

The searchers were also asked whether they had ever used an interactive system for some other purpose prior to using it for bibliographic literature searching. Only 19% of those who responded to the question had had such prior experience. Government and Commercial users seem to have had slightly more prior experience than Educational users had had. About 22% and 24% of the Government and Commercial groups, respectively, reported prior experience, as compared to only 15% of the Educational users. Such differences aside, it is clear that most of the on-line searchers began their on-the-job training for on-line literature searching as terminal-user neophytes without any significant prior experience with this type of computer technology.

CLIENTELE OF THE USER ORGANIZATIONS

To learn what kinds of clienteles were being served by the organizations we surveyed, we showed managers several categories of clientele and asked them, first, to identify those groups for whom their unit or organization performed any kind of literature-searching service (manual, on-line and/or batch) and, second, to indicate the frequency with which those groups used those services. Fourteen categories of end-users, including both group and individual end-users, were listed in the questionnaire to cover the spectrum of clientele. The managers were also given the option of specifying any user type omitted from the list.

Exhibit 18 shows the managers' responses to this section. The largest group of frequent users identified was the researcher/scientist. Approximately 59% of the organizations represented in the study provide literature-searching services for this group on a frequent basis, while another 17% occasionally serve this group. Researchers and scientists seem to be slightly more represented in Commerical and Educational organizations than in Government organizations. Nearly 64% of the managers in Commercial and Educational organizations claimed them as frequent clientele, as compared to 55% of the managers in Government organizations.

The second largest group of end-users of the library/information center's literature-searching services was composed of physicians and other health professionals. Nearly 32% of the organizations were providing literature-searching services on a frequent basis for this group, while 10% provided occasional services. As might be expected, Educational organizations were the ones that most often reported servicing this group. Some 53% of the managers in Educational organizations reported that physicians and other health-related professionals are frequent clientele of their unit, as compared to 30% of the Government managers and only 9% of the Commercial managers.

The third and fourth largest groups of end-users, respectively, were faculty/teachers and graduate students. Not surprisingly, most of these end-users were concentrated in the educational sector. Nearly 75% of the managers in Educational organizations claimed faculty as part of their clientele, while 65% claimed graduate students.

The fifth largest group of users was engineers, for whom approximately 20% of the organizations in the study provide some sort of literature-searching services. Engineers were named as end-users by about 27% of the Government and Commercial user groups.

One of the least served clientele groups appears to be the undergraduate student. It appears that the universities have, by necessity or choice, targeted their services to faculty and graduate students.

		Frequent Users	Occasional Users	Infrequent Users	No Response (not served)
A.	**Group Users**				
	Departments	11.2%	15.4%	13.7%	59.5%
	Project or research teams	15.8%	23.9%	12.9%	47.2%
B.	**Individual Users**				
	Administrative or managerial personnel	6.7%	35.8%	22.0%	35.3%
	Editors/writers	3.6%	9.1%	12.5%	74.7%
	Engineers	20.3%	14.8%	10.1%	54.6%
	Faculty or teachers	28.8%	10.3%	5.5%	55.3%
	Graduate students	26.2%	11.6%	7.2%	54.8%
	Legal staff	2.7%	5.9%	12.2%	79.0%
	Marketing/ sales personnel	5.9%	9.3%	10.1%	74.5%
	Physicians and health practitioners	31.5%	10.3%	6.7%	51.2%
	Policy planning personnel	4.4%	12.2%	10.1%	73.0%
	Program specialists (civil service)	3.3%	3.1%	6.3%	87.0%
	Researchers or scientists	58.9%	17.1%	4.6%	19.2%
	Undergraduate students	5.7%	11.0%	14.6%	68.6%
	Other	3.3%	3.1%	0.6%	92.8%

Exhibit 18. Clientele Served by Organizations in the Study, as Reported by Managers (N=472)

3. INTRODUCTION OF ON-LINE SERVICES

The successful integration of any new service into an organization requires careful planning. A detailed analysis must be made of the requirements and costs of the new service and of the ability of the organization to meet the demands on its resources that may result. The organization that fails to plan may find that it is continually being caught off guard by unanticipated events. Does the experience of the managers bear out the view that planning is needed to initiate an on-line literature-searching service, or instead, can the whole process "just happen" without any special effort on the part of management? The managers were asked to react to the statement that the introduction of on-line services into an organization requires special planning and supervision. Their responses were as follows:

- 84.6% strongly agreed or agreed that special planning is needed

- 6.9% strongly disagreed or disagreed with the statement

- 8.3% either had no opinion or did not respond to the statement

These data leave little or no doubt that in most organizations the on-line service should not "just happen."

There seems to be a relationship between appreciation of the need for planning and both the number of searchers in the organization and the number of on-line searches performed on a monthly basis. The more searchers and the more searches, the more likely were the managers to agree that special planning and supervision are required to introduce on-line services. About 95% of the managers who have three or more searchers in the organization agreed or strongly agreed with the statement, compared to only 79% for organizations with only one searcher; and 92% of those whose organizations perform 56 or more searches a month were in agreement, compared to only 82% of those whose organizations perform fewer than 20 searches per month.

In this section we will discuss three of the system integration areas that were covered in the study. Topics to be examined are:

- Obtaining Initial Approval for On-Line System Use

- Acquiring and Locating Terminals

- Promoting On-Line Literature Searching Services

OBTAINING INITIAL APPROVAL FOR ON-LINE SYSTEM USE

About 18% of the managers experienced significant problems in justifying the use of the on-line services or in getting formal approval to start using them. Asked to elaborate on their problems, approximately one-half of these managers said that funding had been the major barrier to getting approval. Several managers commented that funding new projects or services is always difficult, regardless of the worthiness of the project or the cost-effectiveness of the service. Many managers cited top management reluctance to accept the need for on-line services. Some managers found it difficult to convince top management that the increased speed or precision with which information can be obtained on-line is worth the extra out-of-pocket cost over manual or batch searching.

ACQUIRING AND LOCATING TERMINALS

Once the decision is made to insititute an on-line literature searching service, equipment must be acquired and suitable arrangements must be made. We posed several questions to the managers to elicit information about equipment and facilities.

Acquisition of a Terminal

The managers were first asked whether the purchase or rental of a terminal had been a major barrier for them in starting up their on-line service. For about 87% of the managers, buying or renting a terminal was not a problem, because a terminal was already available to them or because they were able to purchase or lease one. For the rest, however, this was not the case. About one-half of this small group that ran into problems found that funding was the major obstacle. Several managers stated that the library/information center budget had already been determined for the fiscal year when the need for a terminal was determined; thus there was a delay until the budget could be revised to include terminal rental or purchase. A few of them said that they had to wait for a full year before they could even place an order for a terminal. In the meantime, they either used some other unit's terminal, in a location often inconvenient for them, or did without on-line capability for the entire period.

Some managers ran head-on into administrative reluctance to incur the cost of buying or leasing a terminal. Most of this reluctance stemmed from a belief that the service would not be used enough to justify its cost. In some cases, top management was agreeable to using a system on an experimental basis but the experimental period was too short to meet the special lease requirements of the terminal suppliers, which is generally 3 or 6 months. To overcome this kind of resistance to a full-fledged program, managers in a few organizations conducted user surveys, using the results to predict the volume of service, as well as to demonstrate that there was indeed a significant level of user interest in the service.

Those managers who were able to buy or rent a terminal were faced with the decision of selecting from among many makes and models. In keeping with our general study objective of not making specific system comparisons, we did not solicit evaluations of the terminals that had been selected by the responding organizations. We were interested primarily in learning about problem areas in which the on-line suppliers might be able to provide some assistance in the future. A comparative study of terminals relative to on-line bibliographic system usage would undoubtedly be interesting and useful, provided that it took into account characteristics typically used in the selection process, such as terminal speed, intended uses, portability, and the availability of fairly rapid service maintenance.

Approximately 63% of the managers obtained consultation from one or more sources in their selection process. Sources of consultation included the following (since more than one response was permitted, the percentages do not total 100%):

- 50.1% relied on their own computer or data processing staff

- 42.7% received consultation from the on-line service supplier

- 32.8% sought advice from other on-line system users

- 26.4% received consultation from terminal suppliers

- 5.4% relied on other sources

From the survey data, the consultation appears to have been useful. The vast majority of the managers--93%--indicated that the consultation they received was adequate. Only 7% were dissatisfied. This dissatified group was asked to elaborate on the kinds of problems they had encountered as a result of inadequate information. Most of them felt, with hindsight, that the person they had relied on for consultation was not knowledgeable enough about the overall terminal market. Thus, in some instances, potentially better terminals were not evaluated, and the terminal that was finally obtained did not provide the best value, given the special needs of the organization. Others found that there were ramifications of terminal purchase or leasing that were inadequately explained to them. For example, one manager wrote that the terminal his organization ended up with had a peculiar kind of service contract that was not adequately explored before the papers were signed. Another wrote that he had trouble getting full information on all the available options for his terminal.

The fact that on-line users are basically reliant upon advice from sources outside their own units, and that comprehensive and adequate information is not always available from these sources, suggests that there is a need for some group to monitor developments in the computer terminal business and periodically make available a descriptive compilation of available terminals. Although lists of terminals and their characteristics appear from time to time in the computer literature, it would be useful to have a compilation that looks at compatibility with the kind of on-line systems and services discussed in this report.

Selection of a Location for the Terminal

Once the terminal is selected and acquired, another decision needs to be made: Where should the terminal be located? As Exhibit 19 shows, managers have selected several different kinds of locations. (Since more than one response was permitted, the percentages do not total 100%.)

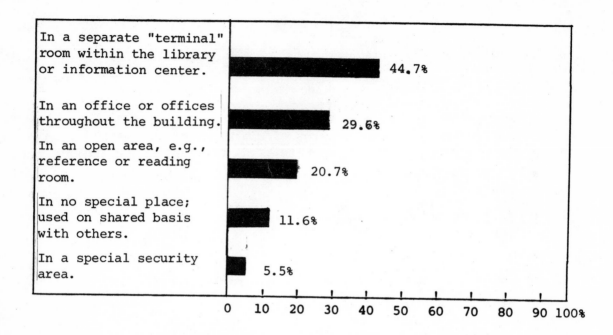

Location	Percentage
In a separate "terminal" room within the library or information center.	44.7%
In an office or offices throughout the building.	29.6%
In an open area, e.g., reference or reading room.	20.7%
In no special place; used on shared basis with others.	11.6%
In a special security area.	5.5%

Exhibit 19.   Responses of Managers to the Question:
Where is the terminal located?   (N=472)

Fewer than 12% of the respondents made no special arrangements for the location of the terminal. The most popular location was in a separate "terminal" room within the library or information center area. Presumably these "terminal" rooms assure a quiet working area for the searchers and those end-users who work with the searcher at the terminal.

Privacy does not seem to be the key factor influencing terminal location for the approximately 21% of the managers who chose to place the terminal in an open area, such as the reference or reading room. For these organizations the desire for high visibility of the service was probably a key factor in their selection process. On the other hand, some 6% of the managers need to keep the terminal under lock and key whenever it is not being used by the searchers.

Two further questions regarding terminal location were posed to the managers. The first asked whether there were any special considerations or problems involved in deciding on the terminal arrangement specified above; the second asked whether the location of the terminal is important. Exhibits 20 and 21 show the responses of the managers to these questions. The disparity between the percentage of managers who indicated that special considerations dictated the location of the terminal and the percentage who believed the location of the terminal was important suggests that many managers who were not greatly concerned with terminal location initially have, with hindsight, decided that it is a very important consideration.

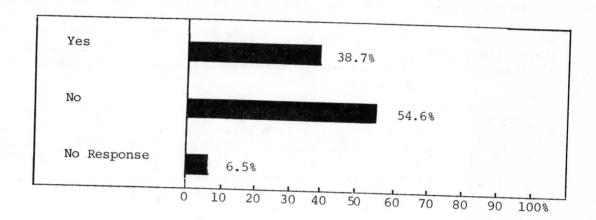

Exhibit 20.   Responses of Managers to the Question:
Were there special considerations or
problems involved in deciding on this
arrangement?   (N=472)

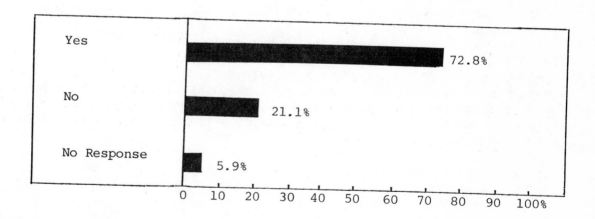

Exhibit 21.   Responses of Managers to the Question:
Is the location of the terminal important?
(N=472)

Several reasons were given to explain the importance that the managers place on the terminal location. The most frequently given reason was the need for easy access by the staff and/or the end-users. One manager wrote that, in his organization, four or five different individuals use the terminal for different purposes every day, but none of them needs it for more than an hour a day. To facilitate sharing the terminal, this organization has installed phonejacks in all the appropriate offices and put the terminal on wheels. In one research organization, the terminals are located within the laboratory areas to facilitate their use by the scientists.

The importance of the easy-access requirement is further borne out by other data elicited from the managers. In a later chapter we show the responses of managers to a question on the different ways in which end-users interact with the searcher and the on-line system. Although in most organizations end-users do not participate in the actual performance of the search at the terminal, this is not by any means always the case. Other alternatives do exist:

- The end-user may sit at the terminal for most or many of his/her searches to provide guidance and feedback.

- The end-user may perform his or her searches in a centrally located area, where assistance is available from an expert searcher-resource person.

- The end-user may perform his or her searches independently in a separate lab or office.

These data suggest that there are a variety of useful interaction modes, and every organization should build some flexibility into its plans when terminal location is being determined.

Other evidence of the need to locate the terminal in an easily accessible place comes from the responses of the searchers to a question asking how they schedule their time at the terminal. Although a majority of the searchers are usually able to go to the terminal either whenever they need to or whenever a request is processed to the point of being ready for the computer search, this is not universally the case.

- 22.6% of the searchers have to coordinate their scheduling of time at the terminal with other staff members or colleagues in other areas of their organization.

- 11.1% must schedule, in advance, the time that they will spend at the terminal on a given day.

Thus with several staff members having to take turns at the terminal and coordinate their usage, placing the terminal in some sort of central location or developing a way for each staff member to get the terminal without wasting time becomes an important consideration in deciding where the terminal should be located.

A second key factor in determining terminal location is noise. Many managers reported that the searchers need a quiet atmosphere so that they can concentrate and work without interruption. Other staff members must also be considered.

Some terminals can be noisy and distracting. Thus, a location must be found that precludes or minimizes disturbance to others in the area.

In addition to access by staff and noise control, the two most important considerations in selecting the terminal location (over 125 managers mentioned either one or both of them), three other considerations were mentioned by a few managers:

- access to other equipment or resources

- the need for security (i.e., classified-information "security" or terminal-protection "security")

- the need for terminal visibility

The first item takes into account that, to perform a good on-line search, the searcher must often first develop a search strategy using, when available, the hard copy indexes that correspond to the data base to be searched. It is thus preferable to have the terminal located close to these materials.

For some organizations the security problem really amounts only to restraining staff and end-users from "playing" with the terminal and perhaps damaging it. In other cases the concern is about potential vandalism and theft. One manager wrote that, in his organization, such items as sinks had been stolen; thus something as valuable and expensive as a terminal would surely disappear if precautionary measures were not taken.

The visibility of the terminal is important for some organizations that are eager to expand the use of their information services and that see the terminal in and of itself as a means for promoting their service. As one manager wrote, the terminal must be seen, not hidden in an office like a rare book.

PROMOTING ON-LINE LITERATURE-SEARCHING SERVICES

Once the on-line service has been instituted, have organizations been informing their current and potential clientele of this new capability and, if so, what procedures have they used? As the reader can see from Exhibit 22 below, about 83% of the managers indicated that they formally announced or promoted their new service in some way.

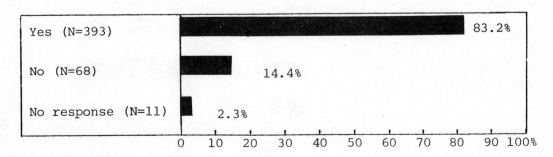

Exhibit 22. Responses of Managers to the Question: Did you
formally announce or promote on-line services? (N=472)

Exhibit 23 shows that Educational organizations exhibited a slightly greater tendency to promote on-line services than Government and Commercial organizations. At least two reasons for such differences can be suggested:

- End-users in Commercial organizations may already be heavy users of the information services available to them; thus, on-line searching is viewed simply as another tool that can be used whenever the need arises, rather than as a special commodity that has to be "sold" to users.

- At the opposite end, use of on-line systems may be the first foray into literature-searching services for many of the Educational organizations. Since their users would not be aware of the new service, there is a special need to push it.

	Yes
Government Users (N=101)	74.3%
Commercial Users (N=152)	77.6%
Educational Users (N=145)	95.9%
Other Users (N=74)	82.4%

Exhibit 23. Responses of Managers, by Type of Organization, to the Question: Did you formally announce or promote the on-line service? (N=472)

Promotional Methods Used

Those that formally announced or promoted the on-line services reported the use of a variety of methods, as shown in Exhibit 24. (Because more than one response was allowed, the percentages total more than 100%.)

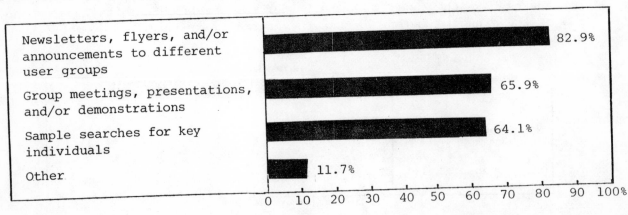

Exhibit 24. Methods Used in Formally Announcing On-Line Services, as Reported by Managers (N=393)

The most popular method for announcing the system involves sending around news-letters or flyers to various users or groups of users. Also heavily used are special presentations or demonstrations, either for groups of users or for important key individuals in the organization or company. Most of the other responses were a variation on the special-presentation theme. For example, in some organizations new faculty members are given one free search; several indi-cated that they have placed special notices in periodicals that claim as part of their readership the clientele of those organizations. One ambitious library went so far as to call a press conference and obtain free advertising on tele-vision.

How successful have these various methods been, in the view of the managers involved? The most successful ones appear to be, first, sample searches and, after that, special group meetings. Newsletters and word of mouth were named by an equal number of people as being methods that had worked effectively in their organizations, but the number naming either of these was only half the number that cited sample searches and group meetings. One manager wrote that, although mailed announcements are necessary, they cannot be relied on as the sole means of publicity; they must be supplemented with demonstrations and word-of-mouth publicity by satisfied end-users.

Whereas 112 managers commented that they had found one or more of the above methods to be successful in spreading the word about the on-line service, only 22 wrote of unsuccessful experiences with these same methods. For this small group, the least effective method seems to be the flyer or newsletter sent out to announce the new service. In too many cases, the managers felt that these were thrown away without being read or, if they were read, the message was quickly forgotten. Several other managers complained that presentations set up for groups and/or key individuals did not seem to be effective.

The managers were asked if they had developed any special materials about on-line searching for users. Their responses are as follows:

- 65.8% had not developed any special materials
- 29.8% had developed special materials
- 4.2% did not respond to the question

The most widely used type of material has been a hand-out or brochure that des-cribes the service. In some cases this description explains what on-line searching is all about; in others, possible search topics and the various data bases that the organization can access are listed. Many other organizations have developed aids for the individuals who perform searches; there are, for example, numerous quick-reference pocket guides that list the commands and special abbreviations used by the system. Others have developed special audio-visual presentations, usually slides used in conjunction with a taped script. Some of these shows have been made in-house, and in other cases they have been borrowed from other users.

It seems clear that promotion is an area in which on-line suppliers and other members of the information industry could be providing more assistance to their users. At the present time, for example, there are no marketing aids (e.g., films or filmstrips) that are oriented toward end-users. Therefore, information service units must develop their own presentations, which--in the absence of other media--require an on-line demonstration. If multimedia presentation materials were readily available on loan or for nominal fees, the service units could introduce larger groups of their users to the technology and capabilities of on-line systems with a minimal amount of extra cost and effort. These could be supplemented with on-line demonstrations to smaller groups after the introductory material had been presented.

One of the reasons we believe that such aids have not been available is that on-line system technology is changing very rapidly, and descriptions of specific systems and features tend to become obsolete within a short period of time. However, if such presentations were developed at a general level, the investment would probably be most worthwhile. As noted above, almost 30% of the users have had to make separate investments, in lieu of being able to obtain any ready-made materials.

Attitudes Toward Promotional Activities

The managers were asked whether they believed a special marketing program was needed to promote on-line services in their organizations. Exhibit 25 shows the results of this question.

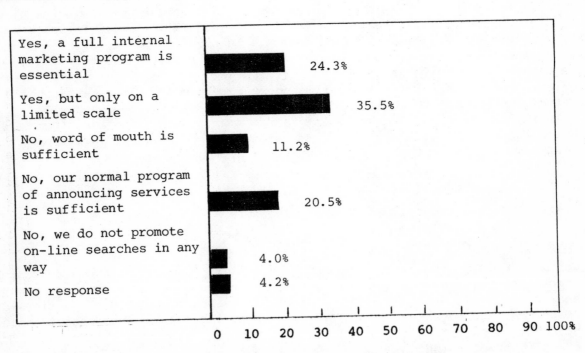

Exhibit 25. Responses of Managers to the Question: Do you believe a special "marketing" program is needed to promote your on-line services? (N=472)

Nearly 60% of the managers believed that some sort of marketing program was necessary. Of this group, over half believed in a limited program, while about 24% thought that all of the stops should be pulled to attract end-users. About 32% seemed content with the publicity that the service was already receiving, either through such means as recommendations by satisfied users to their colleagues or through the channels used by the library or information center to publicize all its services. A small number--4%--did not promote the service at all.

One difficulty that any promotional effort can encounter is the user who is reluctant to allow his or her search request to be performed on-line. Ten percent of the managers have encountered some kind of user reluctance. About 41% of these managers reported that their reluctant users mistrust machine-retrieval, either in terms of precision or recall. Another 29% indicated that users are concerned with security, because their searches are related to new and proprietary ideas or projects with which they are working. Fear that searches run off-line will be sent to the wrong address is especially high in this group. The remaining managers indicated that the cost of the on-line service prevents some of their users from trying it.

What general reservations do managers have about fully promoting on-line searching? About 30 managers expressed concern that the extra workload incurred by an increase in the number of users would be too much of a burden on the already overworked staff. In the same vein, some managers were concerned that an increase in users would bankrupt their budgets; these managers generally represented organizations that did not try to recover the cost of a search. Thus, a large increase in the number of searches performed could pose severe budgetary problems.

Other managers foresaw that an increase in users brought about by a successful promotional program would strain the physical resources of the organization. These managers particularly pointed to the problem of acquiring and providing full-text copies of the source material identified through the on-line system.

A few managers mentioned what they believe to be another problem with a special marketing program for the on-line service: that it would create an artificial separation from all of the other tools and resources that the library or information center has at hand for aiding the end-user. These managers prefer to announce the availability of a literature-searching service, and then let the searcher decide which tools are most appropriate for responding to a specific literature request.

Still other managers believe that the number of data bases that they can access on-line is too small to allow for much publicity of the service. These managers are fearful of announcing the service and then being unable to satisfy clientele who come in with search problems that are not within the range of presently available data bases. The possibility that a bad initial experience will completely turn away potential end-users looms large in their minds.

Attitudes toward the promotion of services may also be linked to perceived
needs for user education. As we saw from Exhibit 23, Educational organizations
have tended to promote their on-line service more than Commercial organizations
have. Exhibit 26 shows additional data that support the same conclusion. About
19% of the Commercial users indicated that a full marketing program was needed
(compared to about 28% of the Educational users), and almost 9% of the Commercial users (compared to only 1% of the Educational users) believed that promotional activities were not needed.

	Yes, Full Program	Yes, Limited Program	Word-of-Mouth	No, Normal Program	No Promotion	No Response
Government Users (N=101)	26.7%	32.7%	16.8%	16.8%	2.8%	4.2%
Commercial Users (N=152)	19.1%	32.2%	14.5%	23.0%	8.6%	2.6%
Educational Users (N=145)	27.6%	37.2%	6.9%	22.1%	1.4%	4.8%
Other Users (N=74)	25.7%	43.2%	5.4%	17.6%	--	8.1%

Exhibit 26. Responses of Managers, by Type of Organization, to the
Question: Is a special "marketing" program needed to
promote your on-line search services?

4. SELECTION AND TRAINING OF STAFF

The rapid growth of on-line services and their adoption in many different settings by users with a variety of backgrounds has raised important questions about who should do the searches and how these searchers should be trained. For both the users and the suppliers, there were initially no precedents to draw from in answering these questions and, even today, principles, procedures, and techniques are still evolving. In this chapter we focus on the experiences of the study population, primarily managers of information service units and information-intermediary searchers, in three general areas:

- Selection of Staff

- Staff Training

- Efficiency in On-Line Searching

We will address the question of end-user vs. information-intermediary searchers in Chapters 10 and 12.

SELECTION OF STAFF

Number of Searchers Initially Selected

Managers were asked to indicate how many individuals were initially selected to be on-line searchers and the basis on which they were selected. The responding managers--of whom only 11% were not involved in the initial startup phase--were asked to restrict their time-frame in responding to these questions to the period of up to 30 days from the time that the organization first began to perform on-line searches.

The actual number of searchers selected initially, shown in Exhibit 27, ranged from one searcher in about 38% of the organizations, to as many as 40 searchers, in one organization. Across all organizations and units, an average of 2.8 individuals were initially selected to become on-line searchers. An analysis of these data by organizational type showed that two or more searchers were selected in over 60% of the Government and Commercial organizations. On the other hand, two or more searchers were selected by about 50% of the Educational organizations, and one searcher was selected by the others. In 14% of the Government organizations, seven or more individuals were chosen, whereas that many were chosen in only 7% of the Commercial organizations and 1% of the Educational organizations. The fact that Educational organizations typically started with only one or two searchers, but now appear to have more searchers than the Commercial organizations (as discussed in Chapter 2), indicates that the growth of service within the academic community has been significant enough to require the assignment of additional staff to the searching function since the services were first implemented.

In 58% of the organizations, the manager was one of the initial searchers. For many of the smaller organizations that have only one professional librarian or information specialist, assisted by clerical workers, the manager was probably the only staff member initially trained for on-line searching. Managers in

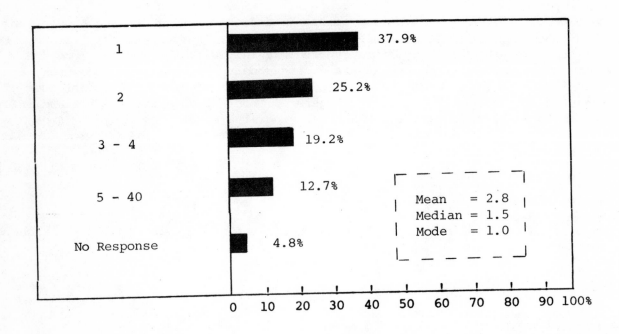

Exhibit 27. Number of Individuals Initially Selected to be Searchers (N=472)

Commercial organizations were the most likely to be found functioning in the dual role of searcher and unit head, and managers in Educational organizations the least likely. Approximately 65% of the Commercial managers and 56% of the Government managers reported that they were included as a searcher, as compared to 47% of the managers in Educational organizations.

A question that was not asked, but one that would probably generate a lively debate, is whether it is important for library managers to have some experience in performing on-line searches in order to plan, budget, and supervise the on-line literature-searching service.

Approximately 12% of the managers indicated that professionals from outside their organizational unit were also included as searchers in the initial startup period. In 42% of the organizations one outside professional was trained; in about 24% of the organizations two were trained; and in 34%, four or more were trained. No differences among organizational types emerged.

Basis for Initial Selection

Managers were asked to indicate why they selected particular individuals as searchers. Eight response choices were provided in the questionnaire. They are shown below in Exhibit 28 along with the managers' responses. (Because respondents could select more than one response, the percentages add up to more than 100%.)

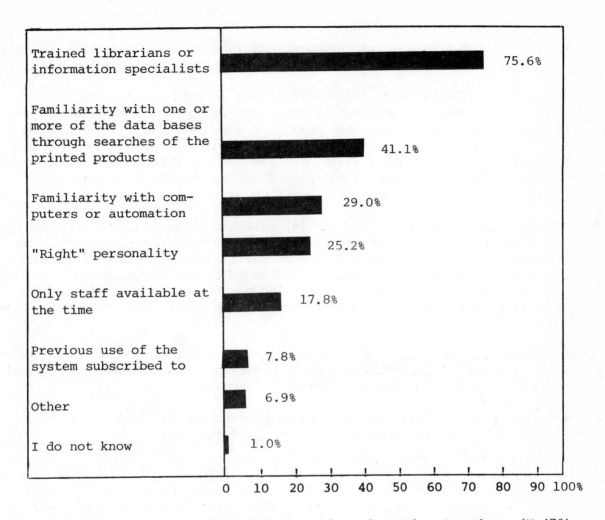

Exhibit 28. Basis for Managers' Selection of On-Line Searchers (N=472)

Across all organizations and units, over 75% of the managers chose individuals who were trained librarians or information specialists. Over 40% of the managers chose individuals who were familiar with one or more of the data bases through coding for batch searches or manual searches of the printed products. About 29% chose those who were familiar with computers, while 25% used the personality of the individual as the chief criterion for selection. Having the "right" personality seemed to include the searcher's having a high level of communication skills and being able to conduct a good reference interview with the end-user.

Some of the responses reported in the Other category (7%) are as follows:

● Seniority among library staff members

● All members of the literature service staff were trained in system's use

● Those chosen were the ultimate users of the information to be searched

- A combination of training and interest
- They [those trained] were in positions where it was reasonable to assume that on-line would be useful in their work

In most cases, organizational type did not make a difference in the reasons given by the managers for selecting individuals to be on-line searchers. One difference that did emerge, however, was that more searchers in Commercial organizations than in any others were chosen because they were familiar with computers or automation. Some 38% of the managers in Commercial organizations chose individuals on this basis, as compared to around 25% in the rest of the population.

To evaluate the usefulness of the initial selection criteria, managers were asked whether some individuals had proved to be much better suited to be on-line searchers than others. Nearly 63% of the managers responded that they had found that there are some characteristics that seem to make some individuals superior on-line searchers, while 22% failed to see any such distinguishing qualities. Another 15% were uncertain and gave an ambivalent response or none at all.

Those managers who had found some individuals to be better suited than others as on-line searchers were asked to list the distinguishing characteristics of these staff members. The two most frequent responses were:

- reference, data base, or subject background in the areas in which the bulk of the on-line searches are performed
- a logical, thorough, analytical mind

Other characteristics of a good searcher were also named, such as curiosity and a desire to learn; flexibility and adaptability; comfort with the machine interaction process and ability to cope with instances of system failure; and patience and persistence.

Finally, there were several other characteristics that were mentioned by only a few managers:

- good memory
- self-confidence
- imagination
- a sense of humor
- spelling and typing skills

The first four traits are certainly important for one to do any job well. But these traits alone, without the ability to think logically through a search and to develop a search statement that incorporates all of the pertinent concepts, will not make one a good searcher. The abilities to type and spell obviously can contribute to efficiency but they do not seem to be regarded as necessary for on-line searching.

The survey did not provide data on the relative importance of reference-work experience and subject-related expertise. We believe that this is an area worthy of study, to determine how the balance of expertise in these two areas contributes to the quality of the searchers' interactions with end-users, their planning and conduct of searches, and end-user satisfaction with search results.

STAFF TRAINING

Once the manager has selected one or more staff members to be on-line searchers, he or she must determine the best way to train them. This training must largely be done on the job. A few graduate schools of library science or information science are beginning to expose their students to on-line retrieval technology, but one cannot yet expect these schools to produce personnel who are trained and ready to do on-line searching.

Many different training approaches are evident in the area of on-line systems, but there has been little or no research on their relative successes. There is probably no one best way to teach all searchers how to use on-line systems. However, certain training patterns have developed as managers and searchers alike attempt to deal with the technology of on-line searching. In this section, we will present and discuss data related to:

- Training methods used

- The number of data bases learned in the early stages of training

- The number of on-line systems learned in the early stages of training

- Views on advanced training sessions

Training Methods

Searchers were asked several questions about the kinds of methods and tools that they had found to be important in learning how to use on-line systems. We asked about formal training sessions conducted by the on-line supplier, as well as other methods that did not involve the on-line supplier. The searchers were asked to indicate the extent of their training for up to four systems. Because it was not an objective of this study to make comparisons between on-line suppliers, searchers were not asked to identify any of the systems by name. Instead, they were instructed to use numbers representing the systems consistently throughout the questionnaire. Searchers who were using more than four systems were asked to confine their response to the four systems that they used most frequently.

Approximately 55% of the searchers in our study received formal training for at least one system. Formal training here refers to supplier-conducted training sessions that generally cover both system and data base use. At the present time, all of the suppliers except one provide new-user training sessions, either on a regular basis (monthly, every six weeks, or annually) or on an as-required basis. Three of the suppliers believe that they have trained between 80% and

100% of their users; the percentages from the others range from 25% to 60%. Searchers in Commercial organizations seem to be those most likely to have received some formal training. Nearly 65% of the searchers in Commercial organizations received training, compared to 55% in Government organizations and 50% of those in Educational organizations.

The level of experience with on-line systems appears to be related to formal training. Over 60% of the searchers with from 1 to 6 months of experience had had no formal training, as compared to 40% each of those searchers with from 6 to 12 months and from 1 to 3 years of experience, and 45% of the searchers with over 3 years of experience. Thus the newest users of on-line searching appear to be the least likely to have formal training. We suspect that this is because there are a growing number of experienced searchers who are capable of providing instruction to new searchers in their organization, and/or because users are not attending training sessions immediately at the time of startup with a system.

We asked the searchers who received formal training to indicate the extent of their training, in relation to the systems and data bases on which they were trained. Their responses are shown in Exhibit 29. The percentages for each system in this figure were calculated on the basis of the number of different on-line systems that the searchers reported using, in the background section of the questionnaire. The number of respondents decreases markedly from System 1 to System 4, because of the decrease in the number of searchers who use multiple systems.

	Trained On One Data Base	Trained On More Than One Data Base	Not Formally Trained
System 1 (N=801)	21.1%	30.8%	48.1%
System 2 (N=339)	13.6%	23.6%	62.9%
System 3 (N=136)	18.4%	16.2%	65.4%
System 4 (N=31)	16.1%	12.9%	71.0%

Exhibit 29.   Percentage of Searchers Who Were Formally Trained on Each of the On-Line Systems Used

Exhibit 29 shows that almost 52% of the total searcher population received formal training for System 1 and that almost 31% received this training on more than one data base. Approximately 37% of the searchers who reported that they use a second on-line system received formal training on it, and nearly 24% received training on more than one data base. In both of these cases, a majority of the group that received formal training was trained on more than one data base. This pattern is reversed for System 3 and System 4. Here slightly more of those who received formal training did so on one data base only.

Nearly 45% of the searchers indicated that they received no formal training from the on-line supplier(s) whose systems they were using, while 13% received formal training on some, but not all, of the systems they use. To understand what alternative learning methods were being used, we asked searchers to indicate from a list of possible training methods the ways in which they first learned to use each of the systems. Exhibit 30 shows the results of this question.

	System 1 (N=801)		System 2 (N=339)		System 3 (N=136)		System 4 (N=31)	
	%	Rank	%	Rank	%	Rank	%	Rank
User's manual	37.3%	1	44.2%	1	41.9%	1	61.3%	1
Instruction from staff member trained by the on-line supplier	29.8%	2	24.5%	3	19.9%	3	25.8%	3
Other (specify)	5.5%	3	2.4%	5	1.5%	6.5	3.2%	5.5
Previous experience with on-line systems on non-bibliographic files	5.2%	4	7.4%	4	5.1%	4	6.5%	4
Previous experience with another on-line literature searching system	3.4%	5	28.6%	2	30.1%	2	45.2%	2
Programmed instruction	2.9%	6	2.0%	6.5	1.5%	6.5	3.2%	5.5
Self-taught without previous experience or reading any documentation	1.6%	7	2.0%	6.5	2.2%	5	0	-

Exhibit 30. Methods Used to Learn On-Line Systems by Searchers Who Were Not Trained by On-Line Suppliers

As the reader can see, a large gap separates the two most frequently used methods for learning to use each of the systems from the other possibilities. On System 1, a majority of the searchers either read the user's manual and documentation provided by the on-line service supplier or received instruction from another staff member who had been trained by the on-line supplier. Other methods were little used. However, by the time the second system was installed, many searchers were able to apply their experience with the first on-line system to the task of learning the new system. Thus, there is a marked increase in the number of searchers who used their previous on-line experience with another on-line literature searching system to learn the second system.

It is not surprising to see that learning through programmed instruction on the computer is ranked so low. At the time the respondents completed the question-naires, only four of the on-line suppliers offered any kind of programmed instruction. This situation does not seem to have changed, although one of the suppliers reports that they are continuing to develop their programmed instruction capability. It is interesting that very few of the searchers taught themselves to operate on-line systems. Although self-instruction may be a suitable learning mode for future generations, these data confirm that other kinds of training are needed now.

We asked the searchers to describe any other ways that they used to learn each of the on-line systems. The various responses can be grouped into the follow-ing categories:

- instruction from colleagues who were not trained by any of the on-line suppliers

- attendance at workshops and courses that provide on-line instruction

- discussion of problems as they occur with the on-line suppliers or colleagues at work

The first two responses suggest that most of the respondents to this question still received instruction in a formal, organized fashion.

Learning methods used by those searchers who were not formally trained were examined by organizational type. Only those methods used for System 1 and System 2 were examined, since there were too few responses to the other two systems for analysis. Searchers in Government and Educational organizations were much more likely than those in Commercial organizations to receive instruc-tion from another staff member who had been trained by the on-line service supplier. Some 30% of the Government searchers and 38% of the Educational searchers learned System 1 in this way, as compared to 19% of the Commercial searchers. For System 2, this method was used by 34% of the Government searchers and 27% of the Educational searchers, as compared to 18% of the Commercial searchers.

Another difference by organizational type is that Educational searchers appear to have learned to use their systems by reading users' manuals and documentation provided by the on-line supplier more than did their counterparts in Government and Commercial organizations. Some 43% of the searchers in Educational organiza-tions, as compared to 32% of the Commercial and Government searchers, learned System 1 in this way. For System 2, 52% of the Educational searchers used manuals and system documentation, as compared to 41% of the Commercial searchers and 32% of the Government searchers.

One final difference is that searchers in Educational organizations learned System 2 by applying their previous experience with another on-line literature searching system far more often than did the other groups. Only about 22% of the Government and Commercial searchers used this method, as compared with 41% of the Educational searchers.

Given the variety of methods used to learn the on-line systems, we asked searchers to indicate which method or methods they would recommend for future trainees. A definition of important training components emerged from their recommendations:

- The new on-line user should first have the opportunity to observe an experienced searcher at the terminal

- A comprehensive manual that has many examples of sample searches should be studied as the second step in the training process

- Next, the searcher should have formal instruction by either the on-line supplier or some other expert; the instruction should include a system overview and cover the mechanics of searching the system and information about the structure of the various data bases that can be used on the system

- The formal instruction should go hand in hand with supervised hands-on experience throughout the session

- At some later date a follow-up training session conducted by either the on-line supplier or some other expert should be held to go over any problems that have emerged for the searcher since the first training session

Many of the searchers were enthusiastic about the idea of programmed instruction, although few had had the opportunity to use it. Several users would like to see an entire course developed that would allow the searcher to proceed on his or her own; others envision various audiovisual aids that would supplement rather than replace formal instruction from an expert in the field.

Another point stressed by the searchers was the importance of having detailed knowledge about the structure of the various data bases used in on-line searching. As one searcher put it, it is essential to the task of formulating search strategies to know how the indexer inputs information into the data base.

The final point emphasized by the searchers is the importance of hands-on experience during the training session. One searcher wrote that the best training consists of "blocks" in which basic classroom information is interspersed with hands-on experience; the worst training occurs when highly detailed technical data about the system and the data bases are presented without any opportunity for terminal practice until the end of the training session. Many searchers also recommended that, along with this hands-on experience at the terminal, paper and pencil exercises be utilized both as a method for testing how well the instructor is getting across the information that he or she believes to be important, and as a way to practice developing search strategies.

During the course of the on-site interviews, the participants were asked several questions about their experiences with learning to use on-line systems. One question asked them to describe the sequence of steps that they had used to master the first on-line system available to their organization, by arranging the following five learning methods in order from first to last used:

- had hands-on practice at the terminal
- read the user's manual or documentation
- used programmed instruction on the computer
- attended a training session held by the on-line supplier
- worked with experienced colleague

There was no clear-cut pattern in the responses for the first learning method used. One-third of the respondents relied first on colleague training, one-third on the user's manual, and one-third on training from the on-line suppliers.

The groups that either worked with experienced colleagues or attended training sessions held by the on-line supplier next read the user's manual, while the group that began with the user's manual either obtained hands-on experience at the terminal or attended a supplier's training session. And, finally, almost all of the respondents who reported using a third learning method depended on hands-on experience.

The interviewees were also asked what they believed the best learning sequence to be. No clear patterns were evident in their responses. Almost an equal number of them chose, as a first step, the following methods:

- working with an experienced colleague
- hands-on experimentation and practice with the system
- attending an on-line supplier's training session
- reading the user's manual

The interviewees were equally divided over the second stage of the ideal learning sequence. Of those who chose either of the first two methods above, one-half of each group thought that a training session with the on-line supplier should come next, while the other half believed that reading the manual would be most helpful. The group that pushed for training sessions with the on-line supplier as a first step thought that reading the user's manual should come next, while the group that believed the manual should be read first split evenly between supplier training and colleague training.

What is the best way, after some initial training, to develop skills quickly in on-line searching in an "on-the-job learning" environment? The following suggestions illustrate the variety of ways in which searching skills can be developed:

- extensive practice as well as thorough reading of all the training aids such as the manual and the keyword indexes (if available)
- learn as much as possible about each of the data bases
- learn by searching a subject that you are familiar with as a means of checking yourself
- users must be reassured that they cannot harm the system so that they will feel free and comfortable enough with the equipment to learn

- practice with assistance after seeing a demonstration

- formal training and refresher courses are extremely important

The availability of special training tools was another topic of discussion. Almost all of the respondents could think of at least one tool that would have made their initial learning experience easier. Representative responses are as follows:

- one-page summary of sample search that is convenient to keep at the terminal

- a thesaurus for each of the data bases

- a quick reference list of the commands

- a "help" line or hot line to the on-line supplier

- better explanations of the data bases in the manuals

- a manual complete enough to enable a person to teach him or herself

- computer-aided instruction

One last area of discussion during the interviews that pertains to staff training was the coordination of search activities and communications among searchers. Most searchers we interviewed did not attempt to specialize in particular types of search activities, but rather, accepted each search request that came their way. Only four of the interviewees had developed some sort of specialization. Of this group, two specialized by data base and one by on-line system, and the last used a subject specialist for developing the search strategy in conjunction with the end-user and a thesaurus specialist for translating the search strategy into terminology that meshed with the thesaurus vocabulary.

Even though most of the interviewees indicated that they did not divide up searching responsibilities, most of them thought that the idea was a good one. Opinion was almost equally divided among those who believed that dividing responsibilities by data base was best, and those who would have preferred to see the division based on systems. Only two interviewees thought that everyone should take every kind of search.

The interviewees were also asked to discuss the kinds of intra-staff communications that they used when they were first initiating on-line services, and to compare them to the communications methods currently used to keep all of the on-line searchers abreast of problems and new developments. About one-half of the respondents started their on-line services with only one searcher, and thus had no opportunity initially for intra-staff communications. Of the group that started with two or more searchers, about one-half met with the entire staff being trained for on-line searching to practice together at the terminal. A few of the respondents not only practiced together at the terminal, but also met with the rest of the staff to work out search strategies, to share information, and to review problems together.

Two of the interviewees who initially used some sort of intra-staff communications methods no longer do so. In both cases, it was felt that staff meetings were no longer necessary. In the other organizations, informal communications channels seemed to predominate. In most cases formal staff meetings were not held, but searchers were able to call or visit with some other staff member whenever they were working on a particularly difficult search.

Learning Multiple Data Bases and Systems

Some controversy surrounds the issue of the optimal number of data bases and systems that can be mastered by the new user in the early months of his or her training. Some believe that learning one data base and one system well enables the searcher to perform expert searches soon, even though the subject scope of the searches that can be attempted is limited. Additionally, it is felt that mastering one data base on one system gives the searcher the confidence needed to learn additional data bases and systems at a later time.

At the other end of the spectrum are those who advocate learning several data bases on several systems, in the early stages of the searcher's training. The assumption behind this position is that, regardless of the data base or system being examined, the similarities of on-line searching far outweigh the differences. Since many of the principles are the same, being exposed to two or more data bases or systems simultaneously supposedly reinforces the learning process for the searcher.

In order to shed light on this controversy, we posed several questions to the searchers about their experience with learning multiple data bases and systems. These questions are from a section of the questionnaire that was to be completed only by searchers who had multiple-system or multiple-data-base experience; thus the responding population for this section was smaller than that for the total questionnaire. Approximately 639 searchers or 80% of the total population answered some or all of the questions in the multiple-data-base section of the questionnaire; 339 searchers, or 42% of the total, responded to some or all of the questions in the multiple-system section.

Multiple Data Bases

The searchers were asked how many different data bases they began to learn during their first three months of on-line experience. As can be seen in Exhibit 31, the responses of those searchers with multiple-data-base experience ranged from one to 13 data bases. Over 60% of the group learned two or more data bases in their first three months of experience. An analysis of these data by organizational type showed that Commercial searchers were the most likely to learn more than one data base. Some 77% of this group, as compared to 59% of the Government searchers and 45% of the Educational searchers, reported multiple-data-base experience in their first three months of on-line experience.

We next asked the searchers to evaluate their learning experience. The nearly 33% who learned only one data base in the first three months of their on-line experience were asked whether they thought that they could have learned more at that time. The remaining group, who learned two or more data bases, were asked whether they thought that it would have been easier or better to have become thoroughly familiar with one data base before learning others. The

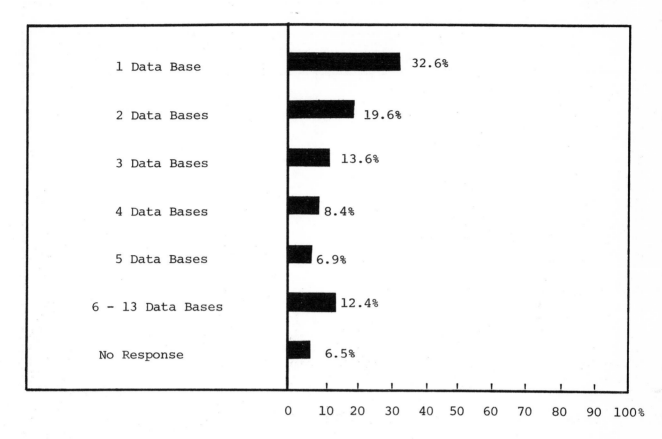

Exhibit 31.   Searchers' Report on Number of Data Bases They Learned Initially
              (N=639)

answers of both groups supports the position of those who advocate learning
several data bases in the early stages of training. Approximately three-fourths
of each group believe that they were capable of learning more than one data base
within their first three months of on-line experience. No differences by organizational type were evident in these data.

How does a searcher learn enough about the contents and coverage of the data
base to decide when to use a particular data base for a particular search
question? Exhibit 32 shows various methods that could be employed to learn
about the data bases, and the frequency with which the searchers used each
method. The most frequently used method, employed by over 80% of the searchers
at some time, was from information provided by the on-line supplier, such as
search aids or training. The most frequent response in the Other category was
that an educational background in several dsiciplines facilitated learning new
data bases.

When these data were analyzed by organizational type, several differences were
noted. Nearly 44% of the Commercial searchers, as compared to 34% of the
Educational searchers and 26% of the Government searchers, learned about most
data bases from previous experience with the file through manual searches of
their corresponding printed indexes. This difference is no doubt related to

	USED FOR:			
	Most Data Bases	Some Data Bases	One Data Base	No Response
From information provided by the on-line supplier	57.7%	19.7%	3.9%	18.6%
Am still learning by experience	36.5%	23.6%	1.9%	38.0%
From previous experience through manual searches	35.1%	30.5%	6.9%	27.5%
From trial and error, or actual experience	32.4%	28.6%	3.8%	35.2%
From information provided by the data base supplier	23.2%	24.9%	6.3%	45.7%
From my colleagues	22.1%	23.0%	3.4%	51.5%
From previous experience through coding searches for batch-processing	5.9%	8.5%	8.5%	77.2%

Exhibit 32. Methods Used by Searchers in Learning to Use Data Bases (N=639)

the fact that Commercial organization libraries, more often than other libraries, operate information services that perform (or performed) literature searches using manual or batch-mode searching.

Another difference was that Commercial searchers tended to rely on information such as descriptions, authority lists, and training provided by the data base suppliers more often than did the other groups. (It should be noted here that this alternative only applied to those for whom an organization other than the on-line service supplier provided data bases.) Over 60% of the Commercial searchers, as compared to 50% of the Educational searchers and 47% of the Government searchers reported using information from the data base suppliers at some time.

A final difference noted was that Government searchers relied on previous experience with coding searches for batch-processing more often than did the others: 13% of the Government searchers used this method to familiarize themselves with most data bases, as compared to 3% of the Commercial searchers and 4% of the Educational searchers.

Multiple Systems

The data regarding multiple-system training show the searchers to be slightly less confident of their abilities to learn to use more than one system during their first months of on-line experience than they were with learning to use multiple data bases. Some 49% of the searchers who responded to the multiple-system-usage section of the questionnaire said that they learned to use only one system during their first three months of experience with on-line systems, while about 29% learned two systems, slightly over 3% learned three systems, and slightly under 3% learned more than three. Approximately 16% of the searchers using multiple systems did not respond to the question.

Those searchers who indicated that they learned only one system initially were next asked if they believed now that they could have learned at least one more within the same "beginner's" period, and those searchers who learned more than one system were asked if they believed it would have been easier or better to have become thoroughly familiar with one system before beginning to learn others. Nearly 63% of those who learned only one system initially believed that they could have learned another, while nearly 57% of those who learned more than one system did not believe that their initial experience would have been better had they learned only one.

An analysis of the multiple-system data by organizational type showed some interesting differences. Searchers in Commercial organizations were less likely than those in any other type of organization to have learned more than one system during their first three months of on-line experience. Only about 42% of the Commercial searchers, as compared to 50% of those in Government organizations and 60% of those in Educational organizations, learned more than one system.

Although learning multiple systems seems to present more of a problem to the searcher than learning multiple data bases, this should not discourage those who want and need to learn several systems. Almost 57% of those searchers who have actually had multiple system experience disagreed with the statement that they would have been better off becoming thoroughly familiar with one system before attempting to learn any others. Thus it seems that learning and using multiple systems is not as difficult as it was originally thought to be. Perhaps by lengthening the 3-month period that we used in our study (e.g., to 6 months and 12 months), we might have obtained an even more positive picture.

We asked the searchers to comment on the positive and negative effects that knowledge of one retrieval system had on learning others. In other words, how did knowing one system help or hinder efforts to learn a second? The positive effect of multiple-system knowledge seems to be that learning how to use one retrieval system provides the necessary background for picking up what is needed to learn others. The searcher develops a general feeling of confidence because he or she knows what to expect the second time around. As one searcher put it, much of the operation of the various systems is identical in theory, if not in form. Thus, after grasping the concept of one system, learning others often necessitates only minor modifications in thinking. Another searcher wrote that he had lost his fear of the machine aspects of on-line searching; instead of feeling hesitant about learning a second system, he was quite enthusiastic.

The negative effects of learning more than one on-line system most often mentioned by the searchers related to confusing the command language and the features of one system with those of another. One searcher wrote, for example, that there are sometimes differences on small details that do not seem worth trying to memorize. Another finding is that many searchers believe that they become biased toward the system that they learn to use first; differences between the first system and all others tend to be viewed as deficiencies in the later-learned systems. Thus the later-learned systems can suffer by comparison and tend to be used less.

Advanced Training Sessions

Another vehicle for developing competency in on-line searching is participation in advanced training or refresher courses. At the time of the initial data collection for this study, 50% of the suppliers were conducting these types of sessions. Now almost all of them do, on either a periodic or an as-needed basis.

The searchers (nearly 39%) who had received any form of advanced training were asked to evaluate the usefulness of that training, and the searchers without this experience were asked if they believed that such training might be useful. Both groups were quite enthusiastic about the positive effects of advanced training or refresher sessions. Nearly 96% of the searchers who had had some advanced training believed that it had been useful, while 81% of those who had not had such training nevertheless believed that it could be useful. When these data were analyzed by organizational type, the only difference to appear was that searchers from Commercial organizations are the least likely to attend advanced training sessions. Only 24% of the Commercial searchers, as compared to 46% of the Government searchers and 47% of the Educational searchers, have attended advanced training sessions.

We asked the searchers to elaborate on their responses about the usefulness, or lack thereof, of training sessions. Most of the searchers who offered further thoughts on this subject were those who had not had any experience with advanced training or refresher sessions but believed them to be useful. The response most frequently made by this group was that advanced training sessions would enable them to learn subtle, sophisticated searching techniques. Other frequent responses were that such training would provide users with a forum for exchanging ideas and would enable them to learn about new features added to the system. The response most frequently made by the group with previous experience was that advanced training provided them with instruction on the newest features of the systems they use.

A small number of searchers commented on why they did not think that advanced training sessions are useful. The prevailing thought was that, by diligent study of an up-to-date manual, the searcher ought to be able to learn all he or she needs to know about on-line searching.

STAFF EFFICIENCY IN ON-LINE SEARCHING

The true tests of the effectiveness of any form of training is how well it prepares and helps searchers to perform high-quality searches, and to do so effici-
ently. It was not within the scope of the present research to evaluate search
effectiveness or training effectiveness, per se. However, useful starting points
for such research are provided by our survey data on the searchers' views of their
own efficiency and the quality of their searches. This section discusses data
from the Searcher questionnaire related to four aspects of efficiency and quality:

- Time needed by frequent users to become efficient searchers

- Time needed by infrequent users to become efficient searchers

- Average time per search

- Quality of search results

Time Needed by Frequent Users to Become Efficient Searchers

To compare the results of formal training by on-line suppliers or by highly
experienced instructors with other training methods, we asked searchers who used
one or more on-line systems frequently about the length of time it took them to
become "comfortable and fairly efficient" at conducting searches on the
terminal. Two sets of questions were posed: one to frequent users who had been
formally trained, and another to frequent users who were not formally trained.
For purposes of this question, a formally trained user was one who received
training from either on-line suppliers or other highly experienced instructors.
Infrequent searchers were asked to answer a separate set of questions on
efficiency at the terminal, which will be discussed later.

Exhibits 33 and 34 show the length of time needed to become efficient at the
terminal for each of the systems used by the searcher (up to four were allowed).
Especially apparent in each exhibit is the large number of non-respondents. The
non-respondents in Exhibit 33 are a mixture of searchers for whom the formal
training or frequency of use, or both, did not apply.

Quite surprisingly, the figures show very little difference in the time estimates
given by the two groups of searchers. For System 1, the time period most often
chosen by both groups was 1 to 4 weeks. For System 2, the formally trained
searchers seemed to catch on to the new system a little faster than those without
formal training; here the largest group of searchers without formal training took
1 to 4 weeks to learn the new system. By the third system, more of the searchers
without formal training were learning the new system as fast as their formally
trained counterparts. The same applies for the fourth system. Thus the data
would seem to indicate that formal training by on-line suppliers or other experts
does not affect the length of time that it takes for most of the frequent searchers
to become comfortable and efficient at the terminal. No differences emerged in
these data when they were analyzed by organizational type.

	System 1 (N=801)		System 2 (N=339)		System 3 (N=136)		System 4 (N=31)	
	%	Rank	%	Rank	%	Rank	%	Rank
1 to 5 Days	10.6%	2	14.7%	1	11.8%	1	6.5%	2.5
1 to 4 Weeks	18.2%	1	9.7%	2	10.3%	2	12.9%	1
1 to 2 Months	9.2%	3	3.2%	4	5.9%	3	6.5%	2.5
2 to 4 Months	4.5%	4	1.2%	5	2.9%	5	0	-
Over 4 Months	2.9%	5	0.9%	6	0	-	0	-
I do not yet feel "comfortable and fairly efficient"	0.6%	6	5.6%	3	3.7%	4	3.2%	4
No response	53.9%		64.6%		65.4%		71.0%	

Exhibit 33. Length of Time to Become Efficient, as Reported by Trained Searchers

	System 1 (N=801)		System 2 (N=339)		System 3 (N=136)		System 4 (N=31)	
	%	Rank	%	Rank	%	Rank	%	Rank
1 to 5 Days	6.7%	2	9.4%	2	13.2%	1	9.7%	3.0
1 to 4 Weeks	13.2%	1	13.0%	1	8.1%	2	19.4%	1
1 to 2 Months	5.7%	3	6.2%	3	2.9%	5	3.2%	5
2 to 4 Months	3.9%	4	2.4%	5	3.7%	4	9.7%	3.0
Over 4 Months	1.2%	5.5	0.3%	6	0	-	0	-
I do not yet feel "comfortable and fairly efficient"	1.2%	5.5	5.9%	4	6.6%	3	9.7%	3.0
No response	68.0%		62.0%		65.4%		48.3%	

Exhibit 34. Length of Time to Become Efficient, as Reported by Untrained Searchers

Time Needed by Infrequent Searchers to Become Efficient Searchers

About 174 searchers, or 22% of the total searcher population, placed themselves in the category of Infrequent Users--those who do not use the system more than once every few weeks or months. We asked them to describe the extent to which they feel "comfortable and fairly efficient" with the system.

As indicated in Exhibit 35, slightly over one-half of the infrequent searchers reported that they were comfortable and efficient at the terminal. This group was asked how long it took them to acquire this feeling of ease and efficiency. Most responded that it took about 5 terminal sessions.

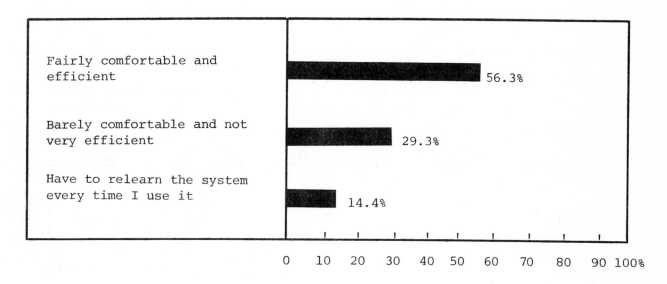

Exhibit 35.   Report by Infrequent Searchers on Feelings of Efficiency in Use of On-Line Systems (N=174)

Those searchers who reported that they have to relearn the system every time that they use it were next asked to indicate how this problem might be overcome. The most commonly given response was that more frequent use of the system(s) was necessary. Other representative responses were as follows:

- More tutorials for the infrequent user, and better indexing of the user manual to handle problems that arise during the search

- Standardize the search syntax between data bases

- The problem is not with machine mechanics but with remembering search strategies that maximize efficiency for the data base being searched

- Search strategies should be planned by the subject specialist but run by the terminal specialist with the subject specialist available in case the strategy breaks down

- Programmed or self-instruction training materials with a number of sample problems

- Better manuals or short outlines of frequently used procedures and changes

Average Time Per Search

To obtain another indirect indicator of efficiency, we asked searchers to compare the time needed to perform an average retrospective literature search at the terminal when they first began searching against the amount of time currently needed. The average searcher reported needing 29 minutes (mean) initially; by the time of the study, that mean time had decreased to 17 minutes. Exhibit 36 illustrates the range of responses for searches in the two time periods under discussion. (Note that different intervals have been used to group the initial and current search times.)

"Initially" (as beginners)		"Now" (as of time data were collected)	
Minutes	%	Minutes	%
3-15	23.0%	1-9	18.2%
16-24	21.2%	10-12	20.2%
25-30	23.5%	13-15	17.6%
31-93	21.5%	16-23	17.4%
94-180	1.0%	24-150	17.2%
No Response	9.8%	No Response	9.1%

Exhibit 36. Changes in Average Search Time for Searchers as Beginners and at the Time Data Were Collected (N=801)

By comparing the "Initially" and "Now" search times, one can see that there has been a marked decrease in the amount of time needed to perform the average on-line search. Initially, only 23% of the searchers spent 15 minutes or less on each search; by the time of the study, 56% of the searchers fell into this category. Another difference brought out in the Exhibit is that, initially, 46% of the searchers spent from 25 to 180 minutes per search; at the time of the study, only 17% of the searchers were in the 24 to 150 minute range.

Searchers in Educational organizations appear to have been spending slightly less time on a search than their counterparts in the Commercial and Government sectors. This holds true for both the time spent initially, per search, and the time spent currently, per search.

The amount of time spent per search was also found to vary with the experience of the searcher and the number of on-line searches that the searcher conducts every week. As should be expected, the less experience a searcher has, the more time he or she currently spends on each on-line search. For example, only 12% of the searchers with less than 6 months of on-line experience spent 9 minutes or less on a search, as compared to 20% of the searchers with from 6 to 12 months of experience, 19% of those with from 1 to 3 years of experience, and 20% of those with over 3 years of experience. Only about 28% of the newest searchers spent 12 minutes or less on each search, compared to 37% of the searchers with 6 to 12 months' experience, 42% of those with from 1 to 3 years' experience, and 50% of those with over 3 years' experience. Strangely enough, however, about the same number of the very least experienced and the most experienced searchers were involved in the truly long searches--24 to 150 minutes per on-line search.

As has already been mentioned, the number of searches that the searcher performs in one week is also related to the amount of time spent on each search. As the number of searches increases, the time spent on each one appears to decrease. This was found to be the case for both initial and current search times. For purposes of analysis, we divided the searchers into two approximately equal size groups, on the basis of the number of searches that they performed in the average week. The group we defined as the "Fewer Searches" group did 5 or fewer searches; the "More Searches" group did more than 5. Examination of the search times for these two groups showed that only 32% of the Fewer Searches group spent less than 15 minutes on each search, as compared to 57% of the More Searches group. When we looked at lengthy search times--from 34 to 93 minutes per search--we found that 27% of the Fewer Searches group had average search times in this range, as opposed to only 15% of the More Searches group.

Quality of Search Results

The data in the previous section that compare beginning and current search times at the terminal indicate that, as the searchers gain experience, there is a decrease in the time needed to perform the average retrospective literature search at the terminal. Of course, a decrease in the time spent performing a search is not in itself evidence of increasing efficiency. For instance, spending less time on each search might be the result of time pressure from an increased volume of search requests, rather than a reflection of increased ability to perform a high-quality search quickly.

In order to shed some light on this issue, we asked the searchers whether they believed that there was any difference in quality between search results they obtained as beginners and their current results. Because another indicator of the quality of the end product is client satisfaction, we also asked the searchers to indicate whether the expressions of satisfaction with search results

from the client or end-user had changed from the time they were novices. The
results of these two questions are shown in Exhibits 37 and 38, respectively.

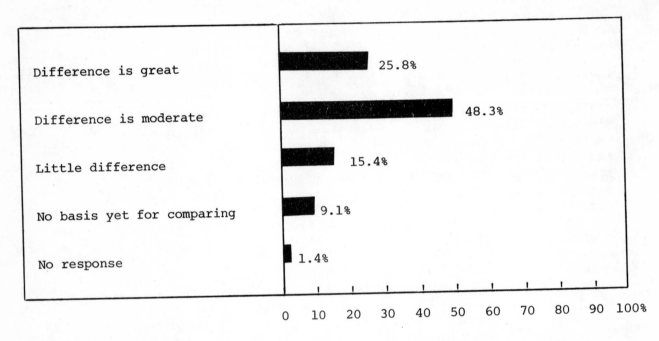

Exhibit 37.   Searchers' Report on Differences in Quality of Searches
"Now" Vs. "Initially"   (N=801)

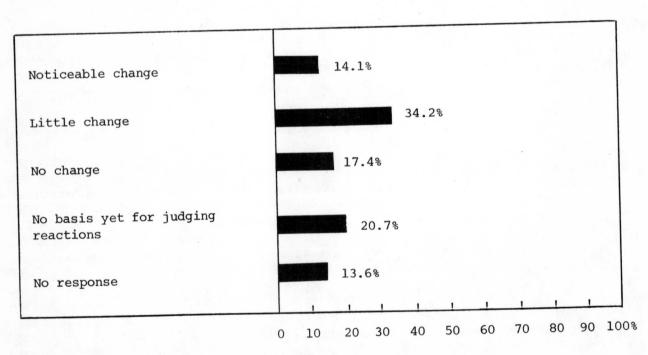

Exhibit 38.   Searchers' Report on Differences in Quality of Searches "Now" Vs.
"Initially," as Expressed by End-Users   (N=801)

A surprisingly high number of searchers, about 48%, reported that they believed there was only a moderate difference in the quality of searches performed now, as compared to those performed when they were beginners. Likewise, 34% of the searchers have noticed little change in the end-users' expressions of satisfaction with search results.

With regard to user feedback, nearly 21% of the searchers indicated that they had no basis on which to judge user reactions. This may be an indication of the relative newness of the on-line search operations, or a reflection of the fact that no feedback mechanism has been developed. The fact that a total of 51% of the searchers reported little or no change in user expressions of satisfaction may well be because there has been no change in the search results; or again, it may be a function of the lack of reporting mechanisms available to end-users.

5. LEVELS OF ON-LINE USE

The data described in the previous chapter on staff training suggest that a significant investment has been made by the using organizations, the on-line searchers, and the on-line suppliers in training for on-line use. That investment has been reflected in the growth in hours of on-line use. Although accurate usage figures are difficult, if not impossible to obtain, we can estimate that during 1975 at least 120,000 hours were spent in on-line searching and over a half million on-line searches were conducted.

In this chapter, we bring together data from several sections of the two questionnaires that dealt with the amount of on-line use at both an organizational level and the level of the individual searcher. We will focus on:

- Number of Systems and Data Bases Used

- Usage as Viewed by the Managers

- Usage as Viewed by the Searchers

In a final section of the chapter, we will examine the data relative to the searcher's requirements for on-line access time--particularly in the context of their levels of use and of their scheduling practices--and the extent to which these requirements are currently being met by the on-line service suppliers.

NUMBER OF SYSTEMS AND DATA BASES USED

Number of Systems Used

We asked both managers and searchers to indicate how many on-line systems could be or were being used for on-line searching. The question to each group differed slightly in emphasis. The managers were asked to specify the number of different on-line literature searching systems to which the organization subscribes or has access, while the searchers were asked to specify the number of different on-line systems that they have actually used in literature searching.

Exhibit 39 shows the responses of managers to the question on how many different on-line searching systems, excluding any internal (i.e., private) systems, the using organization subscribes to or has access to. The responses ranged from 1 system to 12 systems, and the mean was 1.96. About one half of the respondents indicated that their organization subscribed or had access to only one on-line system; the other half subscribed to more than one system. Because so few organizations indicated that they had access to 5 or more systems, we have, for purposes of illustration, collapsed into one group all responses in the 5- to 12-systems range.

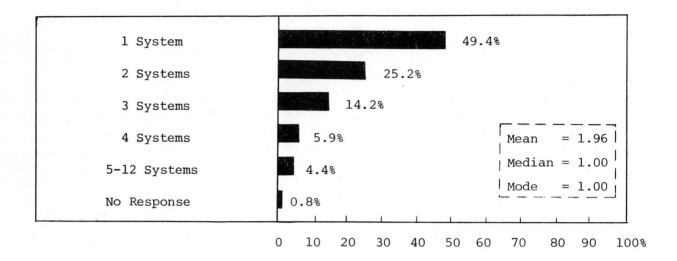

Exhibit 39. Managers' Responses to Question: How many different on-line systems does your organization subscribe to or have access to? (N=472)

Exhibit 40 shows the responses of searchers to the question regarding the number of different on-line systems, <u>excluding</u> internal systems, that they themselves actually used in searching. The responses ranged from 1 to 10 with a mean of 1.68 systems. As with managers, the modal response was 1 system. The vast majority of searchers reported using from 1 to 3 systems, with fewer than 4% using more than 3 systems.

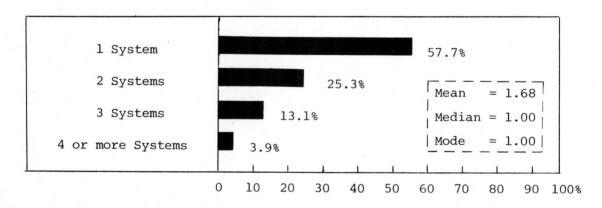

Exhibit 40. Searchers' Responses to Question: How many different on-line systems do you use? (N=801)

We must caution the reader to view the data we have presented on system use
in the organization as a conservative picture of reality today. In conducting
a number of in-depth field interviews following the questionnaires, we learned
that many library/information centers were actively making plans for increased
use of on-line services. Thus we believe that, were the same questions asked
again today, many more than half of the organizations would have access to,
and would be using two or more systems.

Analysis by organization type showed that a majority of the Government and
Other users have access to only one system, while the majority of the Commercial
and Educational users have access to two or more systems. The percentage
responses for each organization type were as follows:

- 62% of the Government and Other users had access to only one on-line
  system, while approximately 38% of each group accessed two or more
  systems.

- 38% of the Commercial users had access to one system, while 60%
  accessed two or more.

- 46% of the Educational users had access to only one system, while 54%
  accessed two or more.

The searcher data were also analyzed by organization type to see whether the
number of on-line systems that the searcher actually used varied by organization. Approximately 60% of the Government, Educational and Other
respondents were using only one on-line system, and 40% were using two or more
systems. On the other hand, a majority of the Commerical users--53% of that
group--were using two or more systems.

Number of Data Bases Used

Most searchers reported that they used more than one data base, with the mean
number of data bases accessed being 6.6. Exhibit 41 shows the searchers'
report on the number of data bases they used. As the reader can see, the
range is between 1 and 34. About 18% of the searchers were accessing only
one data base, while another 60% were accessing between 2 and 10 data bases.

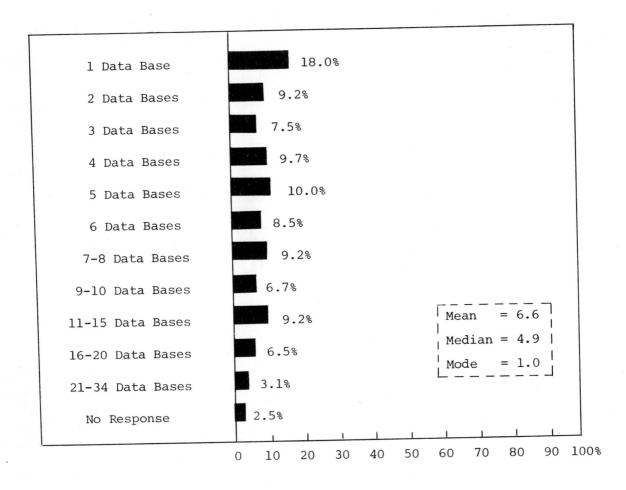

1 Data Base	18.0%
2 Data Bases	9.2%
3 Data Bases	7.5%
4 Data Bases	9.7%
5 Data Bases	10.0%
6 Data Bases	8.5%
7-8 Data Bases	9.2%
9-10 Data Bases	6.7%
11-15 Data Bases	9.2%
16-20 Data Bases	6.5%
21-34 Data Bases	3.1%
No Response	2.5%

Mean   = 6.6
Median = 4.9
Mode   = 1.0

Exhibit 41.   Searchers' Report on Number of Data Bases Accessed
for On-Line Searching (N=801)

The use of a large number of data bases indicated by some searchers is understandable, given that some of the respondents work in information service
centers, organizations that by definition use many information sources to
serve the needs of their clientele. However, there is some possibility of
confusion as to the exact meaning of the question asked; some searchers may
have reported the total number of data bases available to the organization
as a whole rather than the number that they themselves were able to access.

In addition, we must view these data as representing a mix of respondent--and,
for that matter, supplier--definitions of what constitutes a data base. As
we discussed in Chapter 1, some data bases, such as ERIC and COMPENDEX, are
truly quite distinct, while others are members of a family of files. For
example, MEDLINE is a data base developed through the MEDLARS system, and

there are several other MEDLARS-related files that users can access, e.g., SDILINE, the current month's materials. All of these files are sometimes referred to as MEDLINE, the MEDLINE data base, or the MEDLINE system. An even more difficult definitional problem is raised by a data base such as TOXLINE, which actually comprises six different files. Although these differences are not particularly disturbing in terms of tabulating the data that we present here, they do become important in interpreting the data on difficulties that users have in working with more than one data base. This definition problem is addressed further in Chapter 7, where we present the data on usage of multiple data bases.

When the data were analyzed by organization type, we found that Commercial users were the least likely to be accessing only one data base and Other users were the most likely, with 10% and 29% of the users respectively falling into this category. About 20% of the Government and Educational users were accessing only one data base. All the rest of the respondents were accessing two or more data bases.

USAGE AS VIEWED BY MANAGERS

As readers review the next two sections, they may feel tempted to compare the managers' views on some data with those presented by the searchers. We would remind readers that the population bases of managers and searchers are some-what different, as explained in the discussion on methodology in Chapter 1.

The managers were asked to provide data relative to two major time- and amount-related statistics: the average number of searches performed and the average search times. These items of data are reported below. Additional data, e.g., on printing statistics and turn-around time, are provided in later chapters.

Average Number of Searches

It is clear from data provided by the responding managers that the on-line services are being used in both very small and very large amounts and by those with very few and very many search requests. The range in responses for the average number of searches performed per month was from 1 to over 999, the upper limit for our coding system. We also know, both from survey data and our own experience, that on-line searching is being used by both small and large organizations. It is clearly not limited to the very rich and prestigious organizations in the several sectors of our economy.

The median number of on-line searches performed each month by the organizations in our study was 30. From the data shown in Exhibit 42, it appears that Educational and Government users are the heaviest users of the on-line service and that Commercial organization users are the lightest system users.

	1-49 Searches	50-99 Searches	100-999 Searches	No Response	MEDIAN NO. SEARCHES
Government Users (N=101)	45.5%	15.8%	27.7%	10.9%	53.00
Commercial Users (N=152)	75.0%	10.5%	5.3%	9.2%	29.66
Educational Users (N=145)	44.8%	15.9%	33.8%	5.5%	57.68
Other Users (N=74)	60.8%	16.2%	13.5%	9.5%	36.47

Exhibit 42.   Number of On-Line Searches Performed Monthly, as
Reported by Managers, by Organization Type

There is, naturally, a correlation between the number of frequent searchers in an organization and the number of on-line searches being conducted.   The relationship is shown in Exhibit 43.   The more searchers there are in an organization, the more searches that are conducted.

	1-19 Searches	20-55 Searches	56-999 Searches	No Response	MEDIAN NO. SEARCHES
1 Searcher (N=125)	52.0%	29.6%	14.4%	4.0%	17.53
2 Searchers (N=114)	30.7%	36.8%	22.8%	9.6%	34.18
3-50 Searchers (N=186)	10.2%	32.8%	48.4%	8.6%	108.68

Exhibit 43.   Number of On-Line Searches Performed Monthly, as
Reported by Managers with Different Searcher
Staff Sizes

Most one-searcher organizations reported doing between 1 and 19 searches, but in some one-searcher organizations, the individuals were doing 56 or more searches.

Average Search Times

We asked the managers to provide us with their best estimates of the average time spent on a single search, across all systems and across all data bases. The data in this section are taken from the Budgeting and Accounting section of the questionnaire, and the number of respondents to this section was only about 68% of the total number of 472 managers. Although other managers may have had average search-time data available, the search-time-related questions were to be answered only by that subset of respondents maintaining a separate accounting or budgeting system for their on-line searches.

The mean and median times for the managers' report on the average time spent by their staff on a search were:

Minutes per search at the terminal:
Mean = 19.1   Median = 15.3

Minutes per search in pre-terminal work:
Mean = 20.7   Median = 15.1

Minutes per search in post-terminal work:
Mean = 17.7   Median = 10.1

The range for each of these times was from 2 to 99 minutes and, given the skewness of the curve, the medians are probably better indicators of the central tendencies. In general, however, it appears that the total time attributed by managers to on-line-search-related activities is about one hour.

Exhibits 44a, b, and c show managers' responses in each organizational type on average search times at the terminal, in pre-search work, and in post-search work. It appears that Educational users are spending the least time at the terminal but are spending more time in their pre-search work. On the other hand, Commercial users are spending the most time both at the terminal and in post-search work. We can speculate that the data bases with which these user groups are working, as well as their service environments, are contributing to these differences. For example, search-strategy development work by Educational users with the MeSH vocabulary of MEDLINE probably requires a greater level of effort than that required by a data base such as Chemical Abstracts Condensates, which does not have a controlled vocabulary. Post-search work can include the searcher's review and evaluation of search results, location of relevant documents, preparation of a summary report, and/or debriefing on the search with the patron or client. As we will discuss later in Chapter 7, Commercial users are most likely to be involved in these activities.

	2-9 Mins.	10-19 Mins.	20-29 Mins.	30-39 Mins.	40-99 Mins.	No Response	MEDIAN NO. MINS.
Government Users (N=101)	5.9%	29.7%	6.9%	8.9%	6.9%	41.5%	17.8
Commercial Users (N=152)	5.9%	17.8%	16.4%	12.5%	3.3%	44.1%	22.6
Educational Users (N=145)	8.3%	40.7%	19.3%	4.8%	--	26.9%	16.9
Other Users (N=74)	9.5%	31.1%	16.2%	10.8%	4.0%	28.4%	18.0

Exhibit 44a. Number of Minutes Spent at the Terminal on Average Search, as Reported by Managers, by Organization Type

	2-9 Mins.	10-19 Mins.	20-29 Mins.	30-39 Mins.	40-99 Mins.	No Response	MEDIAN NO. MINS.
Government Users (N=101)	10.9%	20.8%	11.9%	6.9%	5.0%	44.6%	18.1
Commercial Users (N=152)	8.6%	22.4%	9.9%	7.9%	7.2%	45.4%	18.4
Educational Users (N=145)	3.4%	29.7%	15.9%	14.5%	7.6%	29.0%	21.5
Other Users (N=74)	9.5%	31.1%	8.1%	9.5%	6.8%	35.1%	17.4

Exhibit 44b. Number of Minutes Spent in Pre-Terminal Work on Average Search, as Reported by Managers, by Organization Type

	2-9 Mins.	10-19 Mins.	20-29 Mins.	30-39 Mins.	40-99 Mins.	No Response	MEDIAN NO. MINS.
Government Users (N=101)	15.8%	26.7%	5.9%	4.0%	3.0%	44.6%	14.4
Commercial Users (N=152)	7.2%	18.4%	4.6%	11.2%	7.9%	50.7%	19.5
Educational Users (N=145)	24.1%	31.0%	4.8%	3.4%	4.1%	32.4%	13.1
Other Users (N=74)	20.3%	27.0%	--	8.1%	5.4%	39.2%	13.8

Exhibit 44c. Number of Minutes Spent in Post-Search Work on Average Search, as Reported by Managers, by Organization Type

It is interesting to speculate on the relationship between costs and time spent at the terminal. Some searchers elect to get off the system quickly with unscreened search hits that will be reviewed for relevance later, off-line. Others refine searches on-line, evaluate for relevance--if they perceive this as their role--and test results against alternate search strategies. An interesting question that we can raise but not yet answer is: What is the relative influence of such variables as searcher experience, users' needs (e.g., for a comprehensive versus narrow search), relative difficulty of the search problem, and cost factors on the searcher's decision as to when a search is completed? Although we do not have data to address this question, we were able to examine the relationship of per-search terminal times to several other study items.

As one might expect, organizations with more on-line experience generally showed a pattern of declining numbers in their median search times. For example, the "at-the-terminal" median time declined from 23.7 minutes for the group with 1 to 6 months of experience to 17.7 minutes for the group with 1 to 3 years of experience. Pre-search time declined from 20 minutes to 18.7 for these same two groups, and post-search time dropped from 16.8 minutes to 14.0 minutes. It is somewhat odd that the group with the most experience (3 years and more) broke the declining pattern and showed higher median numbers: 19.5 minutes for at-the-terminal, 19.0 minutes for pre-terminal, and 15.8 minutes for post-terminal. However, we must recognize that the sheer length of time for which an organization has had access to one or more on-line systems is not necessarily an accurate measure of experience. An accurate measure would need to include the frequency and extent of use and the experience of the particular staff members who are doing the searching.

We also looked at the reported per-search times relative to the volume of searches being done by an organization.

- Those organizations doing between 1 and 19 searches per month spent the following (median) number of minutes per search: 21.9 at the terminal, 25.8 in pre-search activities, and 16.3 in post-search work.

- Those organizations doing between 56 and 999 searches per month spent the following (median) number of minutes per search: 15.6 at the terminal, 15.4 in pre-search activities, and 10.9 in post-search work.

We do not know the cause-effect relationship for these differences, but we can speculate that a two-way relation exists: the pressure of many searches to be done may well be impacting on the time that can be spent on any one search and, at the same time, the more frequent use is helping searchers to increase their skills and efficiency levels.

USAGE AS VIEWED BY THE SEARCHERS

Searchers were asked several questions regarding the amount of time that they were spending at the terminal. For several reasons, including the fact that these questions were not all contained in the same part of the questionnaire, the data cannot be summarized into one simple and comprehensive statement on the amount of time that is being spent at the terminal. The key data on search time are summarized below and discussed further in the following sections*:

> Number of hours spent at the terminal per week:
> Mean = 3.86 hours   Median = 2.1 hours
>
> Number of minutes spent at the terminal per search:
> Mean = 17.3 minutes   Median = 13.7 minutes
>
> Number of on-line searches performed each week:
> Mean = 9.58 searches   Median = 5.2 searches

Several interesting questions must be considered in thinking about search-time data:

- Do most users consider a search to be the interrogation of one data base, or do they consider it to be the interrogation of as many data bases as are needed, or used, to satisfy one search request?

- Where does a search begin and end? For example, is logging-in time included? the entry of mailing information for an off-line printout? the checking of the supplier's electronic mailbox to receive the latest system news or data base currency information? time when the searcher is interrupted to answer a question posed by another staff person or patron? head-scratching time when the searcher is deciding what to do next?

- Does time "at the terminal" include periods when the searcher leaves the terminal to check a vocabulary guide or a user manual? when--as regularly occurs in at least one government agency--the searcher goes home to dinner while a long on-line printout is being produced?

- How many different terminal sessions are required to satisfy a single search request? Some users indicate that they may check their search results with the end-user as an intermediary step before finalizing the search, or that they offer to re-do the search if the end-user feels that it is not exactly what he or she wants. Is the time for such additional terminal sessions considered as part of just one "search"?

---

*The reader may remember that the mean of the products does not necessarily equal the product of the means. Therefore, these three separate items of data cannot be neatly reconciled.

These kinds of uncertainties should be kept in mind as we review the searcher data on 1) number of searches performed; 2) average minutes and iterations per search; and 3) hours spent at the terminal.

Number of Searches Performed Weekly

As indicated in Exhibit 45, the number of searches reportedly carried out each week ranged from none to 322. The effective range was much narrower. Almost 90% of the searchers reported that they personally did from less than one to 30 searches a week. The mean is 9.58 searches. Because of the skewed distribution, the median, 5.2, is more representative of the central tendency in this group.

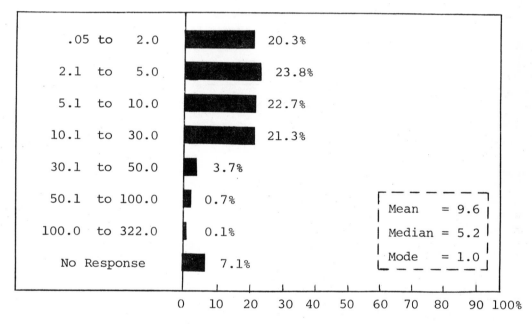

Exhibit 45. Average Number of Searches Performed Per Week by Searchers (N=801)

The reader can see from the data presented in Exhibit 46 that Educational institution searchers were conducting over twice as many searches as Government and Commercial organizations. We also saw some of this same difference in the managers data, but the Government users were second to the Educational users. However, the number of searches reported by searchers should not be compared directly to the monthly total reported by managers because, as indicated in Chapter 2, there are an average of 3.4 searchers per organization and the relative productivity of the searchers participating in this study to other searchers in their organizations is not known.

	NUMBER OF SEARCHES						MEDIAN NUMBER OF SEARCHES
	.05 to 2.0	2.5 to 5.0	5.5 to 10.0	10.5 to 30.0	30.5 to 322.0	No Response	
Government Users (N=192)	13.5%	29.2%	22.4%	21.9%	5.2%	7.8%	5.9
Commercial Users (N=247)	31.6%	27.5%	21.9%	8.5%	0.4%	10.1%	5.4
Educational Users (N=264)	13.6%	16.7%	22.7%	32.6%	8.7%	5.7%	12.9
Other Users (N=98)	2.0%	23.5%	22.4%	25.5%	22.5%	4.1%	10.5

Exhibit 46. Number of Searches Performed Per Week
by Searchers, by Organization Type

Average Minutes Per Search

As noted in the previous chapter, we asked searchers to compare their average
per-search times on the terminal as beginners with the time that it now takes
for them to conduct a search. The importance of on-the-job experience—although the exact period is not defined in this study—seems to be indicated by
the resulting data (see Exhibit 47):

- The mean time per search drops 11.7 minutes between the beginner
  stage and the current level

- The extremes of the range drop from 180 minutes to 150 minutes,
  and from 3 minutes to 1 minute

- There are over twice as many per-search times in the low end of
  the range (in the 3-to-15 minute interval) now than were reported
  for the beginner stage

	MINUTES					
	3-15	16-24	25-33	34-50	51-95	96-180
Time as a Beginner	23.0%	21.2%	23.5%	14.0%	8.5%	9.9%
Time "Now"	56.2%	17.5%	11.5%	5.2%	0.5%	9.1%

Beginner	Now
Range = 3-180	Range = 1-150
Mean = 29.0	Mean = 17.3
Median = 24.7	Median = 13.7
Mode = 30.0	Mode = 10.0

Exhibit 47.   Comparison by Searchers of their Average Search
Time in Minutes as "Beginners" and "Now"

Exhibit 48 provides some comparisons by organization type. Government agency
users, many of whom were, and are, using leased-line, federally subsidized
systems, tend to be more highly represented with Other users in the higher interval of times, i.e., the 24-to-150 minute group, but even more represented
in the lower intervals. Educational institution users tend to be in the low
end of the range, between 1 and 15 minutes, and have the lowest median search
time.

	MINUTES					MEDIAN NUMBER OF MINUTES
	1-9	10-15	16-23	24-150	No Response	
Government Users (N=192)	21.4%	33.3%	10.9%	25.0%	9.4%	14.3
Commercial Users (N=247)	15.4%	36.9%	18.6%	17.0%	12.1%	14.6
Educational Users (N=264)	18.9%	43.6%	21.6%	9.8%	6.1%	13.9
Other Users (N=98)	16.3%	22.4%	12.2%	37.7%	11.2%	19.7

Exhibit 48.   Search Times (in minutes) "Now" (at time study data were
collected), Reported by Searchers, by Organization Type

The direction of the shift made by searchers in the "beginners" and "now" comparison is not apparent in our data, and we must recognize the possibility that some searchers who spent only a few minutes on the terminal as beginners may now be spending more time, particularly as they were able to take on more and more complicated subject searches. It is reasonable to question the skills level required for 1-, 2-, and 3-minute searches, but it is probably not necessary to question their value. Some, perhaps many, of these may be single-term searches--for example, a search on an author's name, on a single subject term, or on a document accession number. Some of these searches may require only a single access point for purposes of finding a citation to confirm bibliographic data for interlibrary loans or document orders.

The searchers' reported times also reflect some of the same patterns discussed in the managers' data with respect to volume and experience of searching. As shown in Exhibit 49, the searchers who were doing over 5 searches per week had lower reported per-search times. As we speculated earlier with the managers' data, the cause-effect relationship for the differences is probably a very complex one.

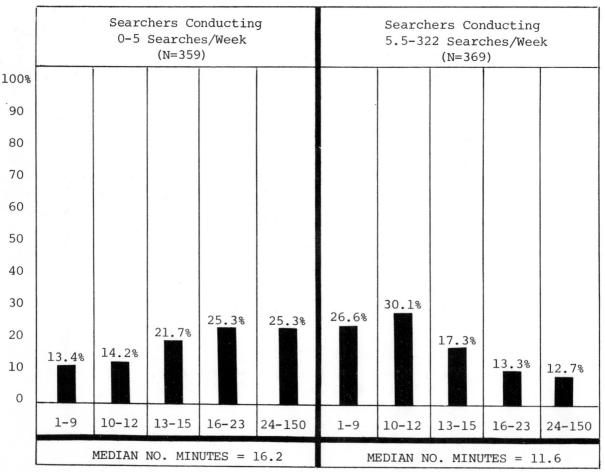

Exhibit 49.   Search Times Reported by Searchers in Two
Different Search-Volume-Per-Week Groups

Experience appears to be somewhat of an influential factor in the overall picture of median search times. We would suspect that a searcher's level of skill with a particular system—and the costs of the system—are the additional influences behind the different percentage rankings for each of the time intervals that are displayed in Exhibit 50.

	1-6 Months Experience (N=171)		6-12 Months Experience (N=223)		1-3 Years Experience (N=343)		3-6 Years Experience (N=58)	
	%	Rank	%	Rank	%	Rank	%	Rank
3-15 Minutes	12.3%	5	20.2%	1	19.0%	2	20.7%	3
16-24 Minutes	15.8%	4	17.0%	4.5	23.3%	1	29.3%	1
25-30 Minutes	19.3%	3	18.4%	2.5	18.4%	3	6.9%	5
31-93 Minutes	20.5%	2	18.4%	2.5	16.3%	4	13.8%	4
94-180 Minutes	21.1%	1	17.0%	4.5	14.6%	5	24.1%	2
MEDIAN NO. OF MINUTES	15.5		14.7		13.6		12.7	

Exhibit 50. Search Times Reported by Searchers in Different Experience Groups (At time study data were collected)

Another consideration in the per-search time statistics is the concept of iterations, i.e., the number of different terminal sessions required to satisfy one search request. The data from the questions that addressed this issue are shown below in Exhibit 51.

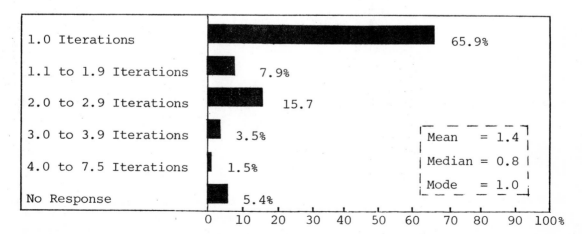

Exhibit 51. Number of Different Terminal Sessions Typically Required to Satisfy On-Line Search Request (N=801)

The data indicate that one terminal session has usually been sufficient to satisfy an on-line search request. When asked to compare this situation with their previous mode of searching (i.e., manual or batch), almost one-third of the respondents indicated the number of iterations was about the same. About 31% indicated that they has no basis for comparison, and only a small group (5.7%) indicated that the number of on-line iterations was greater than the number for manual searches.

Comparisons between manual and on-line searching are inherently difficult, given the possible subtlety of interaction among the variables involved. For example, an on-line system--particularly when accessed at lower baud rates, such as 10 characters per second--can be thought of as providing only a limited "window" into the information, compared to the comprehensive visual scanning that can theoretically take place in the manual process. However, an experienced on-line searcher is likely to have developed compensating strategies, for example, cross-strategy checking and on-line sampling of search results. Any valid comparison between manual and on-line searching would need to take into account the particular data base being searched, and the cost comparisons would need to deal with the very complicated issue of on-line time versus personnel time (either of the searchers or the end-users) in evaluating unscreened search results. Opinion is apparently divided on the role that the intermediary should assume in evaluating search results, as well as on the differences in relevance associated with manual versus on-line searches. Some of these issues are discussed in more detail in Chapter 7, which deals with the search results and the end products.

Exhibit 52 provides data on the number of hours that were being spent at the terminal each week by searchers. Approximately three-fourths of the searchers were spending five hours or less at the terminal each week, and the median number of hours per week is slightly over 2 hours. If we take this median number

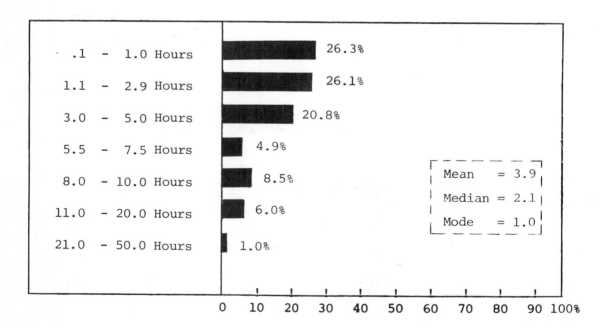

Exhibit 52. Number of Hours Spent by Searchers at the Terminal (N=801)

of hours--or the median number of searches being conducted weekly (5.2 searches) times the median search time (17 minutes)--we can see that the typical searcher has not been spending full time with the on-line services. The searcher may be spending only around 5-10% of his or her time each week. The extent to which these times (plus the pre- and post-terminal times associated with on-line searching) can be absorbed into an individual's weekly schedule depends, of course, on many other factors having to do with the number and nature of other assignments, and productivity expectations of the organization.

The breakdown of data by organization type shown in Exhibit 53 tends to support the data provided by managers relative to the percentages of searches that are performed on-line. Commercial organization users appear to spend a fewer number of hours at the terminal than do other groups and, as we note later in Chapter 11, they also perform a smaller percentage of their searches solely on-line. Educational institutions, on the other hand, have not had a tradition of providing manual or batch-computer-based literature-searching services, and the evidence of more time being spent at the terminal corroborates other data on their greater reliance on the on-line services that are discussed later.

	HOURS					MEDIAN NUMBER OF HOURS
	0.1 to 1.0	1.1 to 2.9	3.0 to 7.9	8.0 to 50.0	No Response	
Government Users (N=192)	17.7%	26.6%	28.6%	19.8%	7.3%	3.4
Commercial Users (N=247)	40.0%	30.8%	15.8%	3.7%	9.7%	1.4
Educational Users (N=264)	18.2%	22.7%	31.4%	23.1%	4.6%	3.1
Other Users (N=98)	29.6%	21.4%	28.6%	16.3%	4.1%	1.3

Exhibit 53. Number of Hours Spent Weekly at the Terminal by Searchers, by Organization Type

Length of Time for Typical Terminal Sessions

We were generally interested in learning how long the typical terminal sessions were. The median number of minutes spent at one terminal session, i.e., at a typical sitting, independent of the number of searches being performed, was 30.2.

The distributions and medians by organization type are shown in Exhibit 54.

	MINUTES					MEDIAN NUMBER OF MINUTES
	1-15	16-29	30-40	41-270	No Response	
Government Users (N=192)	16.1%	17.7%	28.6%	33.3%	4.3%	35.4
Commercial Users (N=247)	29.6%	23.9%	19.4%	19.8%	7.3%	25.8
Educational Users (N=264)	26.5%	20.1%	26.9%	22.3%	4.2%	30.5
Other Users (N=98)	18.4%	19.4%	32.7%	26.5%	3.0%	33.6

Exhibit 54.   Length of Time Spent by Searchers, by Organization
Type, at One Terminal Session

These data show that searchers typically do about two searches in each terminal
session. However, the patterns in these distributions for each organizational-
type user group should not be associated solely with the data on per-search
time and number of searches being performed. The length of a terminal session
is also affected by such elements as scheduling approaches and searchers' interactions with end-users. Some of these additional considerations are discussed
in the next section.

ACCESS TIME REQUIREMENTS OF USERS AND THEIR SCHEDULING PRACTICES

The times during which the on-line services were available to users in late
1974, when the questionnaire data were gathered, are shown in Exhibit 55. Some
of the suppliers have a variable schedule of hours on different days of the
week, but these variations are not included in this display

This Exhibit also shows the changes that have occurred over the intervening
months since the field study. For example, Lockheed and SDC have both expanded
their service into the early morning hours to provide more convenient access to
overseas users.

DAYS PER WEEK OF SERVICE PROVIDED			HOURS PER DAY OF SERVICE PROVIDED		
Days	No. of Suppliers "Then" (Fall 1974)	No. of Suppliers "Now" (Fall 1975)	Hours	No. of Suppliers "Then" (Fall 1974)	No. of Suppliers "Now" (Fall 1975)
5	9	7	7	1	–
6	–	2	8	2	3
7	1	1	9 – 10	3	2
			11 – 12	2	1
			More than 12	2	4

Exhibit 55. Operational Access Schedules of On-Line Suppliers "Then" (Fall 1974) and "Now" (Fall 1975) (N=10)

The actual amount of access time required by users can be derived in a general way from data provided at both organizational and individual-user levels. As discussed earlier in this Chapter, managers reported that the typical number of searches conducted per month, using the median, is about 30. If we take into account the managers' data indicating the typical per-search time to be about 15 minutes, again, using the median and using 21 working days in a month, it appears that the typical organization requires a little over 20 minutes of access time each day.

Another measure of need can be determined from the response of the searchers to several questions concerning their levels of use, data that were reported earlier in this Chapter. Taking the median figure of two hours per week being spent at the terminal, the typical searcher needs about 24 minutes of access per day.

As the reader might suspect, these typical levels of use are not directly correlated with the searchers' perceived needs for access time, which we discuss next.

User Preferences in Access Time

Searchers were asked to indicate the number of days per week that are required or adequate to meet their needs. They were also asked to indicate the number of hours per day that are needed. Data from these two questions are presented in Exhibits 56 and 57. Although the searchers report that they do not use all systems an equal amount of time, the same requirements for access time are generally specified for all systems that are used.

	1-2 Days	3-4 Days	5 Days	6-7 Days	No Response
System 1 (N=801)	6.9%	5.5%	76.3%	7.1%	4.2%
System 2 (N=339)	8.2%	6.8%	71.7%	3.9%	9.4%
System 3 (N=136)	11.0%	10.3%	58.1%	5.9%	14.7%
System 4 (N=31)	3.2%	9.7%	67.7%	12.9%	6.5%

Exhibit 56. Days Per Week of Service Preferred by Searchers on All Systems

	1-4 Hours	5-8 Hours	Over 8 Hours	No Response
System 1 (N=801)	32.1%	45.9%	16.0%	6.0%
System 2 (N=339)	34.8%	42.8%	10.3%	12.1%
System 3 (N=136)	36.0%	33.8%	9.6%	20.6%
System 4 (N=31)	54.9%	32.3%	6.5%	6.5%

Exhibit 57. Hours Per Day of Service Preferred by Searchers on All Systems (N=801)

The majority of on-line searchers prefer a five-day-week service, and 5 to 8
hours of service per day. Commercial-organization users are somewhat more
willing than those in the other types of organizations to accept from one to
four hours of service per day. Perhaps this is because Commercial organization
users are generally doing fewer searches than other kinds of organizations, particularly Educational institutions. The evening and weekend service hours of
academic libraries are probably the main reason why 26% of the Educational-
institution users report the need for over 8 hours of access daily.

It is evident, therefore, that flexibility--the ability to go to the system
at any time--is the key element in the on-line searchers' preferences.

Scheduling Practices of Searchers

The requirement for flexibility can be better understood in the context of the
searchers' responses to a questionnaire item regarding their approaches to
scheduling time at the terminal. Searchers find time-flexibility to be either
necessary (e.g., because of their having other jobs to do) or highly desirable
(e.g., because of the fluctuations in requests, load-balancing requirements
within the library staff, or service to drop-in clients). The variation in
current scheduling practices of searchers is displayed in Exhibit 58.

	FREQUENCY OF USE		
	Most/ Sometimes	Rarely/ Never	No Response
1. I go to the terminal when-ever I need to.	75.2%	10.5%	14.4%
2. I go to the terminal when-ever a request is processed to the point of being ready for the computer search.	71.7%	12.8%	15.5%
3. I have to coordinate my scheduling of time at the terminal with other staff members or colleagues in other areas of my organization.	48.7%	38.2%	13.1%
4. I make appointments with a client or colleague for a specific time.	31.5%	51.3%	17.1%
5. I schedule, in advance, the time that I will spend at the terminal on a given day.	23.8%	57.9%	18.2%

Exhibit 58. Relative Use of Different On-Line Terminal Scheduling
Approaches by Searchers (N=801)

To summarize, most searchers tend to go to the terminal whenever they feel they need to or whenever a request is processed to the point of being ready for the computer search. The searcher does not typically have to make an appointment with a client or colleague for a specific time, or schedule in advance the time he or she plans to spend at the terminal on a given day, except, perhaps, to avoid finding someone else using the terminal or the retrieval service. This typically occurs where users share an access password or a terminal with other organizations.

A breakdown on scheduling practices, by organization type, is presented in Exhibit 59.

		Most/Some Of The Time	Rarely/ Never	No Response
USE TERMINAL WHENEVER REQUEST READY FOR SEARCH	Government Users (N=192)	68.8%	12.0%	19.3%
	Commercial Users (N=247)	69.6%	12.1%	18.2%
	Educational Users (N=264)	73.1%	13.4%	13.3%
	Other Users (N=98)	77.6%	12.2%	10.2%
USE TERMINAL WHENEVER NECESSARY	Government Users (N=192)	76.0%	8.9%	15.1%
	Commercial Users (N=247)	80.2%	6.9%	13.0%
	Educational Users (N=264)	68.2%	15.2%	16.6%
	Other Users (N=98)	77.6%	9.2%	13.3%
MUST COORDINATE USE WITH OTHER PERSONNEL	Government Users (N=192)	51.0%	34.9%	14.1%
	Commercial Users (N=247)	40.1%	44.5%	15.4%
	Educational Users (N=264)	58.3%	29.6%	12.1%
	Other Users (N=98)	38.8%	50.0%	11.2%
SCHEDULE TERMINAL TIME IN ADVANCE	Government Users (N=192)	21.9%	56.8%	21.4%
	Commercial Users (N=247)	20.2%	59.1%	20.6%
	Educational Users (N=264)	29.5%	55.3%	15.2%
	Other Users (N=98)	19.4%	63.3%	17.3%
MAKE APPOINTMENTS	Government Users (N=192)	30.2%	49.5%	20.3%
	Commercial Users (N=247)	25.5%	56.7%	17.8%
	Educational Users (N=264)	39.0%	45.8%	15.2%
	Other Users (N=98)	28.6%	55.1%	17.3%

Exhibit 59. On-Line Terminal Scheduling Practices Used by Searchers, by Organization Type

The variations among the different groups are not great, but those differences that are revealed suggest that working environments also impinge on the scheduling approaches. For example, Commercial organizations are apparently less likely to work by appointment with clients or colleagues than the Educational users. The appointment approach may be the Educational institution user's way of controlling overloads on university and college library staff, or it may be a necessity resulting from the fact that the end-users are often not located close to the library.

In general, the on-line suppliers are meeting the requirement for flexibility with full-day, full-week access, and we would expect that the amount of access provided to users will continue to expand over the ensuing months and years.

6. SELECTION, ACCESS, AND USE OF ON-LINE SYSTEMS

It was not the purpose of this study to conduct a comparative evaluation of current on-line bibliographic systems. The purpose was, rather, to provide a framework for suppliers to assess the on-line users' general perceptions of needs and their preferences and practices. Such an assessment, we believe, can contribute much to the more rapid and rational development of on-line retrieval systems and services.

It is in this context that we asked searchers and, to a lesser extent, managers questions on how they use the systems. In this chapter, we summarize data from both questionnaires in three main areas:

- Selection of Systems by Multiple-System Users

- Access Methods Used

- Use of Various System Features

The intention of the project staff in this chapter, and in the next one on data base use and search results, is to provide a description of how users are using the on-line systems. Problems that users are having in these various areas are described later in a separate chapter.

SELECTION OF SYSTEMS BY MULTIPLE-SYSTEM USERS

In accepting a reference question from a client, the information intermediary has several preliminary things to decide: 1) whether the client's request can be fulfilled in part or wholly by an on-line search; 2) which system (and data bases) to use in accomplishing the search, if on-line is appropriate; and 3) which method to use in accessing the system they have selected. All users do not have to make all of these decisions, but to have a complete picture of on-line searching, one should consider each of them.

After determining that a search should be performed on-line, about 42% of the searchers--those who have access to more than one system--have the next decision to make: which of the two or more systems they should use. Although both decisions in this selection process appear to be made primarily by searchers, some involvement--both direct and indirect--by end-users has been reported.

End-User Involvement

A majority of the managers indicated that their end-users know when a search is to be performed on-line. However, organizations vary widely in the extent of end-user involvement in the actual selection process. The variation probably stems as much from the policies and procedures of the information service facility as it does from the preferences of the end-users.

We asked the managers two basic questions about end-user involvement:

- Do your users ask for searches to be performed by one process or another, i.e., do they ask specifically for either a computerized or a manual search?

- Do users ask specifically that a search be run on a certain on-line system?

The resulting answers are discussed in the following sections.

Requests by End-Users for Specific Searching Processes

Preferences are developing among information consumers with respect to the process(es) by which searches for them are being performed. A majority of managers (55.1%) reported that end-users request a particular process to be used. This is particularly true in Educational institutions, as shown in Exhibit 60.

	Yes	No	No Response
Government Users (N=101)	52.5%	43.6%	6.9%
Commercial Users (N=152)	34.2%	61.2%	4.6%
Educational Users (N=145)	70.3%	25.5%	4.2%
Other Users (N=74)	52.7%	35.1%	8.1%

Exhibit 60. Responses by Managers to the Question: Do end-users request a particular process?

Why there should be greater expression of preferences within Educational institutions is not entirely clear, because we do not know what options, other than on-line searching, are available to users in these institutions. Many academic institutions, unlike Commercial and Government organizations, do not have a tradition of providing literature-searching services, and we do not know from our study data whether the academic libraries have established or expanded manual or batch-mode literature-searching services as a complement to the on-line searches.

Those who responded "Yes" to the question on user specification of the search
process also indicated that end-users generally express a preference for one
particular process. Of those managers who indicated that their end-users
request a specific process, 62% said that their end-users generally expressed
a preference for one particular process. Of those who actually indicated that
on-line was the expressed choice, the percentages, by organizational type, were:

- Government Agency Users: 49.1%

- Commercial Organization Users: 53.8%

- Educational Institution Users: 73.5%

- Other Organization Users: 51.3%

Only two respondents indicated that the expressed preference was generally for
a batch or manual search, and a few did not specify any particular process.

Requests by End-Users for Specific Systems

In the questionnaire, we asked managers about the ways, if any, in which
end-users were phrasing their search requests differently since the introduction of on-line services. In the context of that question, the managers were
asked to indicate the relative frequency with which end-users requested that
their searches be conducted on a specific system:

Most Users	Some Users	Few Users	None	No Response
15.0%	24.7%	11.4%	26.9%	21.8%

The responses indicate that the individuals who request a specific system are
somewhat fewer than those requesting a certain process, such as on-line searching. As shown in Exhibit 61 below, Educational organization users reported the
highest level of system specification, and Commercial organization users reported the lowest.

The indirect involvement of end-users also needs to be considered, particularly
since clients of libraries and information centers are frequently given the
option of selecting systems and data bases to be used from a sheet describing
the services and prices. A special study would be required to determine how
end-users make these judgments, but at least one clue to end-users' behavior
came out in the interviews. One academic librarian indicated that end-users
typically select the cheapest search, even if it means limiting their resources
to only one system, to one data base, or to a small set of data bases. Whereas
convenience has traditionally been one of the major factors, if not the major
factor, in information use, cost factors may be superseding it in the new fee-
for-service environment that on-line systems are helping to engender.

	Most/Some Users	Few/No Users	No Response
Government Users (N=101)	44.6%	29.7%	25.7%
Commercial Users (N=152)	27.6%	48.7%	23.7%
Educational Users (N=145)	53.1%	32.4%	14.5%
Other Users (N=74)	32.4%	40.5%	27.0%

Exhibit 61.   Report by Managers, by Organization Type, on the Question: Do users now ask specifically that a search be run on a certain on-line system?

Searchers' Involvement

About three-fourths of the 339 multiple-system searchers reported that they do not use all systems an equal amount of time. Searchers indicated that there are several reasons why they elect to use one system over another, and why they use one system more than another. These reasons are shown in Exhibit 62. It is evident that the predominant factor in system choice is whether it offers access to more of the data bases that the searcher needs. Also very important is whether the user learned to use the system first and feels more comfortable with it. On the other hand, system reliability and quality customer support seem relatively unimportant in accounting for differences in system use.

In a subsidiary question, the searchers were asked to go back over all the reasons that they had checked and to select the one most important reason. About 95% of the searchers responded to this item, with the following general rankings:

Rank 1: User Needs

Rank 2: Others

Rank 3: Personal Preferences

Rank 4: System/Service Capabilities and Features

The more specific rankings within this overall grouping of searcher priorities are shown in Exhibit 63 below. Again, data base selection predominates, with system familiarity an important additional reason for differences in system use.

	Multiple-system Searchers Using Systems Unequal Amount of Time (N=259)		By Organizational Type							
			Government Users (N=57)		Commercial Users (N=96)		Educational Users (N=81)		Other Users (N=25)	
	%	Rank	%	Rank	%	Rank	%	Rank	%	Rank
A. Learned to use the system first; feel most comfortable with it.	45.1%	2	43.9%	2	53.1%	2	42.0%	3	44.0%	3
B. Offers access to more of the data bases needed.	78.0%	1	75.4%	1	86.5%	1	79.0%	1	48.0%	1.5
C. Greater range of capabilities.	30.1%	3	21.1%	6	44.8%	3	21.0%	6	24.0%	9
D. Better response times.	27.0%	6.5	22.8%	4	37.5%	6	17.3%	8	28.0%	8
E. Supplier offers better customer support.	20.8%	11	12.3%	11.5	30.2%	8	16.0%	11	16.0%	10
F. Uses an interactive language: easier to understand and remember.	29.3%	4	21.1%	6	41.7%	4.5	17.3%	8	40.0%	4.5
G. Supplier's reference materials (e.g., users' manuals) helped more in understanding system features.	27.0%	6.5	12.3%	11.5	41.7%	4.5	17.3%	8	36.0%	6
H. Available on a schedule more convenient to user.	27.4%	5	31.6%	3	26.0%	10	19.8%	4.5	48.0%	1.5
I. Better reliability (i.e., least down time).	13.1%	12	14.0%	10	22.9%	11	2.5%	12	8.0%	11
J. Better structuring by supplier of data bases for on-line use.	23.6%	9	15.8%	9	32.3%	7	16.0%	10	32.0%	7
K. Supplier included greater number of years in data bases.	22.8%	10	21.1%	6	28.1%	9	19.8%	4.5	16.0%	8
L. Others.	25.5%	8	17.5%	8	11.5%	12	43.2%	2	40.0%	4.5

Exhibit 62. Reasons Indicated by Multiple-System Searchers as to
Why Systems Are Not Used an Equal Amount of Time

I.	**User Needs** B. Offers access to more of the data bases needed.	47.9%
II.	**Other**	12.7%
III.	**Personal Preference** A. Learned to use system first; feel most comfortable with it.	8.9%
IV.	**System/Service Features** F. Uses an interactive language: easier to understand and remember.	5.0%
	K. Supplier included greater number of years in data bases.	5.0%
	C. Greater range of capabilities.	3.9%
	J. Better structuring by supplier of data bases for on-line use.	3.5%
	D. Better response times.	2.7%
	H. Available on a schedule more convenient to user.	2.7%
	G. Supplier's reference materials (e.g., users' manuals) helped more in understanding system features.	1.5%
	E. Supplier offers better customer support.	0.8%
	I. Better reliability (i.e., least down time).	-

Exhibit 63.   Ranking by Multiple-System Searchers of Most Important Reasons for Differences in System Use (N=259)

The frequency of Other reasons is particularly important in this question: 1) because of its relatively high ranking; 2) because several reasons not included in the formatted response choices were given by the searchers; and 3) because some of the Other responses that overlap with the structural response choices help to clarify the context in which other searchers may have been responding. Data on the Other reasons are grouped and summarized below in Exhibit 64. Where appropriate, we have given verbatim quotes from respondents; the number of responses is shown in parentheses.

These data highlight the importance of cost and suggest that it might have been an even more important factor, had it been given as a structured response choice. Contrary to the opinion of the respondent who said, "It costs less, which seems a most glaring or deliberate omission," the omission was an oversight, and not a deliberate one. None of our staff or our pre-test users noticed this omission, nor, surprisingly, did any of our reviewers, all of whom are operators of on-line services. The SDC project team fully expected that the two top choices of the respondents would be breadth of relevant data bases offered and "first system used." Only with the increase in availability of the same data bases on different systems, and with price differentials developing in early 1975, after the data were collected, has the importance of the cost factor become so clearly established.

It was not untypical for users to have several reasons for a particular system preference. As one user indicated:

> "We use one system more than others because it's cheaper; it ranks hits in order of importance for display; it can search abstracts and full-text documents; and it's Canadian."

One consideration to be taken into account in reviewing system-preference criteria is the experience of the users. New on-line users may have evaluation criteria different from those of veteran users, and new users may shift their criteria as they progress through successive levels of experience. Some of these differences are illustrated in Exhibit 65.

Although all users, regardless of their experience, concur on the importance of the same first two items that we saw earlier, interesting inversions occur thereafter. The third-most-selected choice of the beginners is Reason F ("It uses an interactive language that is easier to understand and remember"); of the 6-to-12-month group, it is Reason C ("It has a greater range of capabilities"); of the 1-to-3-year group, it is "Other," which, as we learned, covers among several reasons the cost-related factors; and the most experienced group selects Reason J ("The supplier has done a better job of structuring the data bases for on-line use").

We should not underestimate the complexity of system-preference behavior, nor should we expect it to be unravelled within the next few years. The dynamic state of development in the on-line services suggests that any final conclusions about current or future criteria for user preferences would be premature.

COST (29)

"Is cheaper."

"We pay annual rate and system is cheaper per search."

"We pay on contract basis with unlimited usage."

"Available on monthly subscription rather than by hourly rate."

"Supplier is closer and therefore we pay no telephone costs."

"Use more because it is subsidized and therefore cheaper."

"Terminal is hard-wired and no dialup is required."

"Annual subscription covers unlimited on-line access to the primary data base."

"Allows unlimited number of statements for each search."

"Searchers on first system are free, whereas the patron is charged for citations from the second system. More requests for first system as it is government-subsidized."

"Lower cost or no cost to user."

USER NEEDS (22)

"Subject coverage is most relevant to our users' needs."

"Contains data bases in my library and is a location tool for the collection."

"System's data bases are better for most of our requests."

"Content of other systems is peripheral in scope."

"System provides access to data bases requested by more patrons."

SYSTEM/SERVICE-RELATED REASONS (10)

"Logon procedure is much simpler and faster."

"More coherent, easier-to-use manual format." (2)

"Searches can be done in shorter time because several terms can be entered in same search statement."

"Supplier is more knowledgeable about data bases."

"More control over output."

"Data bases accessible all day."

"Familiarity with the program language and features of a particular system because of particularly heavy use of one data base."

"Preferred system has disadvantage of not allowing author entry to test indexing of known key articles."

"Allows use of parentheses in Boolean statements, and am more confident and efficient."

DATA-BASE-RELATED REASONS (4)

"Has free-language terms." (2)

"Has controlled vocabulary."

"Data bases not available anywhere else."

MISCELLANEOUS (3)

"Have not yet received training for System II."

"No choice in the matter."

"Terminal is easier to get to."

Exhibit 64. "Other" Reasons Given by Multiple-System Searchers
for Using Systems Unequal Amounts of Time

	Experience Groups							
	1 to 6 Mos. (N=60)		6 to 12 Mos. (N=223)		1 to 3 Yrs. (N=160)		3 to 6+ Yrs. (N=25)	
	%	Rank	%	Rank	%	Rank	%	Rank
A. I learned to use the system first and feel most comfortable with it.	36.7%	2	33.3%	2	36.3%	2	44.0%	2
B. It offers access to more of the data bases I need.	43.3%	1	60.0%	1	65.6%	1	68.0%	1
C. It has a greater range of capabilities.	21.7%	4.5	28.9%	3	20.0%	6.5	28.0%	5
D. It has better response time.	15.0%	8.5	25.6%	5	20.0%	6.5	28.0%	5
E. The supplier offers better user support.	13.3%	10	20.0%	7.5	14.4%	11	24.0%	7.5
F. It uses an interactive language that is easier to understand and remember.	28.3%	3	23.3%	6	20.0%	6.5	8.0%	11.5
G. The supplier's reference materials helped more in understanding system features.	18.3%	7	27.8%	4	22.5%	4	8.0%	11.5
H. It is available on a schedule that is more convenient to me.	21.7%	4.5	18.9%	9	20.0%	6.5	24.0%	7.5
I. It has better reliability.	13.3%	10	8.9%	12	8.8%	12	16.0%	10
J. Supplier has done a better job of structuring the data bases for on-line use.	20.0%	6	15.6%	10	16.3%	10	36.0%	3
K. Supplier has included a greater number of years in data bases.	15.0%	8.5	20.0%	7.5	16.9%	9	20.0%	9
L. Other	13.3%	10	13.3%	11	24.0%	3	28.0%	5

Exhibit 65. Reasons for Unequal Use of Systems, Reported by Searchers in Different Experience Groups

ACCESS METHODS USED

Several searchers reported that the cost of communications (i.e., the data transmission method by which they access the suppliers' computers) is an important consideration in their decision to use one system more than another. A variety of data transmission, or telecommunications, arrangements, exist for users to access the different computers involved in this study. Although all users do not have all options available to them, the growth of these options has been an extremely important factor in the broad-based acceptance and growth of on-line bibliographic services during the 70's.

Three major kinds of access methods are used:

- Direct Dial: This includes the use of voice- and data-traffic lines of local telephone calls, long distance, commercial calls, WATS, and FTS. Searchers use regular telephones (or dataphones) in their offices and call special telephone numbers that connect them directly with the supplier's computer.

- "Indirect" Dial Through a Network: This includes the use of special data-transmission systems, such as ARPANET, Tymshare's TYMNET, and the Canadian networks (INFODAT or DATAROUTE). Searchers dial special telephone numbers, in their cities or in a nearby city, and are connected to an intervening computer of the data network, which switches them into the host computer that they request.

- Leased (Dedicated) Lines: Users' terminals are generally "hardwired"-- directly hooked--to the host computer, and no telephone calls are required.

A list of the methods available to access the computers of the suppliers involved in this study is provided in Exhibit 66.

	Number of Suppliers "Then" (1974)	Number of Suppliers "Now" (1975)
Leased Line	7	7
Dialup (including local, long-distance, WATS, FTS)	6	8
Communications Networks (TYMNET, ARPANET, or DATAROUTE/INFODAT)	5	5

Exhibit 66. Telecommunications Methods Used to Access On-Line Suppliers "Then" (Fall, 1974) and "Now" (Fall, 1975) (N=10)

The most widely used access method is dialup through the Tymshare communications network (TYMNET). This is not suprising, given the relative preponderance of NLM, SDC, and Lockheed users in the population of respondents. It is instructive, however, to review some of the other methods used across the 472 organizations, as shown in Exhibit 67. The data in this Exhibit include some multiple responses, because organizations can use more than one method. For example, an organization with WATS lines into the supplier's city may permit its on-line users to use this method during certain hours of the day but, at other times, require that they make the hookup through Tymshare or a long-distance call.

	System 1 (N=472)		System 2 (N=236)		System 3 (N=117)		System 4 (N=50)	
	%	Rank	%	Rank	%	Rank	%	Rank
Through Direct Dial to the Supplier's Computer:								
Local call	13.6%	3	10.2%	3	12.0%	3	12.0%	2
Long distance (commercial)	9.5%	4	11.9%	2	12.8%	2	14.0%	1
Leased line	14.2%	2	7.2%	5	9.4%	4	10.0%	3
WATS	9.1%	5	7.6%	4	7.7%	5	6.0%	4.5
FTS	4.7%	6	3.8%	6	3.4%	6	6.0%	4.5
Through a Network to the Supplier's Computer:								
ARPANET	0.6%	8	0.8%	7.5	0.8%	7	--	-
DATAROUTE/INFODAT	1.7%	7	0.8%	7.5	0.2%	8	--	-
TYMSHARE	63.1%	1	67.4%	1	59.0%	1	5.5%	6

Exhibit 67. Relative Use of Telecommunication Methods in Accessing On-Line Systems

Those respondents who use a network for accessing the on-line systems were asked how they accessed the network, e.g., by local call, long-distance, or WATS. For over 60 percent of this subset of respondents, only a local call is needed to access the network that they use for System 1. Another 15% are able to make their connections--at least part of the time--through a WATS line. However, 25% must first dial long-distance to get to the network. For example, a user in Peoria, Illinois, has to dial Kansas City, Missouri, or Chicago, Illinois, to get into the network. Thus they pay two communications costs.

In general, differences among telecommunications alternatives are probably more important from the standpoint of costs than of any technical considerations that impact on the on-line users.

It is clear that direct dialup service, particularly in combination with the Tymshare network, has been largely responsible not only for the growth and acceptance of on-line services but, as well, for the use of multiple systems by organizations throughout the world. As more access points are added, as new telecommunications systems become available, and as communications costs continue to decline, on-line information services are certain to gain even more widespread acceptance.

USE OF VARIOUS SYSTEM FEATURES

Major system features were grouped in three different questionnaire items, two of which are discussed immediately below: 1) system features that are used in entering searches; and 2) system features that are used to aid the user in some way. Searchers were asked to indicate their reactions to different system features and capabilities and to report on any significant problems that they were encountering. (The report on problems is provided in Chapter 9.) The reader who is not familiar with all the systems that are involved in this study should realize that there are probably as many similarities as differences among the general kinds of features that the systems provide. As we mentioned in the introduction to this report, some of the systems even come from the same program "family." Differences in computer resources, peripheral hardware, staffing, and philosophies of on-line system design contribute as much to the differences among the services as the retrieval programs themselves. Systems are converging more and more on a basic repertoire of capabilities, and it is the way in which each capability is implemented that produces some of the major differences.

We would like to recognize, at this point, the contribution of Edwin B. Parker, Stanford University, and Tom Martin, now at the University of Southern California, to the development of these lists of features. We used as a departure point the framework that they used in evaluating several systems in their study, which was reported in A Feature Analysis of Interactive Retrieval Systems.* We also

---

*Martin, Thomas H. and Edwin B. Parker. A Feature Analysis of Interactive Retrieval Systems. 1974. Stanford University, Institute for Communication Research. (Report SU-COMM-ICR-741.)

requested that all on-line suppliers review the features carefully because we were aware that neutral, value-free terminology that we were using to describe the features might make it difficult for respondents to recognize a given feature on the system(s) with which they were familiar.

Search-Input-Related Features

Respondents were given a list of features that are central to the execution of a search. Each of these features is listed in Exhibit 68 below, and the number of on-line suppliers making these features available at the time of the field study ("Then") and the number providing them at the present time ("Now") is also shown.

The percentages and their associated ranks for each of nine searching-related features are reported in Exhibit 69. We asked all searchers to select a response from each of the three Importance choices: Very Useful, Useful, and Not At All Useful. We asked that only the subset of searchers who were familiar with a particular feature respond to its Level-of-Use choices: Heavily Used, Sometimes Used, or Rarely or Never Used. For clarity, we have presented data only for the two extreme positions of Importance and of Use. The percentages of respondents who reported Use information are provided in the far right-hand column of the chart so that the reader can also assess the searchers' level of familiarity with particular features.

There appears to be a strong correlation between levels of importance and use (Most Important/Most Used). The Boolean operators are clearly number one in both cases, and the related feature of being able to combine terms with one or more operators in one instruction received the second highest percentages. The first inversion occurs in the 7th and 8th percentage rankings, with Stored Search (i.e., the ability to save a search strategy that has been entered into the system and to recall it for use at a later time) being considered more important than, but not used as much as, word-proximity operators.

Some readers may believe that the Boolean Operators response choice was an obvious one for the majority of users to make, and that nothing particularly new has been learned from the survey data. We would agree that this number-one choice is not very surprising. However, there are some observers of the on-line scene who have argued that on-line systems are generally being used in a very unsophisticated manner, and that simple author searches and single-term searches are more the rule than the exception. The clustering of high percentages around capabilities that relate to the Boolean processes does not support that view.

The correlation between Least Important and Least Used is not as high as that between Most Important and Most Used. The least important feature is the relational operators, but the least used is the stored search. We would hesitate to recommend these priorities to the on-line suppliers without some caveats, the most important being that these data represent the views of searchers at a given point of time. The technology of on-line systems has

	No. of Suppliers "Then" (1974)	No. of Suppliers "Now" (1975)
The system allows a user to:		
1. Truncate or enter word-stems to retrieve on all possible suffixes.	9	9
2. Specify the data element (i.e., field or category) from which the term is to be searched.	10	10
3. Use relational operators (greater than, less than, between).	4	4
4. Use word-proximity operators.	4	4
5. Use all Boolean operators (AND, OR, AND NOT).	10	10
6. Combine terms with one or more operators in one instruction to the system.	8	8
7. Incorporate previous searches, by number, in new search statements or entries.	7	7
8. Store a search that can be run again at a later time.	4	6
9. Search character strings sequentially or serially in fields or categories that are not directly searchable.	3	4

Exhibit 68. Availability Report from the 10 On-Line Suppliers on Search-Related Features

	IMPORTANCE (N=801)				USE (N=VARIABLE)				
	Very Useful		Not At All Useful		Heavily Used		Rarely or Never Used		Percent Responding to Use Items
	%	Rank	%	Rank	%	Rank	%	Rank	
The system allows user to:									
1. Truncate or enter word-stems to retrieve on all possible suffixes.	55.8%	4	2.0%	7	35.6%	4	8.5%	7	95.0%
2. Specify data element (i.e., field or category) from which the term is to be searched.	43.9%	5	5.1%	6	31.6%	5	10.7%	6	94.1%
3. Use relational operators (greater than, less than, between).	12.9%	9	28.7%	1	4.5%	9	32.1%	2	83.3%
4. Use word-proximity operators.	22.6%	8	10.6%	3	16.1%	7	19.2%	3	80.5%
5. Use all Boolean operators (AND, OR, AND NOT).	93.5%	1	–	9	93.9%	1	0.3%	9	98.0%
6. Combine terms with one or more operators in one instruction to the system.	74.7%	2	1.6%	8	68.8%	2	3.8%	8	94.9%
7. Incorporate previous searches, by number, in new search statements or entries.	58.9%	3	6.6%	5	48.2%	3	14.4%	4	92.6%
8. Store a search that can be run again at a later time.	40.0%	7	12.7%	2	6.4%	8	33.1%	1	91.0%
9. Search character strings sequentially or serially in fields or categories that are not directly searchable.	40.2%	6	7.6%	4	20.6%	6	13.3%	5	85.3%

Exhibit 69. Levels of Importance and Use Associated with Various
Search-Related System Features

been changing rapidly and, with it, user preferences for various system features. While the stored-search capability did not score high on either Importance or Use, we need to interpret this finding in the light of two considerations. First, the stored-search capability was a relatively new feature on some systems at the time the data were collected, which means that all searchers would not necessarily have had actual experience with it (even though some 90% claimed familiarity with this feature). Second, this kind of feature may be important to users when it is needed, but the frequency of that need may be lower than the need for other, more basic capabilities.

An abbreviated display of the organizational-type analysis, with rankings only for three user groups, is provided in Exhibit 70. All three user groups agreed that Boolean operators and the ability to combine terms in one instruction were the most important search-related features. (Dashes in the Not-At-All-Useful column indicate that none of the three organization user groups thought that Boolean Operators was least important.) The inversions occur at the third percentage ranking: more Educational organization users selected Feature 7--the ability to incorporate previous searches by number in new search entries--than the Government and Commercial users, who selected the truncation feature. We suspect that the several differences shown in rankings across groups are due both to differences in organization environments and to differences in the system or systems that any one group most typically uses.

Although searchers did not supply many additional features in the Other response category, their choices, provided in Exhibit 71, are interesting to review.

The features identified by respondents in the Other category include those currently available on at least one system, and also those that were not available on any system in late 1975, i.e., the users' "wish-list" items.

Several items that were not available on any system at the time of the survey are asterisked. These include left-hand truncation (to retrieve terms with variable prefixes) and capability to impose a "weighting" factor on terms included within a search, but after the search is completed. The "weighting" concept referred to by the respondents is really a system/data base feature. On some data bases, developers have provided "central" or "most important" concept indicators, such as the asterisked subject index term. The weighted term retrieves a subset of all citations--presumably, the citations for which the term is of central importance--that are posted to that particular term. Although the system must be able to accommodate this kind of feature, it is data-base dependent and not applicable to all data bases.

The "exploding" capability is also associated with certain data bases, specifically those that have a hierarchically structured vocabulary. The user enters a generic term (or a number representing that term's class), and the system, in effect, automatically ORs all subordinate terms in that hierarchy. In other hierarchically structured data bases, the developers have elected to autopost, i.e., automatically index to broader terms for every specific term that is used as an index term, so that the searcher does not need to enter both specific and generic terms. The point of this comparison is to emphasize what

Search-Related System Features	Importance						Use					
	Very Useful			Not At All Useful			Heavily Used			Rarely or Never Used		
	Gov't. (N= 192)	Comm. (N= 247)	Educ. (N= 264)	Gov't. (N= 192)	Comm. (N= 247)	Educ. (N= 264)	Gov't. (N=Variable)	Comm.	Educ.	Gov't. (N=Variable)	Comm.	Educ.
1. Truncation	3	3	4.5	7.5	8	6	5	4	5	6	7	4
2. Specifying data elements	5	6	7	6	5	7.5	3	5	4	7	5	7
3. Relational operators	9	9	9	1	1	1	9	8	9	2	2	2
4. Word-proximity operators	8	8	8	2	4	2	7	6	7	4	4	3
5. Boolean operators	1	1	1	-	-	-	1	1	1	8.5	9	9
6. Combining terms in one instruction	2	2	2	7.5	7	7.5	2	2	2	8.5	8	8
7. Incorporating previous searches, by number, in new searches	4	4	3	5	3	5	4	3	3	3	3	6
8. Stored search	6	7	4.5	3	2	4	8	9	8	1	1	1
9. Searching character strings sequentially in any category or field	7	5	6	4	6	3	6	7	6	5	6	5

Exhibit 70. Percentage Rankings by Searchers, by Organization Type, of Most/Least Important and Used Search-Related System Features

---

"OTHER" RESPONSES:
SEARCH-RELATED FEATURES

---

*Left (or front) truncation (15)

"Exploding" on terms (or class numbers) to obtain all subordinate terms--hierarchical searching (11)

Weighting of terms (6)

Automatic title searching (3)

Limiting searches--by language, by years, document types, human vs. animal (5)

Use of numbers to search on terms (2)

Recall search strategies for later use or to cross files (2)

Automatic SDI (2)

To select easily from search results only relevant references (2)

Mapping and natural-language inquiries (2)

Break key (2)

Search all categories automatically (1)

*Truncate conditionally, i.e., specify length of the suffix (1)

*Guaranteed response time (1)

Override parentheses (1)

Purge statements after input (1)

Use of variable-character symbol for non-truncation reasons (1)

Receive postings on- and off-line (1)

Deletion of characters and searches before input (1)

*Application of weighting of terms after search is entered and postings are reviewed (1)

(Asterisked features were not available on any system at the time of the survey.)

Exhibit 71. "Other" Important Search-Related System
Features Identified by Searchers

is sometimes not clearly stated: that differences in searching on various
systems are sometimes a function of data-base-dependent features, and the
system features that accommodate these data-base features are not necessarily--
and most likely, are not--applicable across all data bases. When the on-line
supplier is also the data base developer, as is the case with the National
Library of Medicine, the line between system and data base becomes blurred.
In other cases, when the on-line supplier (as with SDC and Lockheed) is providing access to other organizations' data bases, which can have a variety of
formats and vocabularies--uncontrolled vocabularies, controlled vocabularies
from different thesaurus structures, and non-existent vocabularies (i.e., no
human-assigned index terms)--the distinction between system and data base is
important to maintain.

It is surprising that only one respondent pointed out the importance and usefulness of character- and line-correction features, certainly an important
omission from the structured list of choices. Most users, too, apparently take
for granted this very basic correction/deletion system feature.

On-Line-Aid Features

A second set of response choices covered on-line aids that relate to the general
use of the system. This potpourri of features runs the spectrum from those
that are closely related to the searching function (e.g., displaying index
terms on-line or entering several instructions to the system at one time) to
those that are only indirectly related (e.g., communications with suppliers).
The first two items on this list (see Exhibit 72)--the capability to display
on-line the alphabetical index or dictionary, and the capability to display
on-line related or hierarchical thesaurus terms--are probably most closely
associated with the direct searching functions in a system, but the second
item--the display capability for related or hierarchical thesaurus terms--is
also a system/data base interdependent feature. The availability of these
particular features, at the time of data collection and at the present time,
across all of the systems, is displayed in Exhibit 72.

User data from the question on on-line aids are reported in Exhibit 73 in the
same way that data from the searching-related capabilities were displayed
earlier. The comparison between the most-important and most-used features
shows that the importance of aid features is not correlated as strongly with
frequency of use as it was for the search-related features. As mentioned before,
it would appear that a feature can be important to have when it is needed, even
if that frequency of need is not great. An example of this situation is evident
in the second item, "Display on-line the list of related terms of hierarchical
thesaurus."

	No. of Suppliers "Then" (1974)	No. of Suppliers "Now" (1975)
The system allows a user to:		
Display on-line the alphabetical index or dictionary.	7	8
Display on-line the list of related terms or hierarchical thesaurus.	8	6
Obtain explanations of system features on-line.	10	10
Enter comments on-line to the supplier.	2	2
Control the length or form of system messages.	6	6
Receive announcements online from the supplier about important system-related information.	10	10
Monitor elapsed time or CPU usage on-line.	10	9
Display history of search strategy.	10	9
Enter several instructions to the system at one time.	6	7

Exhibit 72. Report from the 10 On-Line Suppliers
on Availability of On-Line Aids

The system allows user to:	IMPORTANCE (N=801)				USE (N=VARIABLE)				Percent Responding to Use Items
	Very Useful		Not At All Useful		Heavily Used		Rarely or Never Used		
	%	Rank	%	Rank	%	Rank	%	Rank	
1. Display on-line the alphabetical index or dictionary.	55.2%	3	5.9%	6	36.2%	3	11.5%	7	95.1%
2. Display on-line the list of related terms or hierarchical thesaurus.	53.6%	4	3.5%	9	25.6%	7	13.1%	6	94.3%
3. Obtain explanations of system features on-line.	29.5%	7	8.6%	4	5.9%	9	39.3%	2	96.0%
4. Enter comments on-line to other terminals.	10.4%	10	36.3%	1	2.7%	10	36.1%	3	87.8%
5. Enter comments on-line to the supplier.	21.8%	9	12.5%	3	6.5%	8	42.1%	1	92.8%
6. Control the length or form of system messages.	25.7%	8	15.9%	2	26.8%	6	13.5%	5	83.5%
7. Receive announcements on-line from the supplier about important system-related information.	60.8%	1	2.2%	10	40.7%	2	7.2%	9	96.6%
8. Monitor elapsed time or CPU usage on-line.	55.6%	2	7.4%	5	56.9%	1	6.6%	10	92.1%
9. Display history of search strategy.	48.8%	5	5.1%	7	29.4%	5	21.1%	4	95.3%
10. Enter several instructions to the system at one time.	46.8%	6	4.6%	8	31.8%	4	9.7%	8	91.8%

Exhibit 73. Levels of Importance and Use Associated With Different On-Line-Aid Features

The on-line thesaurus display capability relates only to those data bases with structured, or controlled, vocabularies, but the strong Importance and Use response raises some interesting issues for the suppliers and users to deal with in the near future. The pre-planning search process was not investigated in this study, but it would be most useful to understand the preferences of users for planning searches off-line with printed vocabulary aids or micro-fiche listings of subject terms, versus the development of searches at the ter-minal with on-line access to vocabulary-related information. The issue is not solely one of "off-line planning," because with on-line searching, the searcher knows immediately how an initially planned search strategy is working. The revision of search strategies on the basis of this kind of feedback poses a searcher decision point: 1) to leave the terminal and start again with off-line planning, using the initial work that was done at the terminal as the basis for rethinking the strategy; or 2) to revise the search by using any on-line vocabulary aids and by scanning terms used in relevant citations. The cost factors associated with different methods must also be considered in this decision-making process, particularly for users of non-subsidized systems.

We believe that differences in working environments and in the systems that are being used introduce some interesting patterns of differences across the various organizational-type responses shown in Exhibit 74. The inversions of percentage rankings begin immediately, with more Educational institution users--in comparison to the other user groups--indicating the receipt of system-related information from the supplier to be of major importance. This group shares with the Commercial organizations the second-most-selected feature on the monitoring of elapsed time at the terminal, which was only the fifth-ranked choice of government agency users. All groups reported that item 8, the monitoring feature, was being heavily used, but the Government agency users, who are primary users of the subsidized services and are less likely to charge back to end-users, did not believe it was as important as some other features.

| | Importance | | | | | | Use | | | | | |
| | Very Useful | | | Not At All Useful | | | Heavily | | | Rarely or Never Used | | |
Feature	Gov't (N=192)	Comm. (N=247)	Educ. (N=264)	Gov't (N=192)	Comm. (N=247)	Educ. (N=264)	Gov't (N=Variable)	Comm. (N=Variable)	Educ.	Gov't (N=Variable)	Comm. (N=Variable)	Educ.
1. Alphabetical index display	1	1	5	5	10	4	3	2	4	6	10	5
2. Related/hierarchical term display	4	4	3	9	9	9	6	7	6	5	6	6
3. On-line explanations	7	8	8.5	6	4	3	8	8	9	3	1	1
4. Comments to other terminals	10	10	10	1	1	1	10	10	10	2	3	3
5. Comments to supplier	8	9	7	3	2	6.5	9	9	8	1	2	2
6. Control length of messages	9	7	8.5	2	3	2	7	4	5	4	7	7
7. System news	2	3	1	9	8	10	5	3	2	8.5	8	10
8. Monitor elapsed time	5	2	2	4	5	6.5	1	1	1	8.5	9	9
9. Display history of search	3	5	6	9	6.5	5	2	5	7	7	4	4
10. Enter several instructions at one time	6	6	4	7	6.5	8	4	6	3	10	5	8

Exhibit 74.   Percentage Rankings by Searchers, by Organization Type, of Most/Least Important and Used On-Line-Aid Features

The "Other" responses to this set of features were not as numerous as those to search-related features, and many of them overlapped response choices from the search-related features or those already included in the on-line-aid set of features. New or explanatory items provided by individual respondents are summarized below in Exhibit 75.

Receive notice at log-on time of files currently unavailable, troubles, etc.

Be notified if system is down.

Clear display of exact strategy used.

Update information.

Capability to store searches indefinitely.

Highlight search terms in the print displays.

Command to free already entered searches to allow more space for additional searches.

Select synonyms in free-text data bases.

Get time and cost of search after you are done.

Be able to retain larger number of searches for a given sequence.

Exhibit 75. "Other" On-Line-Aid Features Identified by Searchers

7. SELECTION AND USE OF ON-LINE DATA BASES

It is important to distinguish between the use of data bases and the use of systems, even though the two blend into a single process from the standpoint of the on-line searcher at the terminal. If we view the system-use part of the on-line-searching process primarily as the skills component, in which fairly fixed principles and rules are to be followed, then the data-base-use part of the task might be characterized more appropriately as the skills-plus component, requiring professional-level knowledge, resourcefulness and, for the multiple-data-base user in particular, strong adaptability to differences.

Many aspects of data-base use that one might want to study deal with questions specific to particular data bases or to a group of data bases that are similar in certain ways. Over 30 data bases, listed below, were available through the 10 participating suppliers at the time the questionnaires were distributed, and it was not practical, nor even possible, to focus specifically on any one or several of these data bases. (The numbers in parentheses refer to the number of suppliers--if more than one--providing access to that particular data base.)

AIM/ARM

API Literature

API Patents

Battelle Energy Information Center (BEIC)

BIOSIS

Chemical Abstracts Condensates (4)

Chemical Abstracts Nuclear Structure File

CHEMLINE

COMPENDEX (5)

ELECOMPS

Energy Research In Progress

Environmental Science Index

ERDA Nonnuclear Energy Data Base

ERIC (3)

Exceptional Children Abstracts

GEOREF

INFORM (2)

INSPEC--Physics, Electrical & Electronic, Computer & Control (3)

METADEX (2)

NAL/CAIN (2)

NASA STAR/IAA

National Referral Center

NTIS (3)

Nuclear Safety Information Center

Nuclear Science Abstracts (2)

PANDEX (2)

Predicasts (Market Abstracts)

Psychological Abstracts (2)

R&D Program Planning (DDC)

R&T Work Unit (DDC)

STIMS

Technical Reports (DDC)

TOXLINE

TRANSDEX

Transportation Research (TRIS)

Water Resources Abstracts

In October, 1975, an additional 29 data bases had been announced or made operational, including: Union Lists of Scientific Serials in Canadian Literature; World Aluminum Abstracts; CA Energy Subset; Cancerline; AvLine (NLM); Journal Authority (NLM); Name Authority (NLM); Predicasts (F&S Index, Domestic Statistics); EIS Plant; CLAIMS/CHEM; CLAIMS/GEM; ISI Social Science Citation Index; MGA; Oceanic Abstracts; Congressional Information Service; Smithsonian Science Information Exchange; LIBON/E, F, S, C; POLLUTION; TULSA; American Statistics Index; RINGDOC; World Patents Index. Two files, PANDEX and MATRIX, have been dropped due to the unavailability of the data bases, and the availability of the NASA STAR, NTIS, ISI, and BIOSIS files was announced by additional suppliers.

In keeping with our objective to develop broad baseline data, we addressed only a selected number of general data-base-use areas. Data from the questionnaires and interviews on these several areas are presented in three major sections:

- Selecting Data Bases for a Search
- Searchers Preferences in Vocabulary Structures
- Searchers' Practices and Preferences: Search Output

Most of the data on data-base use are related to the multiple-data-base user, and it is important to recognize that multiple-data-base use can assume two different definitions. It may mean the use of two or more data bases, each of which is very different in terms of content, coverage, vocabulary structure, and record elements. It may also mean the use of what we might call different "files," or segments of data bases that are closely related, such as those that comprise the MEDLARS data base group--MEDLINE, SERLINE, etc. In interpreting the data provided in this section, we should probably associate many of the Educational institution users--and particularly their MEDLINE-user component-- with the second kind of definition, and consider the Commercial-user data relative to the first definition. Government-agency users and Other users represent a mix of these two kinds of multiple-data-base users.

In a later chapter, we have summarized the study findings relative to problem areas in data-base use, particularly with regard to multiple-data-base use.

SELECTING DATA BASES FOR A SEARCH

Almost 80% of the searchers reported that they have on-line access to more than one bibliographic data base. The composition of this subset of 639 searchers is:

- Commercial organization users: 87.0%
- Government agency users: 78.6%
- Educational institution users: 77.7%
- Other users: 69.4%

For these searchers, one of the key preliminary decisions they must make in handling a search request is which data base or data bases they should use. In some instances, the end-user helps to make that decision. We asked managers whether their end-users were requesting searches to be run on specific data bases. About three fourths of the managers responded.

- 12.9% of the managers reported that _most_ of their end-users request certain data bases

- 25.0% reported that _some_ of their end-users request certain data bases

- 39.1% reported that either _few_ or _no_ users request certain data bases

Some differences exist across the different organization types, as shown in Exhibit 76. More than half of the Educational institutions reported that either some or most of their users were involved in the data base selection process.

	Most Users	Some Users	Few Users	None	No Response
Government Users (N=101)	11.9%	22.8%	21.8%	19.8%	23.8%
Commercial Users (N=152)	5.9%	23.7%	21.7%	25.7%	23.0%
Educational Users (N=145)	22.1%	29.7%	17.9%	11.0%	19.3%
Other Users (N=74)	10.8%	21.6%	18.9%	20.3%	28.4%

Exhibit 76. Managers' Report, by Organization Type, on End-Users Requesting Searches to be Run on Certain Data Bases

We learned from some of the follow-up interviews, and from some of the unstructured responses that are discussed in Chapter 8, that one of the key elements in determining the degree of end-user involvement was whether organizations were charging back to their users. To analyze these data further, we would need to vary the characteristics of the charge-back fees; for example, we would need to compare those organizations that charge flat rates for all data bases with those that have differential prices, and those that let their users select from a price list with those that set up a discussion with end-users about the relative applicability of different data bases. This kind of analysis was beyond the scope of this study, but our data suggest that the selection of data bases has primarily been the searcher's decision, as has been the selection of systems.

Those searchers who had access to more than one data base were asked to select from among several response choices the ways in which they applied the availability of several data bases to a single search, and the frequency with which they used a given approach. As shown in Exhibit 77, a majority of searchers were either using one data base for one search or selecting the different data bases that were relevant to the search and trying the search on each one. Both of these approaches suggest that users were placing a great deal of importance on pre-terminal planning. The other choices, particularly the second and fourth ones, represent "on-the-spot-decision" approaches that are applied after the search results from the first data base(s) are known.

	Most Searches	Some Searches	Few Searches	No Searches	No Response
Use one data base for one search.	48.2%	22.4%	15.6%	6.6%	7.2%
Use a second data base when no success in the first data base.	12.1%	34.2%	29.9%	15.5%	8.3%
Select different data bases that are relevant to the search and try the search on each one.	43.3%	26.1%	15.5%	9.0%	6.0%
When number of hits in search on one file is not as great as expected, try the search on another file.	15.8%	31.5%	30.7%	14.4%	7.7%
Regardless of results from first data base, try search on another just to confirm understanding of its contents or to gamble on finding something relevant.	8.8%	13.8%	34.0%	36.0%	7.5%

Exhibit 77. Frequency of Use, by Multiple-Data-Base Searchers, of Different Approaches to Selecting Data Bases for a Search (N=639)

In Exhibit 78, the data on the first four approaches are displayed for each organizational user group. In general, Educational users were less likely to use more than one data base, and Commercial organization users were the most likely group to use several. Although not indicated in this Exhibit, Commercial users were also somewhat more likely to experiment with additional data bases, simply to expand their knowledge and level of familiarity.

		SEARCHES				
		Most	Some	Few	None	No Response
USE ONE DATA BASE FOR ONE SEARCH	Government Users (N=151)	39.7%	25.8%	17.9%	7.3%	9.3%
	Commercial Users (N=215)	30.7%	32.1%	26.0%	6.5%	4.7%
	Educational Users (N=205)	69.3%	14.1%	3.9%	4.9%	7.8%
	Other Users (N=68)	57.4%	8.3%	10.3%	10.3%	13.2%
USE SECOND DATA BASE WHEN NO SUCCESS ON FIRST	Government Users (N=151)	17.2%	31.8%	23.2%	18.5%	9.3%
	Commercial Users (N=215)	15.8%	39.5%	26.0%	12.1%	6.5%
	Educational Users (N=205)	5.4%	32.2%	36.6%	16.6%	9.3%
	Other Users (N=68)	7.4%	29.4%	35.3%	14.7%	13.2%
SELECT DATA BASES RELEVANT TO SEARCH AND USE EACH	Government Users (N=151)	53.6%	23.2%	11.3%	4.6%	7.3%
	Commercial Users (N=215)	54.9%	27.0%	8.9%	6.5%	2.7%
	Educational Users (N=205)	25.4%	27.8%	23.4%	15.1%	8.3%
	Other Users (N=68)	35.3%	25.0%	20.6%	8.8%	10.3%
USE SECOND DATA BASE WHEN NUMBER OF HITS ON FIRST IS LOW	Government Users (N=151)	20.5%	27.8%	25.2%	17.2%	9.3%
	Commercial Users (N=215)	21.9%	37.2%	24.7%	10.7%	5.6%
	Educational Users (N=205)	6.8%	29.2%	40.5%	14.6%	8.9%
	Other Users (N=68)	13.2%	25.0%	32.4%	17.6%	11.8%

Exhibit 78. Frequency of Use, by Searchers, by Organization Type, of Different Data-Base-Per-Search Approaches

The degree to which these multiple data bases are truly _different_ data bases is certainly a factor in differences of usage. As we noted in the introduction to this chapter, these distinctions in definition are probably contributing significantly to the differences that are reflected in these data. We do not know, however, whether some of the differences across organizations can also be attributed to real environmental differences and to user-need differences.

We asked the interviewees how many data bases they generally used in the average search. Most of them reported numbers ranging from 1 to 6, and the maximum that anyone had used was 29. Some of the typical comments provided by the searchers were:

> "Generally use 2 or 3 data bases for a broad-based or multi-disciplinary question."

> "Sometimes search as many as eight data bases for an author search."

> "Generally use only one data base for specific problems, but for research questions will use as many as I think are relevant."

> "I will use any number of data bases if I can keep the entry time into each one down to 5 minutes."

> "When users want everything, or have the money to pay, will use as many as are relevant."

Comments from other interviewees indicated that some of them believe that any given query can be handled by searching one data base, i.e., the one that is best suited for the query. We do not know how prevalent this belief is, but it raises an important and basic question about how much more information-- and value--is provided to the end-user by searching not only the first-choice, "best suited" data base, but one or more potentially suited data bases.

SEARCHERS' PREFERENCES IN VOCABULARY STRUCTURES

Variations in the format of subject terms can occur within a data base as well as across data bases, even before the on-line supplier decides how to format the data base for on-line use. These general variations can be characterized as follows:

- Provision of controlled vocabulary terms assigned by indexers from a thesaurus or vocabulary-authority listing, that may follow any or all of the following subject-heading conventions: 1) precoordinated terms in natural word order, which may or may not contain punctuation, such as hyphens and parenthetical expressions; 2) precoordinated terms in inverted word order, with commas; 3) precoordinated terms using a major-heading/ subheading system, with separation punctuation that may be commas, slashes, or dashes

- Provision of free-language or identifier terms, which are generally uncontrolled. Indexers select terms from the text of the document, to represent the document by terms that are difficult to control (e.g., acronyms, geographics) and that reflect the more current terminology being developed and applied in the literature

- No provision of any human-assigned index terms

There are variations on these basic themes, as well. For example, the human-assigned subject terms may be applied from semi-controlled vocabulary authorities, or an indexer may work from general guidelines for indexing.

Compounding these differences among the data bases, as they come from their producers, are the ways in which on-line suppliers elect to treat these different variations within, and across the data bases that they make available on their systems. For example, the on-line suppliers can elect to make the controlled vocabulary words available exactly as they appear in the data base input tapes, or they can elect to break up the precoordinated terms into single-word terms in a free-text or keyword approach. They might also elect to separate major headings from their subheadings in addition to retaining the linked major-subheading entry format. The on-line supplier also decides whether to provide access to each single word in the title and/or in the abstract, or in any other subject-related category.

A separate and detailed study would be needed to address completely the impact of this multitude of differences on users, but we did try to examine some of the searchers' preferences by asking them to indicate their choices, under certain conditions, for several general vocabulary structures: controlled vocabulary only; controlled vocabulary plus free-text terms; and free-text terms only. The overall response by searchers to this question is shown in Exhibit 79.

The preferences of searchers under both general and specific conditions seem to lie with controlled vocabularies or a combination of controlled vocabulary plus free-text terms. The addition of free-text terms appears to have a greater impact when users are working with searches in subject areas in which they are most comfortable and when they are working with data bases with which they have had some prior experience. When the searches are in subject areas in which the searchers are not particularly comfortable or knowledgeable, preferences are fairly evenly divided between controlled vocabularies only and the combination of controlled vocabulary plus free-text terms.

	SUBJECT VOCABULARY PREFERENCES				
	Controlled Terms Only	Controlled Plus Free Terms	Free Terms Only	No Difference	No Response
1. I have the most success with searches performed on data bases with . . .	23.2%	48.5%	8.0%	8.1%	12.2%
2. I have learned most quickly about the coverage and scope of data bases with . . .	40.1%	23.2%	6.9%	15.6%	14.2%
3. I am most efficient (timewise) when performing searches on data bases with . . .	39.9%	30.4%	7.4%	7.8%	14.6%
4. When performing searches in subject areas in which I am most comfortable or knowledgeable, I prefer data bases with . . .	16.9%	48.7%	13.3%	7.4%	13.4%
5. When performing searches in subject areas in which I am not particularly comfortable or knowledgeable, I prefer data bases with . . .	34.0%	39.3%	7.5%	5.6%	13.6%
6. When performing searches on data bases with which I have had prior experience (e.g., through coding for batch-system searches), I prefer data bases with . . .	15.6%	33.3%	7.2%	11.6%	32.2%
7. I prepare more for searches on data bases with . . .	32.9%	20.3%	19.9%	11.7%	15.2%

Exhibit 79. Searchers' Preferences for Subject Vocabulary Structures under Different Conditions (N=801)

Those alternative conditions in which some interesting differences occur across organizational user groups are shown in Exhibit 80. In each case, Commercial organization users show a somewhat stronger preference for the free-text terms.

		SUBJECT VOCABULARY PREFERENCES				
		Cont. Only	Cont. Plus Free	Free Only	No Diff.	N.R.
MOST SUCCESS WITH...	Government Users (N=151)	23.8%	44.4%	7.9%	9.3%	14.6%
	Commercial Users (N=215)	17.7%	48.8%	14.9%	11.6%	7.0%
	Educational Users (N=205)	28.3%	50.2%	2.0%	4.4%	15.1%
	Other Users (N=68)	23.5%	48.5%	4.5%	5.9%	17.6%
MOST EFFICIENT WITH...	Government Users (N=151)	31.8%	36.4%	7.9%	7.9%	15.7%
	Commercial Users (N=215)	45.1%	24.2%	13.0%	10.7%	7.0%
	Educational Users (N=205)	41.5%	31.2%	1.5%	5.4%	20.4%
	Other Users (N=68)	36.8%	32.4%	4.3%	5.9%	20.6%
WHEN SUBJECT AREA IS COMFORTABLE, PREFER...	Government Users (N=151)	17.2%	49.7%	13.2%	4.0%	15.9%
	Commercial Users (N=215)	15.8%	41.9%	24.2%	11.6%	6.5%
	Educational Users (N=205)	16.1%	55.6%	7.3%	3.0%	18.0%
	Other Users (N=68)	22.1%	45.6%	10.3%	1.4%	20.6%
PREPARE MORE WITH...	Government Users (N=151)	30.5%	25.2%	15.9%	10.6%	17.9%
	Commercial Users (N=215)	27.0%	17.7%	30.2%	16.7%	8.4%
	Educational Users (N=205)	41.5%	19.0%	12.7%	8.3%	18.5%
	Other Users (N=68)	30.9%	22.1%	14.1%	8.8%	23.5%

Exhibit 80. Differences in Preferences by Searchers in Each Organizational Setting for Subject Vocabulary Structures Under Selected Conditions

In Exhibit 80, one interesting difference is revealed in the last item, related to preparation time. The data show that most Commercial organization searchers believe that they prepare more on data bases with free-text terms, and that most Educational institution users believe that they spend more time in preparing on data bases with controlled vocabularies. The reader may remember from Chapter 5 that Educational users also reported more time in pre-terminal work.

As we stated in that chapter, we believe that this difference is partly an artifact of the groups' experiences with different sets of data bases. The Educational user who thoroughly prepares a search with the highly controlled MEDLINE vocabulary (MeSH) may actually be devoting more time to the pre-terminal planning process with this data base than he or she does with an uncontrolled-vocabulary data base, such as Chemical Abstracts Condensates or NAL/CAIN. If, however, a Commercial user is comparing preparation time across a different set of data bases, with a different continuum of controlled and uncontrolled vocabularies, the greater amount of time spent in preparation with these different data could, particularly excluding MEDLINE, shift toward the uncontrolled-vocabulary data bases. Until the planning processes of subsets of users from different working environments, with different levels of training and experience, are carefully compared on the same sets of data bases, we cannot fully interpret the differences shown in our results.

We asked our interviewees what their favorite data bases were, i.e., those that they felt they could search most easily and effectively, and what special characteristics of these data bases contributed to their sense of success. Opinion was fairly evenly divided between those who believed that controlled vocabularies helped them most and those who believed that title terms or other free-text type terms helped them most.

Although we are not able yet to derive a specific principle for either data base developers or on-line suppliers from the study on vocabulary structures, we can definitely state that differences in preferences do exist. Further study will be needed to relate these preferences to relative levels of searcher efficiency and to the quality of search results. We can speculate, however, that even the best of such studies might have to conclude that no one kind of vocabulary structure is best for all purposes (i.e., for all search requests or for all fields), or for all on-line users. As an indication of what principles, if any, are evolving in practice, it is instructive to see what kinds of vocabulary structures were used in the data bases available at the time the field study was conducted, and what kinds are available now.

As shown in Exhibit 81, the predominant trend over the past year has been toward the provision of both controlled terms and free-text terms. On the basis of our own experiences with user reactions, we would suggest that this trend reflects a kind of resolution to the controlled-vocabulary/free-text argument that has existed for years in the library and information science field. We believe that many, if not all, of the on-line suppliers are being responsive to their users' preferences for having freedom of choice in vocabulary structures, their preferences for comprehensive recall, and their preferences for ease of use that comes from the free-text kind of search-entry format. We feel confident that the on-line suppliers will continue to handle data bases on-line with the provision of this kind of choice in mind.

	No. of Data Bases "Then" (Fall 1974)	No. of Data Bases "Now" (Fall 1975)
Controlled terms only, i.e., those assigned by human indexers.	27	22
Controlled terms plus free-text terms, i.e., those representing non-controlled vocabulary terms assigned by human indexers or "full-text" machine indexing provided by the on-line supplier from titles, abstracts, or other subject-related data elements.	20	48
Free-text terms only.	14	18

Exhibit 81.   Report from 10 On-Line Suppliers of Vocabulary Structures Used in Data Bases Available at the Time of the Field Study ("Then") and Those Available "Now"

SEARCHERS' PRACTICES AND PREFERENCES: SEARCH OUTPUT

After the initial search strategy has been entered into the system and a message has been received that indicates the number of citations matching the particular term or combination of terms, the searcher has several decisions to make:

- Whether to test the apparent relevance of the references by printing some or all of the information in each reference

- Whether to revise the search strategy--to broaden or narrow the strategy by adding terms or limiting the search in some way (e.g., by year or by use of the NOT logic)--or to try an alternative strategy, or to sign off the system and go back to the vocabulary aids or the end-user for more work on the strategy

- Whether to conclude the search, on the assumption that the results are the best that are possible, or are acceptable, given the requirements stated by the end-user of the information

- Whether to print the results on-line at the terminal or to issue a special instruction that means an off-line printout of the results will be generated by the on-line supplier, for later evaluation by the searcher or end-user

Some of these decisions, such as the decision to print on- or off-line, can be made before using the terminal, but the thinking time involved in these decision processes is usually part of the terminal-use time reported by the searchers.

Although a critical-incident-type study would be needed to understand fully the ways in which searchers make the decisions outlined above, there are data from the present study that shed light on current practices and opinions. These data are reported in the following three sections:

- Searchers' Preferences for Search-Output Features

- Use of On- and Off-Line Printing

- Post-Search Evaluation and Packaging of Results

The last section is derived primarily from some items that were covered during the follow-up field interviews.

Searchers' Preferences for Search Output Features

Searchers were asked to indicate the level of importance that they attributed to, and the degree of use that they made of, several system features that are closely related to search output. These data are organized in a way similar to those reported in Chapter 6 for the other groups of system features--search-related features and on-line-aid features. Exhibit 82 shows the availability of each feature from the participating suppliers.

	No. of Suppliers "Then" (Fall 1974)	No. of Suppliers "Now" (Fall 1975)
The system allows user to:		
1. Request standard or predefined print formats.	10	10
2. Tailor or specify his or her own print formats.	6	6
3. Specify sorting of output by designated categories (e.g., author, year).	5	8
4. Specify sorting of output by number of hits.	5	4
5. Specify off-line printing of search results to be run by the supplier.	10	10
6. Have a search strategy entered on-line run in batch mode later by supplier.	4	5
7. Receive citation displays in upper and lower case.	5	6

Exhibit 82.   Report by 10 On-Line Suppliers on Availability, "Then"
and "Now," of Search Output System Features

Exhibit 83 displays the percentage rankings of searchers' responses for each
feature. It is evident that searchers believed the off-line printing capability to be the most important and most used output feature. Some readers may
be surprised that the percentages are not even higher, but as we will show in
the next section, some user organizations were not doing any off-line printing,
and some were doing much less than others.

The system allows user to:	IMPORTANCE (N=801)				USE (N=VARIABLE)				
	Very Useful		Not At All Useful		Heavily Used		Rarely or Never Used		Percent Responding to Use Items
	%	Rank	%	Rank	%	Rank	%	Rank	
1. Request standard or predefined print formats.	58.9%	2	6.2%	4	67.0%	2	5.7%	7	95.6%
2. Tailor or specify his or her own print formats.	42.2%	3	11.7%	3	31.7%	4	16.0%	6	91.4%
3. Specify sorting of output by designated categories (e.g., author, year).	35.6%	4	5.4%	5	15.2%	5	23.6%	3	92.3%
4. Specify sorting of output by number of hits.	20.7%	5	18.6%	2	11.1%	6	31.9%	2	85.8%
5. Specify off-line printing of search results to be run by the supplier.	78.0%	1	1.1%	7	69.3%	1	4.0%	8	95.6%
6. Have a search strategy entered on-line run in batch mode by supplier.	18.7%	6	27.0%	1	6.5%	8	21.6%	4	80.5%
7. Receive citation displays in upper and lower case.	9.6%	7	5.3%	6	8.1%	7	19.7%	5	87.5%
8. Others	2.7%	8	---	---	40.0%	3	33.3%	1	3.7%

Exhibit 83. Levels of Importance and Use Associated with Different Search Output Features

It also appears that, for both on- and off-line printing, searchers were indicating a preference for the flexibility of having predefined formats that can be requested, but, at the same time, being able to specify their own print formats. A format in this case refers to the elements of information that are to be included in the output display. For example, one format might contain only accession numbers and another might contain all of the key bibliographic information, such as author, title, source.

In reviewing the lower-ranked percentages, we see that the cosmetic feature of upper/lower-case displays was considered to be of relatively low value.

Analysis of the feature-preference data by types of organizations shows only slight differences. "Off-line printing of search results" received the highest percentage on use by Educational institutions, but was only second highest for Government and Commercial users, who selected "standard or predefined print formats" as their most used feature. This difference tends to corroborate the data reported on later showing that Educational institution users do more off-line printing than either Government or Commercial users.

Use of On- and Off-Line Printing

On-line printing at the terminal may be used by searchers to determine the effectiveness of their search strategies, or to print some or all of the search results. We will first look briefly at the on-line printing that is done to test search results, to provide a basis for understanding some of the differences in opinions that are seen on the printing done to obtain the search results.

On-Line Printing to Test Search Results

A description of on-line system use would not be complete if we did not recognize that on-line systems can be used in such a manner that they might be considered "on-line batch" systems. This definition is applicable if the searcher enters a search formulation of one or more combined sets or statements and finds out immediately the number of references that meet the stated requirements. This is the on-line part of the definition. The "batch" part of the definition is applicable when the searcher then issues an instruction for the results to be printed off-line, and does not first test the composition of that hit count, for example, by reviewing the titles for relevance.

False drops and material of peripheral relevance are just as likely to occur in the first strategy that is tried in an on-line search as they are in a true batch-mode search. Until the searcher exercises the capability of assessing, at some level, the degree to which the search strategy is yielding the desired results, the differences in search results between the two modes are fairly minimal. Some value remains, however, in using on-line systems in this way, and there are legitimate reasons for this particular mode of operation. The on-line system still produces better turnaround time and reduces the amount of lost time that occurs in batch searches to learn about the costly "no-hit" results. Organizations may elect to use this "on-line batch" approach for a variety of reasons. They may feel that 1) it keeps the per-search direct costs low, but still succeeds in providing a useful information service; 2) it reduces the personnel time involved at the terminal; 3) it allows the organization to accommodate a greater number of searches in a shorter or limited period of time; or 4) their information-intermediary staff cannot really judge relevance of search results, and this assessment must be left to the end-user.

Some observers believe that most on-line searches are being conducted in a batch fashion. We believe that this is not the case, but the issue is sufficiently important and complex that it should be considered in a separate study. We asked our sample of interviewees whether they browsed through the results on-line before requesting a search to be printed off-line. About one-half of them indicated that they always did, and the remainder indicated they did on some searches. Only one indicated that he never did. In most cases, the searchers indicated that they scanned titles or titles and subject-related categories of information. The number of references reviewed on-line varied from 2 to 20, and one searcher said that he scanned all references on-line. Some searchers said that they might review other categories, e.g., the language indicator. Only a few indicated that they reviewed the abstracts.

One user said that he checks his search results by entering a second strategy to see if one or the other nets unique and desirable references. Another user said that if the customer is cost-conscious, he limits the screening that is done on-line, to keep the per-search cost as low as possible. In the same vein, another interviewee said that the searchers in his organization always take more off-line citations than are desired, just to get off the terminal; in other words, they are using the on-line system mostly to ensure comprehensive recall; they perform the relevance assessments, to obtain precision, off-line.

Printing of the Final Search Results

All of the current suppliers of on-line bibliographic information provide capabilities that allow users to instruct the system to print their final search results, the list of citations and abstracts, or summaries, off-line at the supplier's facility, rather than at the terminal.

We asked searchers to indicate how they obtained the final list of references from their on-line searches, and with what frequency.

- Most searchers reported that they use both on-line and off-line printing.

- About one fourth reported that they print either on-line or off-line only occasionally.

- About 16% reported that they never print off-line, and fewer than 10% reported that they never print on-line.

The differences across user groups are displayed in Exhibit 84.

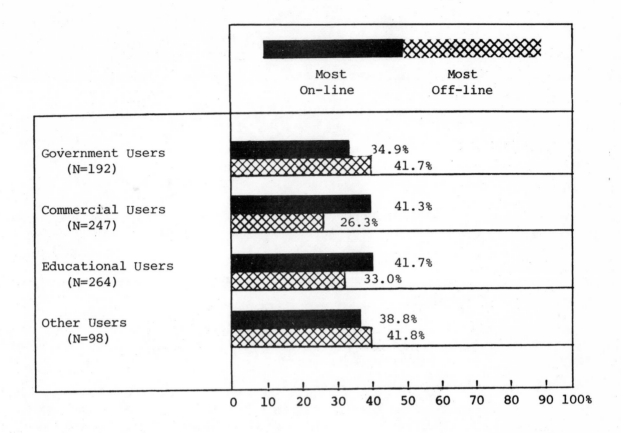

Exhibit 84. Frequency of Use of On- and Off-Line Printing
by Searchers, by Organization Type, to Obtain
Final List of References

Commercial organization users are less likely to do their printing off-line, which can possibly be associated with one or more other characteristics of this group. They spend somewhat more time at the terminal than other types of users, and they provide faster service to their users. These are associated with doing more printing on-line. The additional time spent at the terminal might also reflect greater effort at refining the searches, which would mean that the amount of printing to be done is thereby reduced to a level appropriate for on-line printing. We do not know exactly how these data interrelate, but the possible associations suggest that differences in work environments and in end-user requirements may be very important elements in the decision to print on- or off-line.

We asked respondents to indicate, if they used both printing modes, how they decided which one to use. Over 450 (about 56%) of the respondents provided answers to this unstructured question and reported that they generally used on-line printing only for up to some number of citations; over that amount, they used off-line printing. The numbers of citations that they gave were tabulated and generally fall into the following classes:

Numbers of Citations	Numbers of Respondents
	(N=450)
Few only	112 (24.9%)
(Number not given)	
Up to 10	100 (22.2%)
10-35	200 (44.4%)
40-60	35 (7.8%)
75-100	12 (2.7%)

The comments that accompanied these numbers help us to understand the decision-making process involved. Many of these comments are provided in Exhibit 85.

Cost-Plus Considerations

Sample to decide relevance; do off-line if 4-day delay is tolerable and printout exceeds 50 citations. If on-line print is necessary, print format is cut to include title, source, keywords.

Importance of search plus cost of search.

Number of citations and resulting cost is major factor, as off-line is less expensive. Also important are client's preference, volume of output, and backlog of work at the library.

Other Combinations of Considerations

Off-line is used only for in-house searches or when editing of a client's search is not necessary.

Proprietary searches are generally run on-line, but user's desire is also considered.

Print on-line if user is on premises and picks it up; otherwise, saves searcher's time to print entirely off-line. If abstract accompanies citation, abstracts are always printed off-line.

Nature of Request from End-User

We select each case separately on basis of urgency and disposition.

Dependent upon corporate priorities.

Importance of subject to our firm.

Exhibit 85. Searchers' Comments on How they Decide Whether to Print On-Line or Off-Line to Obtain List of Final Search Results (page 1 of 2)

If the article itself is needed, on-line is often preferred.

Urgent request from top executive is done on-line.

Patient-care type requests are done on-line for a rush.

Patron Decision or Involvement in Decision

It's whatever the user will pay. We charge time and citations.

Depends on whether user wants citations only or citations plus abstracts.

Patron pays so patron chooses.

Patron usually decides, but we encourage off-line printouts for larger numbers of citations. Usually print a few on-line and do the balance off-line.

Other Reasons

Sometimes do off-line if my staying on-line at the terminal prevents someone else from using the terminal.

Presently we have a CRT with no printer.

Off-line prints are of better quality and can be photocopied easily.

Print off-line when "noise" makes on-line printout unreadable.

Data-Base-Dependent Reasons

It depends on the data bases.

On some data bases like Chemical Abstracts Condensates and Engineering Index's COMPENDEX, we get reference numbers to the abstracts on-line and then retrieve the abstracts from the printed products.

Off-line is suggested by the supplier.

Rules are set by the supplier.

Exhibit 85. Searchers' Comments on How they Decide Whether to Print On-Line or Off-Line to Obtain List of Final Search Results (page 2 of 2)

The apparent division of opinion in the area of on- and off-line printing is really not surprising, because the responses must be understood in the context of the system and data bases that are being used. Charges for off-line printing across all systems and data bases (at the time data were collected) ranged from no charge to $.25 per citation. The various elements that must be considered by the user in any complete cost analysis are suggested below (not all elements are applicable for all suppliers):

Cost-Related Factors

- Cost per off-line citation or page

- Cost of computer time

- Cost of communications

- Cost of terminal printer paper

- Cost of postage

- Size of reference (e.g., citation only, citation and abstracts, accession number of abstract reference only)

- Speed of terminal (10 characters per second, 15 cps, 30 cps, 120 cps, etc.)

- Staff time at the terminal

End-User Factors

- Urgency of need and typical turnaround time from on-line supplier, plus postal delays

- Charge-back procedures and record-keeping requirements (e.g., it is easy to state that a flat service fee of some amount includes a fixed number of citations; the cost can be computed in advance for the end-user on the basis of the average connect-time for a search on a particular data base, plus the fixed amount for the proposed number of off-line citations).

Service Factors

- Service goals (e.g., immediate-response image)

- Library staff time

- Shared usage of terminals among several staff members

To illustrate the complexity of this issue with only the direct charges from on-line suppliers, we can look at one example with two different conditions of connect-time and per-citation off-line printing charges. (The terminal speed is also a key factor; we are assuming for purposes of this example that the user has a 30 character-per-second printer terminal.)

Condition A: The searcher is printing only citations, each of which contains key bibliographic information, e.g., title, author(s), source or publication information, and an accession number or reference number to an abstract publication. The average number of characters per citation is 200, and it takes about 10 seconds to print each citation. (One cannot simply divide the number of characters by 30--for 30 cps--because some fraction of time is lost at the time each carriage return is made for each line of the citation, because some number of characters are added for spacing between citations, and for the display format and, for some users, because of variability or delay in the communications network.

Data base price is:	$8/hr.	$25/hr.	$40/hr.	$60/hr.
Off-line printing, per citation, is:	$.10/cit.	$.10/cit.	$.10/cit	$.10/cit.
On-line printing, per citation, is:	$.02/cit.	$.07/cit.	$.11/cit.	$.17/cit.

If readers would like to compute some costs for their own "conditions," they can use the following procedure, which we used to arrive at the above on-line citation charges:

1. Take the data-base price, per connect hour, and divide by 60 to get the price in minutes ($40/60 = $.67 per minute).

2. Use a stopwatch to time several citations from the particular data base, or divide the average number of characters by 30 and add 50% to handle system-formatting overhead, carriage-return delays, etc. (200/30 + 50% = about 10 seconds to print one citation).

3. Take the number of seconds it takes to print one citation and divide by 60 to obtain the time it takes in minutes or fractions of minutes (10/60 = .17 minutes).

4. Multiply the printing time from Step 3 by the connect-time price in minutes (from Step 1), to obtain the cost for printing a citation of a certain size on a specific data base. This figure can then be compared to the off-line printing charge per citation ($.67 x .17 = $.11).

As this one example shows, the on-line printing of key citation information may be cost-effective, given certain connect-hour prices and off-line printing charges. However, if we vary the size of the citation and, say, include a fuller citation, or one that includes an abstract, we have a new series of computations to make.

Condition B: Searcher is printing citations with abstracts. The average number of characters for each reference (citation plus abstract) is 750 and it takes about 40 seconds to print one reference on a 30 cps printer terminal.

Data base price is:	$8/hr.	$40/hr.
Off-line printing, per citation, is:	$.25/cit.	$.25/cit.
On-line printing, per citation, is:	$.09/cit.	$.45/cit.

A comprehensive analysis would also include staff time under each of the conditions, as well as the cost of the paper that would be used at the terminal, particularly for lengthy bibliographies.

Such an analysis for the multiple-system and multiple-data-base users could become a fairly time-consuming project, and some users may elect to set some general guidelines that are flexible enough to accommodate several different pricing conditions and the different requirements of end-users. As one searcher indicated, his organization has no strict guidelines, but the staff simply tries to exercise good judgment. However, since there may be some cost-savings in on-line printing that are not always obvious, the on-line suppliers may need to help users by providing some of the baseline data for these various computations so that users can then more easily determine the most cost-effective printing methods for the several conditions that are applicable in their organizations.

As shown in Exhibit 86, the organizations that have been requesting their final search results off-line vary considerably in their average number of citations per search.   (These data are derived from the Cost section of the Manager questionnaire; some respondents did not contribute to this particular section.)

	NUMBER OF CITATIONS				MEDIAN NUMBER CITATIONS
	2-25	26-50	51-100	101-301	
Government Users (N=43)	27.9%	23.3%	27.9%	20.9%	49.8
Commercial Users (N=62)	32.3%	32.3%	16.1%	19.4%	39.8
Educational Users (N=801)	13.8%	32.5%	32.5%	21.3%	56.8
Other Users (N=39)	5.1%	28.2%	41.0%	25.6%	71.3

ALL RESPONDENTS
(N=224)

Range = 2-301
Mean   = 74.8
Median = 50.5
Mode   = 50.0

Exhibit 86.   Number of Citations in Off-Line
Printouts from the Average Search

The variation in number of citations is probably attributable to a variety of factors, including the kinds of searches that are performed (e.g., retrospective vs. current awareness), the searchers' approach (e.g., with recall vs. precision as the primary objective), fee policies of the using group (e.g., per-citation charges vs. flat fees that include a fixed number of citations) and, perhaps most important, special characteristics of the data bases and their vocabularies (e.g., the degree to which high precision--and fewer citations--in searching can be obtained in a reasonable amount of on-line time). The differences across the various organization-type users most likely reflect primary differences in the fee policies and data bases that are being used.

Post-Search Evaluation and Packaging of Results

Many users, and particularly those in Commercial organizations, spend over 1 hour in post-terminal work. We can understand better how post-terminal time--from 2 minutes to 99 minutes--is being spent from responses to several of the questionnaire items addressed to managers, and from several questions included in the follow-up interviews.

Most of the managers reported that end-users do not request that their search results be either screened or not screened. It would appear that the decision to evaluate the search results in some way, e.g., to eliminate less relevant citations or to organize the citations in some sequence of relevancy, is primarily a decision of the individual intermediaries or is a policy established for all searchers in a given organization.

Although we have no data to show how much evaluation and screening are taking place, we did learn indirectly from the managers what kind of packaging of final search results is taking place. We asked managers whether someone on the staff added any explanatory notes or comments to the final bibliography that is given to the end-user, and a majority of them, 60%, indicated that some material was being added to the computer printout. In Exhibit 87, we can see that Commercial organization users are more likely than other users to do some final packaging of the search results.

	All Managers (N=472)	Government Users (N=101)	Commercial Users (N=152)	Educational Users (N=145)	Other Users (N=74)
Yes	56.4%	46.5%	61.2%	58.6%	55.4%
No	37.7%	43.6%	34.9%	37.9%	35.1%
No Response	5.9%	9.9%	3.9%	3.4%	9.5%

Exhibit 87. Report by Managers to Question: Does someone in your organization add any explanatory notes or comments to the final search product?

We asked managers to describe the kinds of additions that were being made to the final printout. About one-fourth of the managers reported that explanations were given in face-to-face communication with the end-user. In most cases, however, the staff is using preprinted forms or is developing specially tailored cover notes or letters to describe one or more of the following: 1) the different elements of information displayed in the references; 2) the search strategy that was used to accomplish the search; 3) the data base(s) used, including content, time-period, and source coverage; or 4) the availability of full-text documents, e.g., location in the library, interlibrary loan procedures.

Very few managers mentioned that their staff was supplementing the printout by reviewing full-text copies of documents and analyzing these to produce reports or specific "answers" to questions posed by the end-user; making notations of relevancy, e.g., marking the most relevant references or re-organizing the references in some order of relevancy; alerting the end-user that other possible resources were available to supplement the findings of the search; or asking the end-user to complete an evaluation form on the quality and usefulness of the search results.

Some of the comments that were provided by managers and by our interviewees further illustrate the kinds of packaging that are being done:

> "Although we can't always do it, most patrons would like to be spoon-fed and would like to have, in order of preference: 1) full-text copies of relevant documents; 2) abstracts saying that articles will follow on request; 3) abstracts; 4) printout with relevant citations."

> "We will delete items from the printout if they are particularly bad ones."

> "We add a caveat that says we are not responsible for the contents of the article being referenced, and also include any applicable copyright restrictions."

> "We prepare a final report that has a summary of the search, a number of selected abstracts, and some abstracts from the printed document; any 'garbage' citations are removed."

> "We send a descriptive sheet only when we are first introducing the on-line search service to a patron."

One searcher who was interviewed indicated that his organization's searchers do not make any relevancy judgments because they feel it would be arrogant to do so. We do not know how prevalent this attitude is, but for whatever reasons, it appears that most of the organizations are not involved in extensive evaluation, screening, and packaging of on-line search results.

8. COSTS OF USING ON-LINE SERVICES

We asked the managers a number of questions to obtain information on the cost elements associated with the use of on-line services. Our major purposes were:

- to see whether, and how, organizations were keeping track of on-line search costs

- to learn the average cost for the typical on-line search across all systems and all data bases

- to determine what cost elements organizations were including in their estimates of the cost of an average on-line search

- to determine what portion of the cost of on-line service the organizations were recovering from the end-user of the on-line search results

The data in this section were compiled from the Manager questionnaires and from the field interviews. Approximately 31% of the managers either were unable to, or did not choose to, respond to the Cost section of the questionnaire. Thus the data that will be reported describe the operations of approximately two-thirds of the organizations that participated in the study.

MAINTENANCE OF A BUDGETING AND ACCOUNTING SYSTEM

The first question that we asked managers, in the Cost section of the question-naire, was whether a separate budget or accounting system was maintained for the on-line services. Those managers who responded negatively to this question were asked to skip the remaining items in the section. During the review of the draft questionnaires, we had been advised by several of the U.S. Government on-line suppliers that many of the items on time and cost could probably not be answered by their users because the on-line service was not a part of their users' budgets; most (or all) of the costs were being absorbed by the suppliers themselves. Therefore we decided that we would be able to obtain more reliable cost-related data by gathering these data only from organizations that had accounting systems from which estimates could be derived.

Exhibit 88 shows both the total response of all the managers to this question and a breakdown of the responses by organization type. About 67% of the organizations were maintaining a separate budget and accounting system for all or some of the on-line services being used, while 31% were not. This exhibit also shows that no one organization type predominates in the group of on-line users that were not maintaining a budget and accounting system. This fact suggests that, although some portion of the no-budget group was probably using one or more of the fully subsidized services, other reasons were behind the "No" response from the 31% group. We learned from our follow-up interviews that some of the 31% group were units that were recovering from their end-users all of the out-of-pocket costs incurred in on-line searching. Because they were recovering the "extra" costs associated with the service, such as the computer-connect time and communications, they believed there was no requirement for maintaining a separate budget system.

	Yes, All Systems	Yes, Some Systems	No	No Response
All Managers (N=472)	62.9%	4.0%	30.9%	2.2%
Government Users (N=101)	57.4%	5.0%	37.6%	
Commercial Users (N=152)	53.0%	6.5%	37.5%	3.0%
Educational Users (N=145)	73.7%	1.4%	21.3%	3.6%
Other Users (N=74)	67.5%	5.4%	27.0%	

Exhibit 88. Managers' Responses to Question: Do you maintain a separate budget and accounting system for on-line services?

It seems likely that others in this group were units that were drawing upon fixed funds that were originally earmarked for some other department or budget item, rather than for on-line services. From our own experiences in talking with users, we know that for many organizations the startup year has been considered experimental and that creating a new line-item in the budget can take a long time.

COSTS OF ON-LINE SEARCHING

Average Costs per Search

Managers were asked to estimate the cost of their average on-line search, computing it across all data bases and systems for which they maintained records. Exhibit 89 shows their responses to this question, collapsed into $10.00 increments. The chart reveals that 62% of the group that provided data for the cost section estimated their cost per search to be under $30.00. The responses ranged from $1.00 to $99.00, with the mean being $23.83 and the median $17.16.

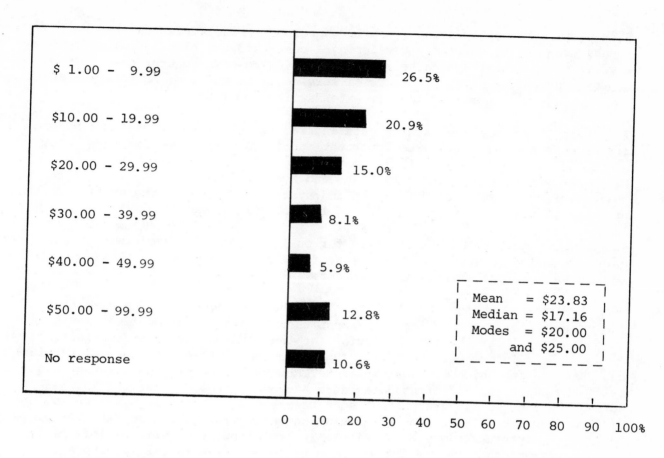

Exhibit 89. Cost Per Search Across All Systems and Data Bases
as Reported by Managers (N=320)

In keeping with our overall study objective, we did not ask managers to associate the cost data with any particular system or group of systems. Prices and pricing policies of the 10 suppliers vary considerably, however, and it was probably difficult for some of the users to compute an average cost. At the time that the questionnaires were being completed, the pricing policies included the following variations:

- The U.S. government suppliers were providing partially or completely subsidized services; users were paying either a nominal fee per computer-connect hour or monthly charges for leased lines.

- The commercial suppliers were charging for computer-connect time (from $25 to $90 per hour, depending upon the data base); for Tymshare communications (about $10); and for off-line printing (from $.05 to $.25 per citation, or $2.50 per 1000 lines).

- The other suppliers were providing subscription services, with the user paying for leased lines or other direct communications and, in some cases, a per-page off-line printing charge or data-base royalty charge.

This picture has changed and is still changing. For example, one federal agency supplier is currently developing a cost-recovery pricing policy, and several of the subscription services are moving toward computer-connect time charges, as well. For the commercial services, the range of computer-connect time charges has increased and now extends from $25 to $150.

To interpret the cost-per-search data and relate it to the "today" costs, the reader must keep in mind three important considerations. The first is that, since the managers averaged their cost per search across systems and data bases, federally subsidized data bases and systems have been pooled with the charges of the commercial data bases and systems. The resulting average is probably high for the former group and low for the latter.

A second consideration is that costs for on-line services have risen in the one-year period between the completion of the questionnaires by the respondents and the preparation of this final report.

The third consideration has to do with how the respondents define a search. The project staff, and--we believe--most users, think of an on-line search as encompassing all of the time and effort at the terminal necessary to fulfill an end-user's information request. The search may necessitate several terminal sessions, during which the searcher redefines his or her search strategy and tries the search on different data bases and/or systems. After the initial data gathering, we discovered that some users tend to think of a search in more limited terms, such as a single formulation run against a single data base. Such an interpretation may be particularly prevalent in commercial information service centers that charge users on the basis of per-data-base searches. It is not possible to determine from our survey data how frequently the more limited definition of search was used by respondents, but the reader should be aware of the possibility that the average per-search times and per-search costs may underestimate the true values.

The cost-per-search data for each organization type are shown in Exhibit 90. Some of the differences across organization types can be attributed to the fact that each group tends to be associated with a particular system or set of systems. The lowest per-search costs were reported by the Educational users, many of whom are users of partially subsidized systems. Commercial users, on the other hand, are primarily users of the commercially available systems, and they reported the highest per-search costs. The Government users represent a mix of federally subsidized system users and commercial system users, and their median per-search costs lie between the two groups. The spread, however, between the lowest and highest median costs is still only about $14.

	AVERAGE COST						MEDIAN COST
	$1.00 to 9.99	$10.00 to 19.99	$20.00 to 29.99	$30.00 to 39.99	$40.00 to 49.99	$50.00 to 99.00	
Government Users (N=63)	27.0%	22.2%	12.7%	1.6%	7.9%	15.9%	$17.60
Commercial Users (N=92)	7.6%	20.6%	26.0%	11.9%	6.5%	17.2%	$26.52
Educational Users (N=111)	37.8%	25.2%	11.7%	7.2%	1.8%	5.4%	$12.70
Other Users (N=54)	35.1%	11.1%	5.5%	11.1%	11.1%	16.5%	$19.28

Exhibit 90. Cost Per Search Reported by Managers, by
Organization Type

Components of Search Costs

Some of the within-group and across-group differences also stem from the particular elements of cost that were included in the average search costs reported by managers. Exhibit 91 shows that most of the respondents included in
their cost figures those direct, out-of-pocket costs for which they were being
charged by most on-line suppliers: off-line printing costs, computer-related
costs, and communications. (All of the percentages in this Exhibit were calculated on a base of 286 managers, those who had estimated their average costs.)
A surprisingly high percentage of managers (44%) indicated that they included
some portion of the staff time necessary to perform an on-line search. We can
speculate that an even greater percentage of organizations would have included
some or all of the staff time in their costs if the on-line services had generated a need for additional staff and if staff salaries had not already been
covered in the units' budgets. As we will learn later, most of the respondents
did not believe that additional staff had been required.

Exhibit 91 also shows that almost half of the managers who reported on their costs included the terminal rental or purchase price in this cost. Much less often included were subscription fees for the on-line system, probably because most of the on-line suppliers do not use the subscription-fee method of charging for on-line use.

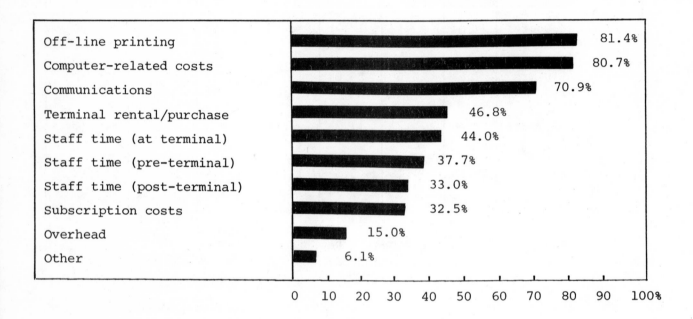

Exhibit 91. Elements of Cost Included by Managers in Computing Average Search Costs (N=286)

The overhead and "Other" categories were used least often by the managers in computing on-line searching costs. Few managers actually included any share of the organization's facilities or overhead that the on-line operation was using.

The "Other" category included:

● paper for the terminal

● staff training for on-line searching

● photocopy charges incurred to obtain a copy of the journal articles, etc., listed in the printout

● postage costs incurred when the printout is mailed to the end-user or when printouts run off-line are mailed to the searcher

Exhibit 92 shows the cost elements included in the managers' per-search costs, broken down by organization type. Some of the differences between groups are understandable. For example, the availability of the Federal Telecommunications System to Government users is one reason why the Government user group had a lower percentage in communications costs. The reasons for some of the other differences are not so clear. In the area of pre-terminal staff time, we might speculate that Educational users, who, as we saw in the earlier data, are spending considerable time in pre-terminal planning, have felt a greater impact on their staffing from the on-line services than the Commercial user group has felt. For university libraries that had not previously provided a literature searching service, pre-terminal planning time might be considered an "extra" cost, comparable in some respects to the out-of-pocket costs represented by the charges of the on-line suppliers. On the other hand, in the Commercial organization libraries, where literature searching services have traditionally been provided, the pre-terminal planning time may be considered comparable to the time spent with other methods of providing their literature-searching services; therefore, they may not view the staff-time costs as being something new for which staff-related funds had not already been budgeted. It is clear that we can go only so far in interpreting these data, and that additional study is needed to understand more fully the basis for these differences.

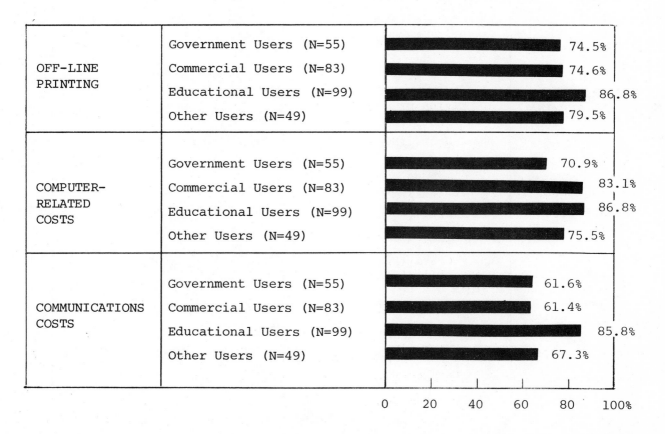

Exhibit 92. Cost Elements Included in Average Search Cost Reported by Managers, by Organization Type (page 1 of 2)

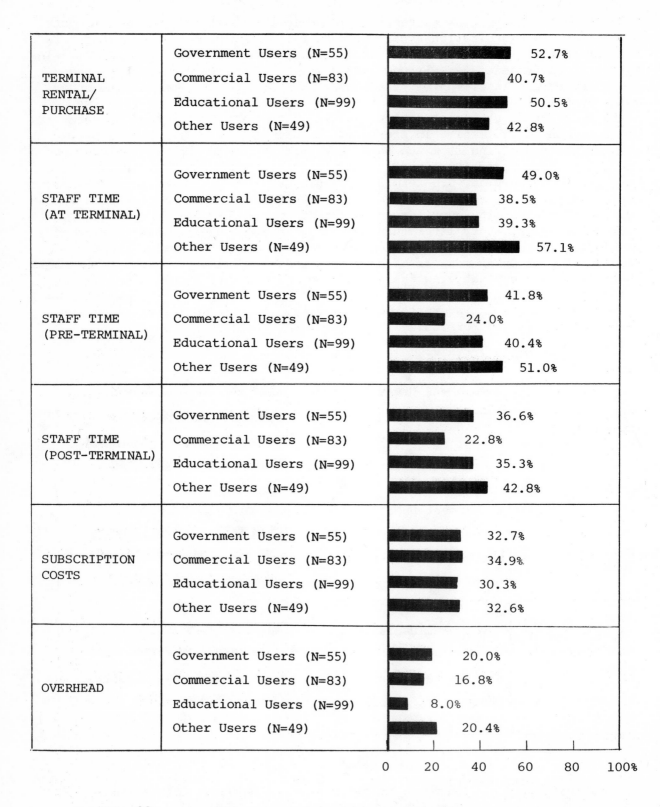

TERMINAL RENTAL/ PURCHASE	Government Users (N=55)	52.7%
	Commercial Users (N=83)	40.7%
	Educational Users (N=99)	50.5%
	Other Users (N=49)	42.8%
STAFF TIME (AT TERMINAL)	Government Users (N=55)	49.0%
	Commercial Users (N=83)	38.5%
	Educational Users (N=99)	39.3%
	Other Users (N=49)	57.1%
STAFF TIME (PRE-TERMINAL)	Government Users (N=55)	41.8%
	Commercial Users (N=83)	24.0%
	Educational Users (N=99)	40.4%
	Other Users (N=49)	51.0%
STAFF TIME (POST-TERMINAL)	Government Users (N=55)	36.6%
	Commercial Users (N=83)	22.8%
	Educational Users (N=99)	35.3%
	Other Users (N=49)	42.8%
SUBSCRIPTION COSTS	Government Users (N=55)	32.7%
	Commercial Users (N=83)	34.9%
	Educational Users (N=99)	30.3%
	Other Users (N=49)	32.6%
OVERHEAD	Government Users (N=55)	20.0%
	Commercial Users (N=83)	16.8%
	Educational Users (N=99)	8.0%
	Other Users (N=49)	20.4%

0   20   40   60   80   100%

Exhibit 92.   Cost Elements Included in Average Search Cost Reported by Managers, by Organization Type (page 2 of 2)

Estimating the On-Line Searching Budget

During the on-site interviews with selected managers and searchers, we asked
several questions about how an organization decides how much money will be
needed to cover the expenses of the on-line services for a given period of
time. The responses to these questions indicated that most managers have been
using very rough approximations of the out-of-pocket costs.

Managers in 22 organizations were asked specifically how they had decided on
the amount of money that would be allocated for the on-line services, prior to
initiating the service. About half of the group estimated the cost of the
on-line service on the basis of the major out-of-pocket cost elements mentioned
above and multiplied an average search cost against the number of estimated
on-line searches the organization or organizational unit expected to perform
in one year's time. This figure then became the amount of money budgeted for
the on-line service. In only one case was the cost of staff time also included
in this figure.

In all cases the initial allocation covered the first year of the on-line
operation. When asked if the initial allocation was adequate, almost all of
the managers responded that it had been. Thus, even though a very rough
method was used to estimate the total cost of the on-line service during its
first year of operation, most of the organizations found this method to be
satisfactory. The managers have apparently been successful in selling top
management on the idea that the service can basically be supported with present
facilities and staff and that extra funds are needed only for the new, direct
costs. Most managers cited stable costs and good guessing as the keys to their
success in being on target with the budget.

Of the two organizations that did experience financial problems in the first
year of operation, one had difficulty with the accounting procedures, rather
than with a shortage of funds. In this case a terminal budgeted for and
ordered during one fiscal year did not arrive until the next. Because the
organization was not allowed to carry over unspent funds into the new fiscal
year, a new budget item had to be approved for the late-arriving piece of
equipment. The second manager indicated that the money allocated for on-line
service had been inadequate, but he was able to continue spending beyond the
budgeted amount.

Several of the managers indicated that they were not required to develop any
kind of on-line budget at all, and instead were given money from other funds
as expenses came up. Other managers were able to bypass the budget stage
because they already had the terminal needed for on-line searching and were
able to pass all the other direct costs onto the end-user.

During the on-site interviews, the managers were asked whether they believed
that they had a solid basis for estimating the budget requirements of the
on-line service in the coming year. A majority of the managers answered this
question affirmatively. Illustrative responses, both positive and negative,
were:

- yes, if it becomes necessary

- yes, because only equipment is charged (budgeted for)

- yes, for one (totally subsidized) system, but more information is needed for ones that change (e.g., commercial and partially subsidized systems)

- yes, using past invoices

- no, the costs are now changing too much

- no, because good statistics on searcher time are not available

During the interviews the managers were asked how best to maintain records or logs of system use. All but one of the managers agreed that careful record-keeping is essential. The one exception, a manager who was working with a partially subsidized system, did not keep records because his organization paid a yearly flat rate for unlimited use of the system.

Those who were keeping records indicated that the main purpose was to keep track of the time spent by the searcher on-line in performing a search. Other data, such as the date, the requester of the search, the data base used, the number of citations (both on-line and off-line), and charges to the requester were, in many cases, also being recorded. These records were often used to verify invoices received from the on-line supplier and were maintained as part of a file of searches done for end-users in case any questions or problems were to arise. In general, we did not sense that the records being maintained were sufficiently detailed to permit managers to calculate the total amount of time used to complete a search, from initial request to delivered results. Given the multipart nature of the complete searching process, the time lapses between any of several of these parts, and the variability in any searcher's daily schedule, we should not be too surprised that recordkeeping and account-ing are not entirely systematic or complete. We believe that some guidelines, drawing particularly upon managers' experiences, are needed, and that the management aspect of on-line searching is only beginning to be developed.

COST-RECOVERY: GOALS, PRACTICES, AND ATTITUDES

Two major conclusions can be drawn from the managers' responses to a number of questions about their cost-recovery practices:

- There has been a definite trend toward charging the end-user for on-line searches

- Those organizations that have been charging end-users have generally been attempting to recover only direct costs

Cost-Recovery Goals

Of the 320 managers who answered the Cost section of the questionnaire, about 56% represent organizational units that have been charging their end-users for on-line searches. In Exhibit 93, the percentages for each organization-type group are displayed, showing that Educational users have been the most active group in establishing fee structures to support the adoption of on-line literature-searching services.

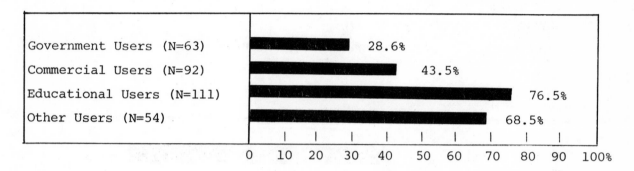

Exhibit 93. "Yes" Responses of Managers, by Organization Type, to Question: Do you charge users for on-line searches?

For those organizations that have established a fee structure, the method most often used for recovering costs (see Exhibit 94) has been the variable charge-- the amount of which has depended on the search, the data base, or the end-users. Much less often used has been the fixed-charge or subscription-type fee. Some of the most common practices reported by managers in the "Other" category were:

- there is a fixed charge for up to 100 pages, then a variable charge for each additional page

- we charge those who have a contract that can absorb the charge

- there is a fixed charge per search plus a variable charge for off-line printing

- only end-users not affiliated with the organization are charged

- the prices for most searches are fixed, but if a search is found to be extremely costly, the charge is passed on to the end-user

During the on-site interviews, we asked how those organizations that were charging end-users for on-line searches had decided upon a certain charge method.   The most commonly given responses were:

- we take the actual charge and add an overhead factor

- we use the guidelines established by the National Library of Medicine

- we recover all costs

- we break even on our data base costs by calculating a standard break-even charge per search

- we charge all expenses against the end-user's department

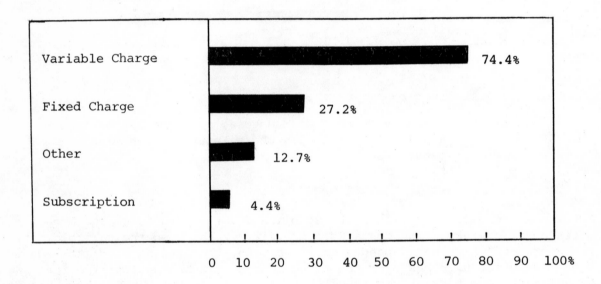

Exhibit 94.   Methods of Charging for On-Line Searches, as
Reported by Managers (N=180)

In an effort to detect any evolution of thinking about charging the end-user for on-line searches, we asked the managers to compare their cost-recovery goals when on-line services were first introduced into their organizations with the cost-recovery goals in effect at the time of the survey.   The data on initial cost-recovery goals can be summarized as follows:

- 50.0% of the respondents had no cost-recovery goals; instead, they planned to absorb the full cost of on-line searching

- 31.8% of the respondents planned to recover some portion of the costs

- 15.9% of the respondents hoped to recover all costs from the users of the on-line services

- 1.2% of the respondents hoped to make a profit

The organization-type data in Exhibit 95 shows that a majority of Government agency users and Commercial users had apparently been able to implement on-line literature searching services without an initial commitment to some kind of cost-recovery goal, but that a majority of the Educational institution users (almost 65%) viewed the recovery of costs as a necessity from the start.

	Recover All Costs	Recover Some Costs	Make A Profit	No Cost-Recovery Goal	No Response
Government Users (N=63)	7.9%	17.5%	--	74.6%	--
Commercial Users (N=92)	14.1%	19.5%	1.4%	60.8%	4.2%
Educational Users (N=111)	14.4%	50.4%	0.9%	33.3%	--
Other Users (N=54)	29.6%	31.4%	2.0%	37.0%	--

Exhibit 95. Responses of Managers, by Organization Type, to the
Question: What was your cost recovery goal when
you first introduced on-line services? (N=320)

We asked managers whether their original cost-recovery goal had changed since the on-line service was first introduced. Approximately 71% responded that no change in cost-recovery goals had been necessary, while 25% said that there had been a change. The other 4% were uncertain or did not respond to this question. About 41% of the Educational users, in contrast to 12% of the Commercial users, indicated that their original cost recovery goals had changed.

The majority of those who changed their cost-recovery orientation had moved toward recovering some portion of the costs incurred by on-line searching. For the most part these respondents found that the entire costs could not be absorbed in their present budgets. Many other respondents began their on-line program using grant funds and hoped that their grants would continue to be renewed. As the grant funding ended, they found that continuation of the service dictated that the end-user pay for some portion of the search costs. Another smaller group of managers responded that they had always intended to initiate some sort of end-user charge as soon as the searchers were able to perform high quality on-line searches. This latter group felt strongly that the end-user should not be required to pay for the "training" of the searchers.

The group of managers and searchers who participated in the on-site interviews were also asked whether they believed that their current position on cost recovery would change over the next year. The group split evenly between those who foresaw no imminent change and those who believed that some sort of change would occur. Most of the latter group were managers from organizations that at that time did not charge the end-user for on-line services; these managers believed that completely free service would be ending soon. The reasons most often given for instituting user charges were increasing costs and increasing use of the on-line services.

The managers who participated in the on-site interviews were also asked whether any limitations or pressures were placed on their service by their current policies on recovering costs. Most replied that they could think of no limitations that they themselves placed on service (e.g., establishing a maximum time to be spent on an individual search request). However, two managers reported that end-users sometimes placed a limit on the amount that they were willing to pay for an on-line search, thus making it impossible for the on-line searcher to perform a high-quality search if the search turned out to be a particularly difficult one. Of the group that did place limitations on on-line searching, most of them were not charging end-users for on-line searches. The most common limitations in these cases seemed to be a maximum time allotment for performing the on-line search and a limit to the number of citations per search.

Given the fact that libraries, the type of organization most heavily repre-sented in the study, have a tradition of offering service without charge to the end-user, the initial efforts on the part of over half of the respondents to the Cost section to maintain that tradition should come as no surprise. In a separate analysis, we learned that those organizations that did not offer literature-searching services before having access to on-line services were somewhat more likely that the rest of the study population to try to recover some or all of their costs. About 17% of this group of 114 organizations reported that they wanted to recover all costs when their service was first initiated, and 41% tried to recover a portion of their costs. For the overall study population, the corresponding figures were 16% and 29%.

During the on-site interviews, managers were asked whether the question of charging clients for on-line services had been a major issue in their organiza-tions. For most of the interviewees, it had not. Some of them expressed the belief that library services should be free, because charging discriminates between those who can pay and those who cannot. Others felt that the library is overhead and, since all departments pay into this, they should get all the service they need. On the other hand, others felt that cost recovery through user fees was a necessity and/or that a minimum charge restrains casual users from "playing" with the system.

Cost Recovery Practices

Cost Elements

The cost elements used by organizations to compute the service fees are shown
in Exhibit 96. (All the percentages shown in this table were calculated on a
base of 180 managers, those who reported that their units were charging end-
users for on-line searches.) The rankings of the cost elements used to compute
the charges to the end users are quite similar to the previously shown rankings
(Exhibit 90) of the elements used to estimate the average cost of an on-line
search. In both cases, the out-of-pocket costs for off-line printing,
computer-connect time, and communications are ranked first, second, and third.
The only differences in the two are that the fourth- and fifth-ranked elements
in Exhibit 91 (staff time at the terminal and terminal rental/purchase) are
reversed in Exhibit 96, as are the seventh- and eighth-ranked elements (subscription costs and post-terminal staff time).

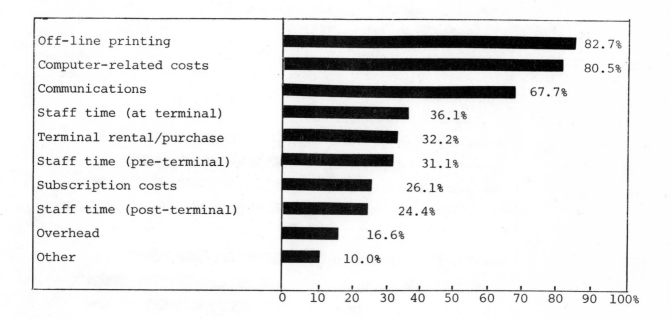

Off-line printing	82.7%
Computer-related costs	80.5%
Communications	67.7%
Staff time (at terminal)	36.1%
Terminal rental/purchase	32.2%
Staff time (pre-terminal)	31.1%
Subscription costs	26.1%
Staff time (post-terminal)	24.4%
Overhead	16.6%
Other	10.0%

Exhibit 96. Elements of Cost Included in End-User Fees for
On-Line Searches (N=180)

As already mentioned, the cost elements most commonly included in computing
end-user fees are the direct or out-of-pocket costs of off-line printing,
computer connect time, and communications, reported by about 83%, 81%, and 68%
of the managers, respectively. After that, there is more than a 31% drop to
the next group of cost elements. We do not know whether the majority of
organizations were not including pre- and post-terminal staff time in their
fees because they did not believe that they should be included or because they

were finding that the record-keeping associated with monitoring these activities was so difficult. A slightly greater percentage of organizations were including staff time _at_ the terminal in their fees, perhaps because this time is directly associated with searching costs and lends itself more easily to maintaining records.

Some of the responses reported by the managers in the "Other" category were:

"The charge is based on the difference between our operating grant and the actual operation costs, excluding staff. This figure is divided by the estimated number of searches performed in one year."

"The photocopy charges of some lending libraries are passed on to the end-user (if copies of any of the articles cited in the on-line printout are obtained for the end-user)."

"There is a $1.00 service charge for all end-users."

"There is a nominal charge for all end-users to avoid abuse of the on-line service."

In Exhibit 97 we have displayed the percentages of users, for each organization type, who were including the various cost elements in their search fees.

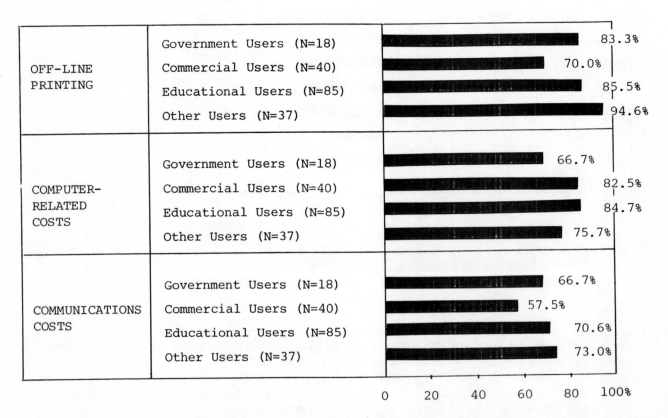

Exhibit 97. Cost Elements Included in Charges to End-Users by Organization Type, as Reported by Managers (page 1 of 2)

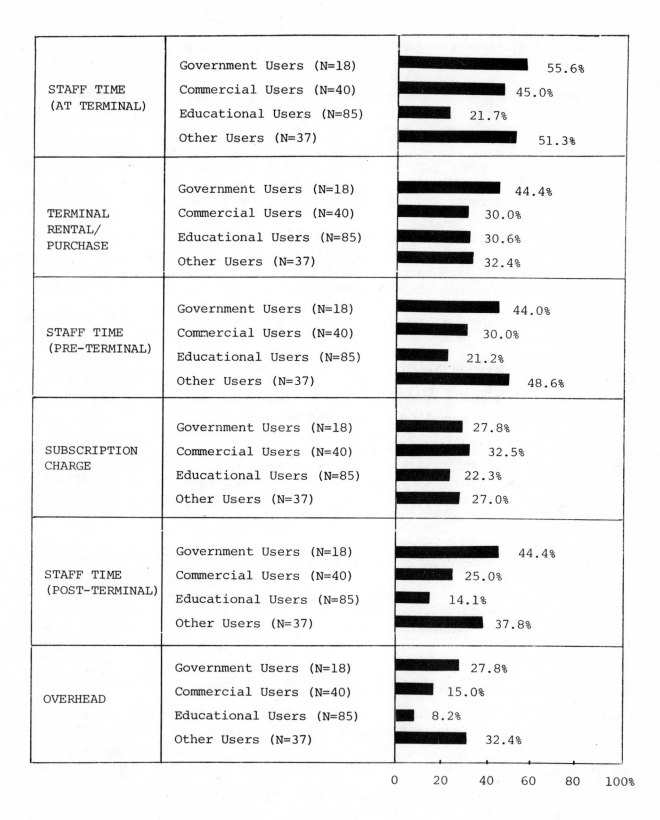

Exhibit 97. Cost Elements Included in Charges to End-Users by Organization Type, as Reported by Managers (page 2 of 2)

In spite of some unanswered questions raised by the data, we can summarize the results as follows:

- The obvious, out-of-pocket costs--computer, printing, and communications costs--have been the elements most likely to be included in the fee structures of each organization-type group

- Other elements of cost, such as terminal rental/purchase, subscriptions (applicable only to certain systems), and overhead are more likely than not to be omitted from consideration as costs associated with the service, and they are even less likely to be included in fee structures

- The staff-time-related costs present the greatest variability in both costs and fees, and it would appear that staff time is an area in which true costs have been the least understood and cost-recovery goals have been the least clearly stated

These data support the data presented earlier that showed that most organizations with established fees have not been attempting to recover all of their costs.

Comparison With Other Services

Another question in the area of user charges, shown in Exhibit 98, asked the managers whether the accounting or charging procedures for on-line services differed in any important ways from those procedures used for the other literature-searching services offered by the organization. Of the group who responded to this question, almost 42% indicated that the question was not applicable to their situation. Although other reasons may have been involved in this response, we believe that a significant number of managers were unable to make a comparison because they were not offering any other kind of literature-searching services.

Only a minority of the respondents, about 19%, reported that they had different accounting and charging procedures for the various literature-searching services provided by the organization. From the open-ended responses associated with this question, it appears that most of this group were charging end-users for on-line and batch searching (if offered), but not for manual searching:

- In 45 of the organizations, there were no fees for manual literature searching but there were fees for on-line searches

- In 3 organizations, charges were being assessed for both batch and on-line searches, but at different rates

- In 2 organizations, fees were associated with both manual and on-line literature searching, but again at different rates

- In 1 organization, fees were associated only with batch searching; on-line literature searches were free

Another 38% of the managers responded that their organizations were not differ-
entiating accounting and charging systems on the basis of the type of literature-searching method used.

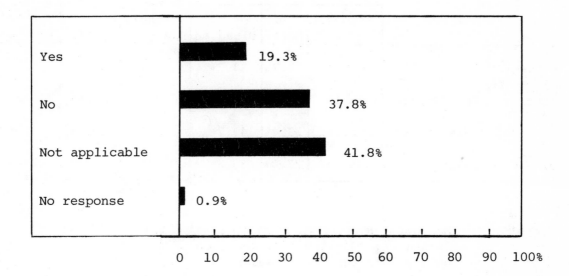

Exhibit 98.   Managers' Responses to the Question: Do your
accounting or charging procedures for on-line
services differ from the procedures used for
your other literature-searching services?
(N=320)

Attitudes Toward Cost-Recovery Practices

To assess current attitudes toward cost-recovery practices, we asked managers
to react to the following statement: "On-line services should 'pay their own
way' in an organization." The results were as follows:

- 42% of the respondents agreed or strongly agreed with the statement

- 37% of the respondents disagreed or strongly disagreed with the
statement

- 17% had no opinion, and 4% did not respond

These responses show that the user community is split fairly evenly between
those who believe that on-line services should pay their own way, and those who
do not, with approximately 17% of the survey population being undecided about
this issue.

In Exhibit 99, the attitudes on this question are shown for each type of organization.

	Strongly Agree	Agree	Disagree	Strongly Disagree	No Opinion	No Response
Government Users (N=101)	2.0%	27.7%	33.7%	6.9%	25.7%	4.0%
Commercial Users (N=152)	15.1%	37.5%	20.4%	2.7%	18.4%	5.9%
Educational Users (N=145)	5.5%	32.4%	40.7%	7.6%	10.3%	3.5%
Other Users (N=74)	16.2%	27.0%	36.5%	2.1%	16.2%	2.0%

Exhibit 99. Managers' Responses, by Organization Type, to the Statement: On-line services should "pay their own way" in the organization.

Over 48% of the Educational users disagreed or disagreed strongly with the statement but, as we previously indicated (Exhibit 93), over 76% of the Educational users reported that they had instituted service fees. The contrast in these two responses, and across the user groups as a whole, suggests the kind of tug-of-war that prevails in the library and information services community relative to the traditional philosophy of free service and the practical requirements of implementing on-line literature-searching services for end-users.

9. PROBLEMS IN USING ON-LINE SERVICES

The two previous chapters reported study results on how the systems and data bases were being used. In this chapter we will report the results from various sections in the Searcher questionnaire dealing with problems associated with accessing the systems, with use of the data bases, and with off-line printing. A final section will cover questionnaire items on communications between on-line suppliers and users.

Although it would be helpful to the industry if we could isolate the source of problems encountered by users in terms of specific system components, e.g., the telecommunications systems, computer hardware, terminals or retrieval programs, it is not possible to obtain precise or highly reliable data through a questionnaire survey. The total system involved in providing on-line services is so complex and interrelated that even the most experienced user may often not be able to isolate the source of a particular problem. Therefore, our objective in studying the reliability issue was relatively modest and limited: to identify the general problem areas associated with the use of the on-line technology, to learn something about their frequency and severity, and to determine what areas merit more detailed and careful study.

GENERAL SYSTEM-RELATED PROBLEMS ENCOUNTERED BY SEARCHERS

System-Related Malfunctioning

When the on-line light goes out at the terminal, or the searcher's internal time-clock says that the response from the computer is taking longer than normal for a particular system, he is encountering a problem. The source of the difficulty may be a malfunctioning in any one of the components of the total system: the terminal, the telephone, the coupler or modem, the telephone lines, the network computer(s) or telephone lines, some part of the supplier's computer, or the retrieval program itself. People in the system may also be involved. For example, if the user is dialing through a switchboard operator, he may have been disconnected. By dialing again, the user may "eliminate" the problem, but he may never know exactly what caused the difficulty. If the difficulty continues, the user has several choices. One is to engage in some diagnostic procedures, e.g., try a different telephone or, if it is available, a different terminal. Another alternative is for the user to call the supplier to see if the particular system is functioning properly, so that the number of possibilities is reduced before additional diagnostic steps are taken. Still another alternative is to leave the terminal and try later, or to do the search in some other way. Some searchers do this, hoping that the problem will be gone the next time they decide to use the terminal.

Exhibit 100 shows the frequency with which searchers reported system-related problems.

	Frequently	Occasionally	Rarely/Never	No Response
1. With supplier's computer system	13.1%	37.8%	36.9%	12.2%
2. Disconnection from host computer	10.7%	36.5%	45.8%	7.0%
3. Apparent loss of control of the program (i.e., nothing seems to work right)	4.8%	14.4%	70.8%	10.0%
4. Loss of data (i.e., incomplete transmission)	6.1%	13.5%	72.9%	7.5%
5. Intermittent transmission of "garbage" characters	12.1%	21.1%	60.4%	6.4%
6. Totally unintelligble transmissions	4.1%	7.1%	78.4%	10.4%

Exhibit 100.   Frequency of Occurrence of System-Related Problems Reported by Searchers (N=801)

Many of the problems itemized in the questionnaire were intended primarily to apply to the suppliers' systems. However, to interpret the data in Exhibit 99 solely in relation to the suppliers' system reliability we must assume that users generally know the source(s) of any difficulties. For items 2, 4, 5, and 6, however, the source could easily be elsewhere in the total system, particularly in the communications system. Therefore, if the data are not entirely reliable in terms of source identification, they do represent some initial measurement of the degree to which the users attribute problems to different sources.* In general, these data suggest that the systems are indeed quite reliable or the users' tolerance for sporadic system problems is fairly high.

---

*The data groupings in Exhibits 100, 101, and 109 have been developed from the original quantified response choices as follows: "Frequently" is an aggregation of About Once During a Terminal Session and About Once Every 2 or 3 Sessions; "Occasionally" was defined as About Once Every 6 or So Terminal Sessions. The data for each original response choice are provided in Appendix B.

Additional data from this section of the questionnaire also indicate that the equipment being used by organizations has been fairly reliable. As shown in Exhibit 101, terminals and couplers or dataphones have been the source of problems only infrequently.

	Frequently	Occasionally	Rarely/Never	No Response
Terminal Problems	4.2%	8.9%	76.2%	10.6%
Coupler Problems	2.1%	4.2%	64.4%	29.2%
Dataphone Problems	1.1%	1.9%	52.9%	43.9%

Exhibit 101. Frequency of Occurrence of Equipment-Related Problems Reported by Searchers (N=801)

Users' levels of tolerance for various problems cannot be measured adequately through a questionnaire survey. However, one aspect of on-line system use for which we believed it was important to establish some attitudinal data is response time, i.e., the elapsed time that occurs between the users' signaling input to the system and when the response is received at the terminal. Differences between systems in response time occur because of any number of factors, including the computer hardware that is used (including the data storage hardware) and the design of the retrieval program itself. Variations within one system from time to time can be a function of user load, of the particular operations that are being performed by users at the time--since some search processes are more demanding of Central Processing Unit (CPU) time--and of the general "health" of the computer system. Some response-time variation can also be introduced by the intervening communications network system.

Searchers were first asked whether variations in response time bothered them, and then were asked to identify the courses of action they generally take on response-time problems. As shown in Exhibit 102, almost 80% reported that they were bothered by variations in response time. In a separate analysis, we learned that those with more experience were even more vocal in indicating that variations in response time bothered them: of those with from 1 to 3 months' experience, about 63% said Yes to this question, and of those with from 1 to 3 years' experience, almost 87% said Yes. The subset of respondents who said Yes to this basic question appear to react in one of several ways when these variations occur.

	All Respondents (N=801)	BY ORGANIZATIONAL TYPE			
		Government Users (N=192)	Commercial Users (N=247)	Educational Users (N=264)	Other Users (N=98)
Yes	79.7%	79.2%	71.7%	87.1%	79.6%
No	19.1%	19.8%	26.7%	11.4%	18.4%
No Response	1.2%	1.0%	1.6%	1.1%	2.0%

Exhibit 102. Searchers' Responses to Question: Do variations in the response time from the system generally bother you?

The data displayed in Exhibit 103--based on the percentages responding Yes to the question above--show that most users seem to have been "putting up with it," and very few have been turning to a different mode of completing the search. This suggests that, given a short-term problem, the searchers may very well have an adaptable, if not totally tolerant, approach to "waiting time." Since we did not pursue the distinction between infrequently occurring variations and consistent variability within terminal sessions, we cannot draw any conclusions about the general level of tolerance among on-line users. We can clearly establish, however, that users are relying on the suppliers to "fix" their problems so that the users can, in turn, perform their service function.

		Usually	Sometimes	Rarely/ Never	No Response
TERMINATE TERMINAL SESSION AND TRY AGAIN	All Users (N=638)	19.6%	57.2%	22.7%	0.5%
	Government Users (N=152)	15.8%	52.6%	30.3%	1.3%
	Commercial Users (N=177)	16.9%	55.9%	26.6%	0.6%
	Educational Users (N=230)	21.7%	61.3%	17.0%	--
	Other Users (N=78)	26.9%	57.7%	15.4%	--
TERMINATE TERMINAL SESSION AND COMPLETE SEARCH IN SOME OTHER WAY	All Users (N=638)	1.3%	18.0%	80.3%	0.5%
	Government Users (N=152)	2.0%	19.7%	77.6%	0.7%
	Commercial Users (N=177)	1.7%	16.4%	81.4%	0.5%
	Educational Users (N=230)	0.1%	16.5%	82.6%	0.8%
	Other Users (N=78)	--	23.1%	75.6%	1.3%
PUT UP WITH IT	All Users (N=638)	48.7%	34.0%	16.8%	0.5%
	Government Users (N=152)	49.3%	28.9%	21.7%	--
	Commercial Users (N=177)	46.9%	36.7%	15.3%	1.1%
	Educational Users (N=230)	51.7%	34.8%	13.5%	--
	Other Users (N=78)	43.6%	35.9%	19.2%	1.2%
CALL SUPPLIER TO ASK WHAT'S HAPPENING BE-FORE MAKING DECISION	All Users (N=638)	11.0%	36.2%	52.2%	0.6%
	Government Users (N=152)	21.1%	40.8%	37.5%	0.1%
	Commercial Users (N=177)	10.2%	39.5%	49.2%	1.1%
	Educational Users (N=230)	3.9%	34.8%	61.3%	--
	Other Users (N=78)	12.8%	24.4%	61.5%	1.3%

Exhibit 103. Reactions by Searchers to System Response-Time Variations

Undiagnosed Difficulties

Only about one-half of the searcher respondents elected to respond to a final
item--on the frequency with which they were encountering "undiagnosed" problems--
in the list of problem areas that they were given. Of those, 37% rarely or
never had problems that they considered undiagnosed. In a separate part of
the questionnaire, the respondents were asked to indicate the degree to which
they were having difficulty in actually diagnosing different kinds of problems--
those that appeared to be system-related problems and those that appeared to
be their own errors:

- Only about 4% of the searchers were having any difficulties in
  diagnosing what appeared to be system-related problems in most
  searches or terminal sessions, and about 38% were having difficulties
  in some sessions. Over 50% reported that they were having difficulties in diagnosing system-related problems in very few sessions
  or never at all.

- Only about 3% of the searchers were having difficulties in diagnosing
  what appeared to be their own errors in most searches or terminal
  sessions, and 28% in some sessions. Over 67% reported that they
  were having difficulties in diagnosing their own errors in very few
  sessions or never at all.

As shown in Exhibits 104-A and 104-B, the responses across user groups are
fairly consistent. In a separate analysis, we also learned that differences
in degrees of difficulty do not appear to be related to either experience
levels or to use of different numbers of systems.

	SEARCHES/TERMINAL SESSIONS				
	Most	Some	Very Few	Never	No Response
Government Users (N=192)	2.6%	31.3%	54.7%	9.4%	2.0%
Commercial Users (N=247)	4.3%	30.8%	53.0%	9.7%	2.2%
Educational Users (N=264)	0.8%	25.0%	61.4%	11.4%	1.4%
Other Users (N=98)	4.8%	24.5%	51.0%	16.3%	3.4%

Exhibit 104-A.   Frequency of Problems Reported by Searchers, by Organization Type, in Diagnosing What Appear to be System-Related
Problems

	SEARCHES/TERMINAL SESSIONS				
	Most	Some	Very Few	Never	No Response
Government Users (N=192)	5.7%	38.0%	44.3%	11.5%	0.5%
Commercial Users (N=247)	5.7%	31.6%	51.4%	9.3%	2.0%
Educational Users (N=264)	1.2%	41.7%	48.9%	6.4%	1.8%
Other Users (N=98)	4.1%	40.8%	41.8%	11.2%	2.1%

Exhibit 104-B.   Frequency of Problems Reported by Searchers, by Organization Type, in Diagnosing What Appear to be Their Own Problems

Although it is quite remarkable that the level of difficulty with undiagnosed problems is so low, the unstructured responses to the general question of problem-areas, diagnosed and otherwise, that were provided by about 25% of the searchers, help to illuminate, in the users' language, the general problems of concern to them. Tabulated responses and illustrative comments are provided in Exhibit 105. The number in parentheses after each group heading shows the total number of responses for that particular problem area. Representative comments follow each major heading, and the number (if greater than one) of respondents who provided similar comments is shown in parentheses after the comment. The language of the respondents is sometimes quite colorful, but it is heartening to note that some common system terminology is being adopted.

<u>System Performance:</u> <u>Response and Transmissions</u> (26)

Slow response.

No response.

Inordinate delays without a disconnect.

Response-time changes in mid-search (from 5 to 20 seconds); is irritating.

Occasionally receive no response after an extended time and must decide whether to disconnect or not.

Delay in response time--1 to 2 minutes, sometimes longer. Occurs frequently.

End of each user-generated message fails to be received by computer, and user waits endlessly for processing to be completed.

Slow response time: system dies during session, and no indication whether system went down or network in difficulty.

Slow response; unable to log-off or do anything.

<u>"Garbage" Transmission and Telephone Line Problems</u> (25)

Use government telephone lines; phone hookup very bad.

Transmits garbage characters--costly in terms of time and money.

When typing there are <u>un</u>transmitted garbage characters.

Garbage-characters.

Terminal is sensitive to line noise; irritating during training activities.

Telephone line noise.

Poor quality telephone lines. Correctly typed terms will be rejected first time then accepted when retyped.

Don't get garbage characters every day, but when it occurs, it continues all day.

Exhibit 105. Problem Areas Identified by Searchers in Unstructured Questionnaire Item (page 1 of 5)

Line problems; leakage and garbage transmission; neither phone company nor communications network will take responsibility.

Terminal "dies" because of a "blurp" or something in the FTS system which knocks me out of system.

Incorrect transmission of characters.

Problem seems to be going through switchboard.

Line interference.

Telephone operators interrupt or monitor lines.

Lightning and thunder.

'Ghosts' or transients, e.g., an end of search transmitted and effected from outside.

Undiagnosed problems we believe to be caused by phone company lines, as we have to call long distance to the nearest network node.

We frequently have problems with obtaining a static-free line on the company tie-line network.

Fluctuation in accuracy of print letters.

On dedicated telephone line, no response from supplier for brief periods when trouble is not with supplier's computer.

The Retrieval Program   (18)

Having difficulty getting a certain feature to work right.

Have been returned to the beginning of search with no discernible reason.

System occasionally just stops when a category is indicated which is not available from that data base.

Occasional loops; reentry into another user's search.

Strange unexplainable results appear.

If system fails after extensive combining of searches there is no way to recover the lost time and money.

Instruction confused the computer--it skipped to middle of search.

Difference in posting message when the same statement is re-run.

Rejects or wipes out legitimate entries.

Improper reponse to commands.

Exhibit 105.   Problem Areas Identified by Searchers
(page 2 of 5)

Related to software--e.g., data cell loops.

Software problems, e.g., program loops; data cell malfunctions.

A command may yield no hits but the reentry yields 20 or 30.

Manual-suggested means/rules of searching are not followed by the system.

Bugs in program that programmers haven't fixed.

Program seems to ignore part or all of a search strategy; doesn't get all citations.

General   (17)

Numerous difficulties each time it's used; takes many hours to accomplish what should take a short time. Have checked the terminal, the coupler, the phone, phone lines, Tymshare, and suppliers all say their segment is working fine.

Two searchers simultaneously trying to use same password.

Lack of knowledge of commands, format, etc.

Problems usually go away on retry.

Unsuccessful search--now what?

Inexperienced in deciding whether logging in problem is due to system or communications network.

Don't have the technical background to determine problems. I try again or call supplier.

Intermittent terminal, telephone, network, host computer problems. Each says it isn't their equipment.

System not up when scheduled, or the computer crashing while on-line. Occurs often enough to be faintly ulcerogenic.

Carrier tone changes and nothing works until the tone is normal. Unable to diagnose problem.

General computer failures.

Software problems.

Programming errors.

Each technician for a piece of equipment in a given system...only understands the characteristics of his equipment and never seems to have an understanding of the whole system--human problems trying to pass the buck are the ugliest.

Operator errors.

Occasional parity errors on information from computer.

Difficulty in distinguishing equipment problems and supplier's problems.

Exhibit 105.   Problem Areas Identified by Searchers
(page 3 of 5)

System Availability (12)

Get "No ports" message and can't get in.

Log in, only to find system is down. (Time of availability not given.)

Due to heavy use, computer "out of ports" or network "out of channels"; 3 hours time difference between location of computer and terminal lessens on-line time.

Communications network down.

Sometimes communications network and host computer appear to go down simultaneously.

Establishing Connections (10)

Log-on in half-duplex, but continue to get double characters. Control H does not make a difference. Do searching in full duplex to get single characters. Logging on in full duplex doesn't work--does not accept password and invariably the communications network sends error message. No problems logging on when half-duplex used.

Most problems due to interfacing between net and host--almost all due to identification.

At times, after logging in there is no response and one must hang up and dial again. A given password is often rejected continuously.

Difficulties logging in with a 2741-type terminal, but few with a 10 cps teletypewriter.

Trouble logging in.

Can't establish connection--line, dataphone problem or computer down.

Cannot log in--no diagnostic messages.

Occasionally, system refuses to accept legal entry code.

The "Bump" (7)

Average about 3 to 4 disconnects per month; in middle of search.

Enter message appears in midsearch.

Dropped midsearch.

Cut out of system in middle of a print.

Interrupted; goes back to log in.

Asked to log in again during search about 2 times per month.

Interjection of request for password after having logged in and having been accepted. Happens far too often.

Exhibit 105. Problem Areas Identified by Searchers
(page 4 of 5)

<u>Crossed Wires</u> (6)

Get logged into 'another user's environment.'

Receiving results of someone else's search; someone else illegally using project code.

Crossed-wire type responses on the terminal.

Once got disconnected because got someone else's search.

I have twice received someone else's data.

Twice received another searcher's data.

<u>The Terminal</u> (5)

Paper doesn't advance.

Inevitable shut down of connection (keyboard locks) after on-line printout of any length (on 2741-type terminal).

Terminal goes into total vibration and disconnects.

Keyboard problems.

<u>Intermittent Transmission</u> (4)

Jerky print movements.

Typing quits mid-citation.

System stops during printout, must repeat instruction to system.

Exhibit 105. Problem Areas Identified by Searchers
(page 5 of 5)

The groupings established for these responses could vary considerably if we had more details on the problems at the time they occurred and could associate the problems with their actual sources. For example, some problems in establishing connections may be due to system availability status, system performance, or transmission problems. System performance can mean the performance of the supplier's computer or of its retrieval program, or it can mean the performance of components in the communications network.

In general, we interpret these comments, and the responses to other system-problem-related areas, to mean that there is no one major weak link in the chain that underlies the on-line services. However, we believe that the un-structured responses--in particular, the combination of responses for establishing connections, getting bumped, and garbage transmissions--suggest that many of the problems are associated with the transmission of data through the telephone system. This is the one element that is least under the control of the supplier, and is a key to understanding the "finger-pointing" dilemma that some of the respondents reported.

The "finger-pointing" dilemma by various suppliers was one of the main reasons that many of the on-line suppliers who use the Tymshare communications network (TYMNET) created a formalized user group. This group provides a forum for the on-line suppliers to bring to the attention of one of their key suppliers any problems that are being experienced by many users of different systems. More of this kind of cross-supplier communication--with terminal suppliers and "Ma Bell" representatives--would be very advantageous for the further advancement of on-line services.

In a later section of this chapter, we discuss users' communications with their on-line suppliers. The fast-contact methods (by terminal and telephone) were not being used as frequently as we might have expected, but we would hope that individuals who were experiencing the complicated log-in problem with half- and full-duplex, or whose terminal paper was not advancing properly, have at least written to their on-line supplier(s) for help. This second problem could, for example, be the result of the paper's not being loaded properly, or of the roll's not being in the correct position, or the roll's having become uneven. If checking these possible conditions does not help to solve the problem, it may be that the terminal itself has a line-feed problem, in which case a call to the maintenance supplier for the terminal is required.

The retrieval programs themselves emerge from this picture with rather high marks. Although the basic programs are well field-tested, some problems are to be expected, since most of them are in a dynamic state of development. Some of the general problems that were identified by users in the course of our survey have already been alleviated or removed, and others will disappear as the communications systems and teleprocessing hardware and software are improved. We expect that there will always be some number of system-related problems but that significant improvements in teleprocessing systems will be made in the next several years to reduce their "ulcerogenic" nature for users.

Searchers were asked to indicate the degree of impact that the several kinds of problems were having on their work pattern. As shown below in Exhibit 106, over half of them indicated that they interferred either "not very seriously" or "hardly at all."

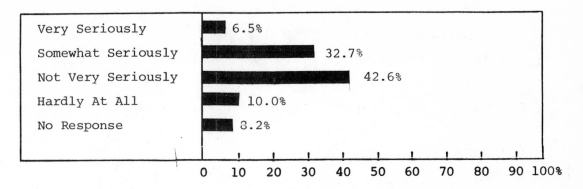

Very Seriously		6.5%
Somewhat Seriously		32.7%
Not Very Seriously		42.6%
Hardly At All		10.0%
No Response		8.2%

Exhibit 106. Searchers' Responses to Question:
How seriously do these problems in-
terfere with your work pattern?
(N=801)

When asked to indicate which kinds of problems interfered most with their work patterns, 560 respondents reported on several areas, particularly in system performance and transmission areas, as shown in Exhibit 107.

A. GENERAL AREAS

System Response Time (slowness and variability) (100)

Getting and Staying Connected (including logging in, busy telephone numbers) (214)

Disconnects or "getting bumped" (110)

Garbage Transmission (43)

Program Problems (27)

  Overflow or disk storage overflows (9)

  Loss of control of program (7)

  Rejection of instructions (5)

  Invalid or unintelligible error messages (2)

Terminal Equipment (20)

  Internal scheduling problems (8)

  Location (3)

  Malfunctions (9)

Exhibit 107. Searchers' Unstructured Response on Kinds of
Problems That Most Interfere With Work Patterns
(page 1 of 3)

Off-line printouts--delays and losses (6)

Lost data, particularly on on-line printouts (5)

Preparation of search strategies (4)

Multiple data base and system use (3)

Keeping track of frequent changes in operating rules (2)

Lack of good manual to answer all problems (1)

Duplicate citations across data bases (1)

Regular reference work (1)

Inconsistent search results (1)

Frustration (1)

Coping with uncontrolled vocabularies (1)

Search efficiency and quality of results sometimes low (1)

Lack of staff (1)

Establishing relevancy of search results (1)

Own mistakes (1)

Insufficient time for searches (1)

B. VERBATIM COMMENTS

"In order of frequency, my major problems are: 1) no ports open into host computer; 2) data bases needed and unavailable; 3) Tymshare line problems; 4) host system problems."

"The most disruptive problems are those system problems that interrupt searches, search time, and techniques."

"Any problems which cause me to repeat a search or spend extra time and money."

"Any problem which keeps me from finishing a search."

"Total loss of previous work accomplished."

"Any problem which prevents accessing host computer when doing a rush search."

"When a combination of factors prevents any on-line searching for more than 2 days running."

"System saturating: so many channels are occupied during day that response time is 'great'; best time to run a search is not best time in library, so I come in at 6 AM."

Exhibit 107.   Searchers' Unstructured Responses on Kinds of Problems that Most Interfere With Work Patterns (page 2 of 3)

"24 hour wait to perform a searching during regular working hours."

"Failure of the computer to respond in expected manner (computer and user errors)."

"Any that require rescheduling of work plan to redo a search."

"Problems occur rarely according to your choice of frequency. May log in several times a day and have problems once every two weeks. Problems occur when users are rushed or when users have free time."

"Problems after a period of time are usually worked out by the supplier. Most problems not usually system-related, but are staff problem."

"Because we schedule appointments, it's difficult to know whether to sit out a down problem, or to terminate and schedule another session. Supplier can rarely notify us of nature or magnitude of difficulty; we must telephone supplier."

"Fear of disconnection with keyboard lock which causes me to avoid using on-line display features. Deciding when slow response: should I keep waiting or should I hit an Attention Key, and perhaps the Key will interfere with the response as it is beginning."

"Difficulty in accurately defining universe of search--lack of thesauri, lack of understanding data base contents. Need better way of identifying, selecting relevant data from hits."

Exhibit 107. Searchers' Unstructured Responses on Kinds of Problems That Most Interfere With Work Patterns (page 3 of 3)

The problems identified by the respondents as most seriously interfering with their work patterns know no boundaries with regard to systems or countries. System down-time clearly has an impact on the searchers' performance of their work and in their scheduling of searches, but a bigger irritant, which is not necessarily related to the computer system of the supplier, is the "getting-into" and "staying-connected" aspect. The responses suggest that the mystery of a disconnect or a slow-down in response time is as irritating as the problem itself. On-line service suppliers can help to reduce user frustration by helping the users to understand why such problems occur and how to handle or plan around them.

More comprehensive trouble-guides, on-line aids, and "hot-lines" are undoubtedly also required to help users. We attempted to learn, through one question, what methods users had found to be effective in helping them learn how to diagnose problems. The responses, reported in Exhibit 108, show that the two most frequently used methods are telephone calls to the on-line service supplier and the elimination, one at a time, of each of several possibilities. The heavy use of the latter alternative suggests that users are in fact learning better how to diagnose problems.

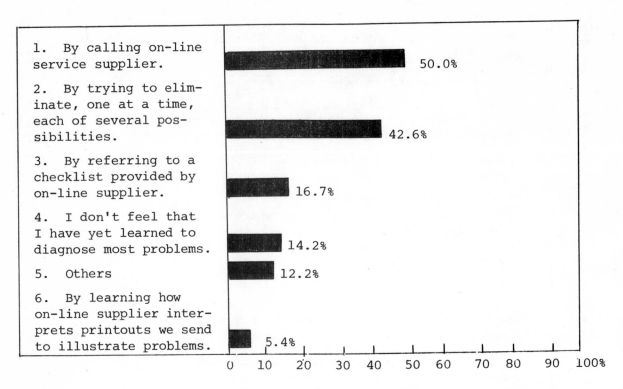

Exhibit 108. Searchers' Report on Different Methods Used
to Diagnose Problems (N=801)

Some differences exist in the ways that different user groups diagnose problems.

- A larger percentage of Government users (61.5%) call suppliers than those in Commercial or Educational organizations (47.0% and 46.6%, respectively.) This is most likely due to the availability of FTS lines in government facilities.

- Educational users (51.9%) tended to diagnose by eliminating, one at a time, each of several possibilities. Other percentages were: Commercial, 39.7%, and Government, 37.0%.

- More Commercial users (23.5%) reported that they did their problem diagnosis by referring to a checklist provided by the on-line service supplier. Other percentages were: Educational, 17.4%, and Government, 7.8%.

For those users who do not feel that they have learned to diagnose most problems, the percentages are similar across all types of organizations.

Other methods were suggested by searchers in their unstructured response
choices:

>Leaf through the manual.

>Consult another in-house user.

>Consult outside user or expert.

>I learned in training and refresher classes.

>Use manufacturer's testing system for terminal.

>Call phone company.

>I rely on terminal messages sometimes to suggest what is wrong.

>Trial and error.

>Common sense.

>By thinking.

>Experience.

>I disconnect and try again later. Always works.

Some users reported that the nature of the problem was usually obvious, and one
said that there was seldom anything that could be done about the problem. The
try-again-later approach was the most frequently given unstructured response.
There was one individual who offered a slight variation on this theme: he or
she screams first, and then tries again!

PROBLEM AREAS IN ACCESSING SYSTEMS

As mentioned earlier, some differences in telecommunications services impact
on searchers. All searchers were asked to report on the frequency of problems
in accessing the different systems, and multiple-system searchers were specifically asked to report on the degree to which the different logging-in procedures were a source of confusion to them.

Reliability in the Telecommunications Area

There are several links in the chain of access to a host computer, some of which
are not under the direct control of the on-line supplier. These include tele-
phone-related services (local telephone companies, AT&T, and data networks) and
equipment (terminals, couplers or dataphones, and the data networks' computers
and related hardware/software).

It is not always easy to identify the source of a difficulty and it may take considerable time and effort to narrow down the possibilities. An example will help to illustrate the potential complexity of the diagnostic process. A user in New York, working with a 2741-type terminal (i.e., non-ASCII code, and operating at approximately 15 characters-per-second) and a dataphone, was unable to get to the SDC computer on her terminal. This same terminal was being used successfully by the data processing department in the organization to access another interactive, non-bibliographic system, but none of the information or data processing specialists could make it work through Tymshare's network.

The user called several vendors, including representatives from Tymshare, the local telephone company, and the terminal supplier. In the meantime, this searcher was constantly being asked by suppliers and her colleagues the same questions, such as, "Are you sure you are dialing correctly?" As we discussed the problem with the searcher over the telephone, it became clear that individual consultations by each supplier were not being productive and that remote diagnosis was impossible. Each supplier was, in effect, pointing the finger at the other suppliers. Therefore, we scheduled a group meeting, on-site, with all vendors present in the same room to diagnose the problem. The searcher, in the meantime, was feeling that, when all the "doctors" were in the room, the symptom would not occur, and continued to work at the problem. She asked the data processing staff person who used the terminal for the other non-bibliographic on-line system to watch her dial--one more time. After several tries, he noticed one difference between her procedure and his: she pressed the dataphone button labeled "DATA" before she put the telephone in the cradle; he was used to doing it after the phone was in the cradle. Simply reversing the steps solved the problem, ending a month of inability to use on-line service. In spite of puzzling and frustrating problems like this, the data in Exhibit 109 show that searchers rate the reliability of the components in the access chain as fairly high, and that no one component is regarded as a major problem.

	Fre-quently	Occa-sionally	Rarely/Never	No Response
1. Can't get a telephone line out of my own organization.	5.6%	6.1%	73.3%	15.0%
2. Have trouble in logging into the communications network.	14.7%	30.7%	43.8%	10.7%
3. Have trouble logging into the host computer.	15.6%	41.7%	33.3%	9.4%
4. Get disconnected by our own switchboard.	0.8%	3.4%	77.9%	17.9%
5. Problems with lines or computers of the communications network.	12.4%	29.1%	41.0%	17.4%

Exhibit 109. Searchers' Report on Frequency of Occurrence of Problems with Equipment and in Establishing Connections (N=801)

The three areas with more than 10% of the problems have to do with logging into either the network or the host computer, but the possible sources of these
difficulties can vary from time to time, and can include terminals, couplers,
telephone connections, and computers.

No objective data on the reliability of the computer networks or suppliers'
computers are available, but the subjective responses from the respondents
suggest that 1) the total systems have been working about as well as the
respondents expect, and/or 2) the problems users have been encountering are
sporadic enough, or the signs of continuing improvement visible enough, that
the overall feeling they have is one of fairly high satisfaction.

Different Logging-In Procedures As Sources of Confusion

Multiple-system users must learn how to log into each of the computers, using
one or more different access methods. Those multiple-system searchers (51.6%)
who reported that the use of multiple systems had been a source of confusion for
them were asked to indicate the degree to which the different login procedures
were a source of confusion.* The response data are provided in Exhibit 110.
As the Exhibit shows, the majority have experienced either little or no confusion in this area. Most Educational and Commercial users do not seem to be
having a problem, but nearly 40% of the Government users report that it is
either a "great" or "moderate" problem for them.

	Great	Moderate	Low	None	No Response
All Users (N=175)	5.7%	21.7%	42.3%	27.4%	2.9%
Government Users (N=29)	3.4%	34.5%	41.4%	13.8%	6.9%
Commercial Users (N=72)	6.9%	15.3%	43.1%	31.9%	2.8%
Educational Users (N=52)	3.2%	19.2%	44.2%	30.8%	2.6%
Other Users (N=22)	9.1%	31.8%	36.4%	18.2%	4.5%

Exhibit 110. Degree of Confusion Among Multiple-System
Searchers in Procedures for Logging into
Different Systems (N=175)

---

*These data are derived from Section D of the Searcher questionnaire. The
total number of multiple-system-searcher respondents to this section was 339.
Most of the data from this section are reported in Chapter 10. A particularly
important piece of data is the background response for this question: 47.8%
of the 339 searchers reported that using more than one system was sometimes
confusing but the problems were not insurmountable nor did they generally
affect efficiency, and 3.8% reported that using more than one system was a
major problem. Both of these respondent groups (a total of 175 searchers)
are included in this login procedures report.

The login area is one in which the on-line suppliers might be able to help eliminate much of the confusion. For example, if the problem stems primarily from the different terminology for logging into the host computers, the suppliers might conceivably work toward a more uniform, agreed-upon interactive language.

Some of the confusion, of course, may reside in areas outside their control, e.g., in the procedures for logging into the communications network or in areas that are integral to the differences in teleprocessing hardware and software resources being used by the suppliers. Yet, even here, the on-line suppliers can play a useful role by forming network-user groups and calling the attention of network suppliers to problems associated with different network protocol.

GENERAL PROBLEMS ASSOCIATED WITH DATA-BASE USE

Searchers were asked to indicate the degree to which they were having difficulties in three major areas related to data-base use: 1) identifying the appropriate data base(s) for a given search; 2) preparing search strategies; and 3) assessing the relevance of their search results. The respondents indicated that none of these areas presented problems in all searches, but, to varying degrees, they did pose problems in some or very few searches:

- About 8% of the searchers encountered problems most of the time in preparing their search strategies (including selecting terms and deciding how they should be combined) and about 47% encountered this difficulty in some searches. The remainder of the searchers had this problem only rarely or not at all.

- Only about 2% reported that identifying the appropriate data base(s) for a given search was a problem that they encountered in most searches; about 17% encountered it in some searches, and the majority believed that it was a problem in very few searches or never.

- Most users (about 55%) indicated that they rarely or never had problems in assessing the relevance of their search results and in deciding that the search was actually done. About 36% of the searchers encountered this difficulty in some searches, but fewer than 10% encountered it most of the time.

These data are displayed by organizatonal user group in Exhibit 111. In general, the responses are similar, except in the first area: identifying the appropriate data base(s) for a given search. Commercial organization users have a slightly greater tendency to encounter difficulty in this area than users in other groups. We believe that this difference probably reflects the fact that, as we saw in Chapter 7, these searchers are more likely to use a multiple-data-base approach and, perhaps, they are working with more complex search problems that are potentially cross-disciplinary in content.

		Searches/Sessions				
		Most	Some	Few	None	No Response
IDENTIFYING APPROPRIATE DATA BASE(S)	Government Users (N=191)	1.5%	17.3%	46.6%	34.6%	--
	Commercial Users (N=247)	1.8%	22.3%	52.2%	21.1%	2.6%
	Educational Users (N=264)	0.3%	12.9%	54.5%	32.2%	0.1%
	Other Users (N=98)	2.3%	14.3%	43.9%	36.7%	2.8%
DEVELOPING SEARCH STRATEGIES	Government Users (N=191)	11.5%	45.0%	34.6%	8.9%	--
	Commercial Users (N=247)	8.5%	44.1%	39.7%	5.3%	2.4%
	Educational Users (N=264)	3.1%	53.0%	39.0%	4.8%	0.1%
	Other Users (N=98)	8.2%	45.9%	35.7%	8.2%	2.0%
ASSESSING RELEVANCE	Government Users (N=191)	8.4%	39.8%	38.7%	13.1%	--
	Commercial Users (N=247)	9.3%	32.8%	48.2%	7.3%	2.4%
	Educational Users (N=264)	5.3%	35.6%	52.7%	5.7%	0.7%
	Other Users (N=98)	5.1%	38.8%	44.9%	9.2%	2.0%

Exhibit 111. Searchers' Report on Frequency of Problems with
General Data-Base-Use Areas (N=801)

We also looked at the searchers' responses in terms of level of experience and
the number of systems that they were using. A greater percentage of the less-
experienced user group, particularly those with only 1 to 6 months of experience,
were having problems in each of the areas, and fewer of the experienced users,
particularly the veterans of three years or more, were having difficulties
in any of the three areas.

The only difference in responses between single-system users and multiple-system
users occurred in identifying the appropriate data base(s): multiple-system
users have somewhat more difficulty. This is not surprising, since multiple-
system users also have access to more data bases.

USERS' PROBLEMS WITH OFF-LINE PRINTING

Since off-line printing is clearly a very important part of the on-line retrieval services, it is important to review the kinds of problems that users have been encountering with this aspect of the services.

According to our study results, users are fairly satisfied with the off-line printing services of the suppliers. About 15% indicated that they have experienced significant or frequent problems with off-line printing, but the vast majority reported that they experienced no problems. Among those respondents who indicated, in an unstructured question, that they were encountering problems, approximately 100 specified the nature of the problems. The most frequently mentioned problem was delays in the mail. The range of turnaround time reported was from a few days to over three weeks. Some users who are getting three-to-five-day service were still not satisfied; they indicated that they wanted one-day service.

There was no particular concurrence on the other types of problems, samples of which are illustrated below:

> Printouts lost by supplier (or as one respondent reported: "On occasion, printouts have been eaten by the computer").
>
> Receive only partial results.
>
> Mailed to wrong user.
>
> Occasional duplications. *(There was not enough explanation provided here to know whether the user was referring to duplicate printouts or duplicate citations from several data bases.)*
>
> Print quality and format are poor.
>
> Rising costs.
>
> Cannot address directly to user.
>
> Takes too much time to enter mailing information.
>
> Would like to receive notification of its being sent.
>
> Want configuration message that the off-line action has been accepted by the system.
>
> Occasionally get dropped from the communications network right while I am entering off-line information.

One user indicated he or she would like to receive notification that the off-line printout had been sent. This is not an unfair request but, most of the time, the user would probably receive the printout before they received the notification.

COMMUNICATION BETWEEN USERS AND ON-LINE SUPPLIERS

An important contribution to the users' being able to deal with system problems and differences among systems is the support that they receive from on-line service suppliers. We asked the searchers several questions about both their direct communications with suppliers for obtaining assistance and their indirect contacts through newsletters and system documentation.

The first question asked searchers to indicate the level of importance they placed on the availability of telephone or interactive, terminal-to-terminal consultation with the supplier's staff regarding questions about system usage or problems. Two thirds of the searchers reported that telephone assistance is essential, but fewer than one fourth of them believed that terminal-to-terminal consultation is essential. Interestingly, the more experienced searchers were somewhat more likely than the less experienced ones to consider telephone contact an essential part of the on-line service.

The responses of searchers in each organizational user group are displayed in Exhibits 112 and 113. These data show that there is a fair amount of consensus on the need for direct contact, although Educational users place a slightly higher premium on terminal-to-terminal communication.

	Essential	Important	Not Needed	No Response
All Searchers (N=801)	68.8%	25.1%	3.0%	3.1%
Government Users (N=192)	77.1%	18.2%	3.9%	0.8%
Commercial Users (N=247)	70.0%	23.9%	1.2%	4.9%
Educational Users (N=264)	65.2%	29.2%	3.7%	1.9%
Other Users (N=98)	58.2%	28.6%	6.1%	7.1%

Exhibit 112. Searchers' Report on Level of Importance of Telephone
Contact with On-Line Suppliers

	Essential	Important	Not Needed	No Response
All Searchers (N=801)	21.0%	52.6%	17.9%	8.6%
Government Users (N=192)	15.1%	46.4%	26.0%	12.5%
Commercial Users (N=247)	13.8%	59.9%	17.0%	8.1%
Educational Users (N=264)	29.2%	52.3%	9.5%	9.1%
Other Users (N=98)	25.5%	46.9%	23.5%	4.1%

Exhibit 113. Searchers' Report on Level of Importance of User-Terminal-to-Host-Terminal Contact with On-Line Suppliers

From a special analysis of these data, we learned that those who indicated that some kind of assistance was essential also indicated that they had some amount of direct contact with their suppliers. The amount of contact for each of the organizational user groups is shown in Exhibit 114.

	Some	Very Little	None	No Response
All Searchers (N=801)	56.4%	32.7%	9.1%	1.8%
Government Users (N=192)	63.5%	28.6%	6.8%	1.1%
Commercial Users (N=247)	55.9%	28.3%	12.6%	3.2%
Educational Users (N=264)	53.4%	38.6%	6.4%	1.6%
Other Users (N=98)	50.0%	34.7%	12.2%	3.1%

Exhibit 114. Searchers' Report on Amount of Contact They Have With On-Line Suppliers by Telephone or Terminal

Although the differences are not particularly dramatic, it would appear that Government agency users have somewhat more direct contact with their suppliers. The greater contact may not reflect a true difference in their need for assistance but may, rather, be an artifact of their location (i.e., of being close to federal on-line suppliers in the Washington, D.C. area) and of their having the use of the FTS service.

All of the on-line suppliers send some kind of newsletter or bulletin to their users. Almost 80% of the searchers indicated that they received these notices from all of their suppliers. About 14% indicated that they received them from only some of them, and 6% said that they did not receive any such notices. Since all of the suppliers were providing some kind of bulletin at the time of our study, we must assume that the searchers who did not receive any notices were either new searchers or were not receiving copies from the key contact in their organization. From our own experience, we know that getting information directly to the searchers is not always easy, particularly in large organizations.

Of those who had received newsletters or notices, almost three fourths found them to be very useful, and another 20% found them somewhat useful. Only one respondent indicated that they were not at all useful.

A final question in the area of communications concerned the user manuals that are available from the on-line suppliers. The vast majority of searchers reported that they had purchased or received some kind of user manuals from all of their suppliers, but a small group either did not have manuals for all of the systems or had none for one or more systems that they use.

We also asked searchers to indicate what kinds of approaches and formats they believed were most useful in the user manuals, and to identify any information that they would like the suppliers to provide. A summary of their responses is provided in Exhibit 115. Their comments are grouped into three sections, relating to content, style and writing, and format.

The most frequently expressed needs for information related to the content area and particularly to searching hints and sample searches. Another frequently mentioned need was for more vocabulary guides (e.g., thesauri, dictionaries, cross-reference listings, and scope notes for terms). Searchers also commented on the need for additional tools or services:

- A quiz to take on-line or by mail

- On-line news

- Subject guides to data bases

- Toll-free numbers to suppliers

- "Vest-pocket" guides (i.e., summaries of system commands or summaries of searchable data elements)

CONTENT (GENERAL)

From a non-CRT user: make instructions easily adaptable to any terminal.

Discussions on when and how use features optimally; include "tricks of the trade" or searching hints; show samples of search strategies; provide hints from other searchers.

Include statements on limitations (data base or system not specified).

Include troubleshooting guides.

Show command and search strategy charts/dictionaries.

Give accurate information about diagnosing problems.

Be thorough and comprehensive.

Need detailed explanation of error messages.

More emphasis needed on techniques to make cost-accounting easier.

Show flow chart for conducting searches.

Provide more on data base supplier's selection and indexing procedures.

Characterize unique characteristics of record elements.

Describe data base construction; show sources where original articles can be obtained.

Need more subject authority lists.

STYLE AND WRITING

Conciseness if required.

Pictorial approach useful.

Tutorials needed for different levels of sophistication.

Programmed instruction approach more useful.

Need to be written by a user of the system in conjunction with the supplier.

Should provide step-by-step explanations.

Should be user-oriented, not programmer-oriented.

Should be written by, or with technical editors who can communicate.

FORMAT

Supplements for each data base are better; keep system information and data base information separate.

Tabs for ready reference.

Indexes are important.

Differentiate in color between user entries and computer responses.

Exhibit 115.   General Comments from Searchers On Suggestions
for User Manuals

- Audiovisual aids

- Simplified manuals for infrequent users

- Listings of data base postings (frequency counts) to provide pre-search assistance

Some of these items were available from some suppliers at the time the questionnaires were completed, and some changes and additions in user aids have since been made. All of the suppliers report that they provide a user manual containing a description of the system and the data base(s). For most of the current manuals, the system description is contained in one manual and the database descriptions are in separate manuals or sections. The suppliers report that they have designed their manuals primarily as reference guides, and only one supplier reports that the manual is both a programmed text and a reference guide. As mentioned earlier, all of the suppliers send out some kind of newsletter or bulletin that contains news about their system and data base(s). Some of these are regular monthly, quarterly, or bimonthly publications; others are prepared at irregular intervals. The suppliers also report that they have at least one full-time staff person who is assigned the responsibility of providing telephone or host-terminal-to-user-terminal assistance to their system users.

It is important to point out that data base suppliers and users have also been developing user aids. For example, Chemical Abstracts Service has since developed a package of microform materials that is designed "to help the user select the search terms that will be most effective in obtaining information from Chemical Abstracts Condensates...." It contains a word frequency list, a key-letter-in-context index, and a title phrase list. Two users of on-line systems, Barbara Lawrence of Exxon Corporation in Linden Hills, New Jersey, and Barbara Prewitt of Rohm & Haas, Springhouse, Pennsylvania, collaborated to prepare a one-sheet reference guide to the major commands that were available on selected on-line systems. The National Federation of Indexing and Abstracting Services has assumed responsibility for updating this tool. Given the dynamic state of movement in the technology, this will be an important service.

We expect that with the growing needs of both frequent and infrequent users for additional reference guides and aids, more and better searching tools and products will be developed over the next several years.

10. SPECIAL CHALLENGES

Chapter 9 dealt with the detection and solution of problems in using on-line services. This chapter deals with two areas of activity that might also be viewed as problems but are more properly discussed as challenges. They are, respectively, the definition of an effective interface with end-users and the use of multiple systems and multiple data bases.

THE END-USER INTERFACE

Our study clearly shows that most on-line bibliographic searches are performed by information intermediaries. In the early days of on-line systems, there was a strong belief among many designers and planners that these systems should be designed for, and used by, end-users. This belief is still held by some but it has not been translated into practice. However, on-line systems permit--and, some would say, demand--a new relationship between the end-user and the information intermediary, and the challenge today is to define the kinds of interfaces that take full advantage of the potential of the on-line, interactive technology.

Description of Current Interfaces

In one questionnaire item, we asked managers to characterize the ways in which their end-users interacted with the on-line system and to indicate the degree to which each of the alternative interactions we listed was being used. The results of this question are shown in Exhibit 116.

A review of these data suggests that the traditional interaction between intermediary and end-user has carried over into on-line service, but that some new interactions are being defined. Over three fourths of the managers reported that traditional reference interviews or written descriptions were used in many or most searches, and that the end-user was not actually participating in the conduct of the search. However, some new interface modes have been developed. In about 45% of the cases, the end-user is actually present at the terminal while the search is being conducted, for most or many searches; in another 8% of the cases, the searcher and user are in contact (generally by telephone) during the conduct of the search. As our data indicate, the percentage of cases in which end-users perform their own searches is very small.

	SEARCHES			
	Most	Many	Few or None	No Response
User discusses problem with searcher or provides written statement, but is not at terminal during search.	63.1%	15.6%	16.9%	4.4%
User works with searcher at terminal.	18.4%	26.4%	47.8%	7.4%
User is in contact with searcher during search, but is not at terminal.	1.7%	6.4%	80.1%	11.9%
User performs search for self in centrally located area.	4.3%	5.3%	78.4%	12.1%
User performs search independently.	3.0%	2.5%	80.5%	14.0%

Exhibit 116. Alternative Searcher/End-User Interactions Used, as Reported by Managers (N=472)

Exhibit 117 shows that Educational searchers are more likely to have their users present at the terminal, and Commercial organization searchers are the least likely.

		SEARCHES			
		Most	Many	Few or None	No Response
REFERENCE INTERVIEW/ WRITTEN DESCRIPTION	Government Users (N=101)	55.4%	21.8%	14.9%	7.9%
	Commercial Users (N=152)	65.1%	15.1%	16.4%	3.3%
	Educational Users (N=145)	64.8%	14.5%	17.9%	2.8%
	Other Users (N=74)	66.2%	10.8%	17.6%	8.1%
USER PRESENT AT TERMINAL	Government Users (N=101)	12.8%	26.7%	49.5%	10.9%
	Commercial Users (N=152)	18.4%	17.8%	55.9%	7.9%
	Educational Users (N=145)	23.4%	33.1%	40.0%	3.4%
	Other Users (N=74)	16.2%	31.1%	44.6%	12.2%

Exhibit 117. Use of Two Searcher/End-User Interactions, as Reported by Managers, by Organization Type

One of the newer modes of user/intermediary interaction, found in all groups, is one in which the user is not physically located at the searcher's terminal but is nevertheless in contact with the searcher while the search is being performed. All of the managers whose organizations were using this kind of interaction indicated that the user remains in his or her own office throughout the search, talking with the searcher over a telephone. One manager reported a particularly innovative approach. The end-users stay in their offices and view the progress of a search on a terminal that is also logged into the computer as a "slave" terminal to the searcher's "master" terminal. The searcher and end-user communicate at the same time on other telephones.

During the on-site interviews, we pursued the interaction issue further with searchers. About one half of those we interviewed preferred a face-to-face conversation with the end-user before they performed the search. Only a few members in this group considered telephone conversations to be an adequate substitute for a personal interview. All of this group agreed that a good interview is required for a good search. After the initial interview, the user leaves and the searcher performs the search when time permits. If problems occur during the search, the searcher logs off and checks additional resource materials. Almost all of these searchers indicated that, if this step is not sufficient, they telephone the user and elicit additional information or guidance. These searchers found that having the end-user at the terminal during the search was too distracting, too time-consuming, and added to the costs. One searcher said: "The system behaves poorly in front of users, but is always fine when I am alone."

The next largest group of interviewees indicated that they preferred to discuss the search with the user and then have him or her remain at the terminal throughout the search. These interviewees preferred this method because of the instant feedback that end-users could give and the subject expertise that they could lend to the search. Some of the searchers in this group occasionally performed searches alone, but they only felt comfortable doing this when they knew very well the subject area or the special interests of the person for whom the search was being conducted.

The interviewees were also asked whether their users were doing their own searches at the terminal. In only three of the organizations that participated in the interviews was this occurring. One searcher told us that most of the users who conducted their own searches were the younger researchers and scientists; the older ones claimed either that they did not have the time or that it was not an appropriate role for them to assume. In all three cases, the users were trained by the library staff, usually in just one or two terminal sessions. If problems occurred after that period, the user was free to consult one of the library staff members for help.

The remaining interviewees told us that users were not doing their own searches at the terminal. When asked if they could envision their users eventually doing their own searches, 60% said that they could, while the remainder could not. Several of those who could envision end-users performing their own searches were not happy about this possible arrangement. One interviewee stated that the user even now too often believes that a machine search can produce all the relevant information about a topic, and that further digging is unnecessary. On their own, users might never go beyond an on-line search, to the detriment of finding the best answer to their search request. Another interviewee wondered whether someone who was not familiar with a data base could perform an effective search.

Most of the group who could not envision their users eventually performing their own searches felt that their users were uninterested in performing searches for themselves or that the high cost of training end-users would pose a major barrier.

Reactions of End-Users

Over 63% of the total manager population reported that they believed there had been some changes in the behavior of their users, as a result of the availability of on-line service. About 28% did not believe that any changes had taken place. The most frequently observed change reported by the 63% group was that end-users were preferring on-line searches to manually done searches. Many managers also reported that there had been an increase in the use of other information sources and of the backup services of the library or information center. Some other representative comments on the nature of the observed changes were:

"Many users accept a machine search as an exhaustive, definitive product and believe that further manual searching is unnecessary."

"Users are more reluctant to conduct manual searches themselves, even for one-term searches."

"Users expect faster and more complete search methods."

"They use library resources with more enthusiasm and satisfaction."

"Requesters are willing to settle for only the information in the data bases and rarely ask for older literature or other resources."

"Users are more inclined to look for pertinent information than they were before."

"Users depend more on the library for information as they gain confidence in the ability of the searcher."

"There is more current-awareness reading."

"When time is short, users are willing to seek out information, as provided by the on-line service, rather than not doing any literature searching at all."

Although the comments given to us were rather brief, they imply both positive and negative changes. For example, the first comment suggests that this manager is critical of this new behavior and that perhaps the end-users are settling for less than they should, by overestimating the comprehensiveness of the on-line search. However, other comments support the belief that services are contributing to increased use of available information.*

MULTIPLE-SYSTEM AND MULTIPLE-DATA-BASE USE

The availability of multiple systems and multiple data bases presents, at the same time, both an important opportunity and a potential problem. As we will see in the next chapter, the expansion of information resources available to an organization is perceived by the on-line using community as an important benefit of on-line services. On the other hand, the multiplicity of now-available resources poses a special challenge to searchers in developing an appropriate level of technical mastery of the various protocols and procedures.

---

*A study being undertaken at this time by Dr. G. Jahoda at Florida State University, under a grant from the National Science Foundation, may help us to understand further the impact on end-users' behavior. In their study on introducing on-line systems to end-users, they will be exploring the relationship of pre-on-line information-seeking behaviors to post-on-line behaviors.

The trade-off between potential benefit and potential problems is truly complex. In our questionnaires, we attempted to obtain the searchers' perceptions on the degree of difficulty associated with this challenge. The relevant data are reported in the following two sections.

Multiple-System Users

One of the questionnaire items for searchers who use more than one system begins: "It is generally believed that using more than one system can be confusing...." The question is, how confusing is it?

Response data for the question in which users were asked to indicate their general reaction to using more than one system are shown in Exhibit 118.

	All Multiple-System Users (N=339)	Government Users (N=76)	Commercial Users (N=132)	Educational Users (N=99)	Other Users (N=32)
Using More Than One System:					
Is a major problem and seriously affects my efficiency.	13(3.8%)	4(5.3%)	6(4.5%)	2(2.0%)	1(3.1%)
Is sometimes confusing but the problems are not insurmountable nor do they generally affect my efficiency.	162(47.8%)	25(32.9%)	66(50.0%)	50(50.5%)	20(62.5%)
Has not been a source of confusion for me.	106(31.3%)	30(39.5%)	40(30.3%)	28(28.3%)	8(25.0%)
No response.	58(17.1%)	17(22.4%)	20(15.2%)	19(19.2%)	3(9.4%)

Exhibit 118. Degree of Confusion Reported by Searchers in Using Several Systems

It appears that the use of multiple systems has not been a major problem, except for about 4% of the responding population. This 4% group comprises searchers from each experience group, from beginners to the very experienced. Somewhat less than half of the multiple-system searchers considered it to be sometimes confusing, but the problems were not insurmountable nor did they generally affect their efficiency. About one third of the searchers reported that multiple-system use had not been confusing.

Because the Commercial user group is probably most representative of those who are using truly different systems, i.e., those from different retrieval program families, their responses are particularly important in validating this overall pattern of responses. As shown in the same Exhibit, their response percentages were quite similar to the overall response pattern.

The 52% who reported that use of different systems was either a major problem or one that was sometimes confusing were asked to indicate the degree of confusion that they experienced in each of several areas. Their responses are summarized in Exhibit 119, which shows percentage rankings of collapsed groupings, "Moderate to Great" Confusion versus "Low to None."

	Moderate to Great		Low to None	
	%	Rank	%	Rank
1. Procedures for logging in	27.4%	5	69.7%	3
2. Relating capabilities or features with the correct system	54.2%	1	42.9%	7
3. Procedures for expressing Boolean combinations	28.5%	4	68.6%	4
4. Understanding messages from the system	24.6%	6	70.8%	2
5. Procedures for entering searches	44.0%	3	52.0%	5
6. Procedures for issuing printing instructions	46.8%	2	49.7%	6
7. Relating schedules for access time to the correct system	21.7%	7	73.8%	1
8. Others	8.0%	8	1.1%	8

Exhibit 119. Most and Least Confusing Areas for Searchers in Using Multiple Systems

The two most frequently indicated areas of confusion--relating capabilities or features with the correct system, and procedures for issuing printing instructions--are clearly associated with system use. The third most frequently selected area--procedures for entering searches--may very well overlap somewhat into multiple-data-base use, because the procedures for entering searches encompass the entry of search terms and, as we will report in the next section, the entry of search terms is an area of some confusion for the multiple-database user. In fact, when the "Great" responses are reviewed alone, as shown in the breakdown by organization type in Exhibit 120, the entering of searches becomes the number-one percentage ranking for some groups.

		Great	Moder-ate	Low	None	No Response
RELATING CAPABILITIES TO CORRECT SYSTEM	Government Users (N=29)	4.5%	34.5%	48.3%	10.3%	2.4%
	Commercial Users (N=72)	8.3%	48.6%	31.9%	6.9%	4.3%
	Educational Users (N=52)	9.6%	44.2%	42.3%	1.8%	2.1%
	Other Users (N=21)	19.0%	47.6%	19.0%	14.3%	--
PROCEDURES FOR ENTERING SEARCHES	Government Users (N=29)	13.8%	27.6%	48.3%	3.4%	6.9%
	Commercial Users (N=72)	8.3%	34.7%	44.4%	6.9%	5.7%
	Educational Users (N=52)	11.5%	23.1%	42.3%	21.6%	1.5%
	Other Users (N=21)	14.3%	61.9%	14.3%	9.5%	--
PROCEDURES FOR ISSUING PRINTING INSTRUCTIONS	Government Users (N=29)	10.3%	24.1%	48.3%	6.9%	10.4%
	Commercial Users (N=72)	8.3%	50.0%	26.4%	13.9%	1.4%
	Educational Users (N=52)	5.8%	32.7%	38.5%	19.2%	3.8%
	Other Users (N=21)	23.8%	23.8%	42.9%	9.5%	--

Exhibit 120. Most Confusing Areas of Multiple-System Use Reported by Searchers, By Organization Type

In general, it appears that the use of more than one system has been quite manageable. Thus it is not surprising that the number of multiple-system users has probably increased significantly since the questionnaires were completed. But, even though multiple-system use is manageable, how much impact does it have on the searchers' efficiency, i.e., on the time it takes to perform a search? As indicated by the data shown in Exhibit 121, the searchers' answer is little or none.

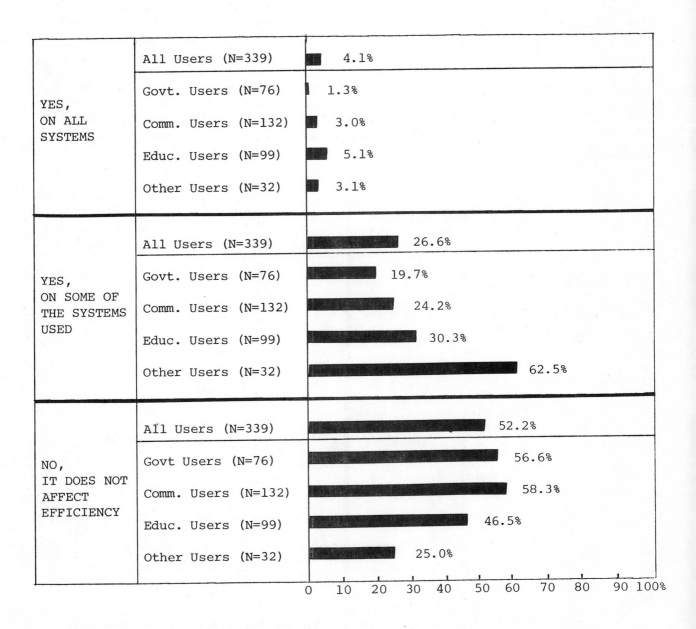

Exhibit 121. Searchers' Responses to Question: Do you believe that your use of several systems reduces your efficiency, i.e., increases the time it takes to perform a search?

Multiple-Data-Base Users

There are a number of potential sources of difficulty for multiple-data-base users. They must learn, understand, and remember (or have quick reference-access to) the content coverage of different data bases, the time-span of each, the access points that are made available on the system or systems that they are using, the element names and print formats that are available, and the way to use different vocabulary aids and resources. The argument is frequently made that these potential sources of difficulty constitute a major problem and that considerable standardization in nomenclature, formats, and on-line handling should be imposed either on, or by, data base developers and on-line suppliers.

Although there may be some merit in this argument, the majority of searchers who use more than one data base reported that such usage has <u>not</u> been a source of major confusion for them. As shown in Exhibit 122, only about 2% reported that searching on more than one data base was a major problem that seriously affected their efficiency.

	All Multiple Data-Base Users (N=639)	Government Users (N=151)	Commercial Users (N=215)	Educational Users (N=205)	Other Users (N=74)
Searching on more than one data base is a major problem and one that seriously affects my efficiency.	1.7%	0.6%	1.4%	2.9%	1.5%
Searching on more than one data base is sometimes confusing, but the problems are not insurmountable.	39.0%	39.7%	35.8%	40.0%	44.1%
Searching on more than one data base has not been a source of confusion for me.	51.5%	49.7%	60.5%	46.8%	41.2%
No response.	7.8%	9.9%	2.3%	10.2%	13.2%

Exhibit 122.   Searchers' Report on the General Degree of Confusion Caused by Using More Than One Data Base

The majority reported that searching on more than one data base had not been a source of confusion at all. If we make the assumption again that Commercial users are the most representative users of different data bases, then their responses to this question in particular confirm that the degree of the problem has not been as great as has been suspected.

In a separate analysis, we learned that those searchers who have also been using multiple systems are somewhat more represented in the "Some Confusion" category, but the "Major Confusion" category shows equal representation of single- and multiple-system users. If we interpret the multiple-data-base problem partly as a frequent- versus infrequent-user problem, we might expect that the searchers who do more searches are less likely to experience confusion. The data do not bear this out. There is almost equal representation in each of three response choices--Major Confusion, Some Confusion, No Confusion-- by searchers who do fewer than five searches, and those who do more than five searches a week.

Experience appears to be somewhat of a factor, but not as much as we might expect. The lack of an experience level influence may be related to the fact that multiple-data-base use is actually a fairly recent phenomenon--less than three years old--and those who have been using on-line systems for a longer period of time have primarily been using only one data base, or several related files from one data base family.

A total of about 41% of the searchers who indicated that the use of several data bases was either a major problem or, at least, sometimes confusing, were asked to identify the specific sources of their confusion. The response choices identified a number of possible areas of confusion. When the "Great" and "Moderate" responses are collapsed, the areas of confusion in order relate to:

- Form of subject term entry (67.3%)

- Fields of information that are searchable (47.0%)

- Fields of information that are printable (40.0%)

- Vocabulary aids or resources (34.6%)

- Subject/content coverage (25.7%)

- Time coverage (21.1%)

The percentage responses for each of the four user groups are shown in Exhibit 123 for selected problem areas. These data indicate that there are, indeed, some areas that are worthy of attention by both the on-line suppliers and the data base developers. One area in particular that should be noticed by the on-line suppliers is the potential confusion with entry formats of subject terms, which were defined in the questionnaire, by example, as single terms, precoordinated terms, inverted index terms, and main headings/subheadings. Most of the variation that users see among data bases stems from vocabulary differences, from one data base to the next. Perhaps the on-line suppliers need to do a

better job of helping users to relate a given data base to a class of data
bases that are alike in subject-term entry formats. They may also need to
provide users with quick-reference tools that can help in this association
process.

		Great	Moder-ate	Low	None	No Response
FORM OF SUBJECT-TERM ENTRY	Government Users (N=70)	8.6%	50.0%	17.1%	7.1%	17.1%
	Commercial Users (N=80)	15.0%	56.3%	18.6%	5.0%	5.0%
	Educational Users (N=88)	17.0%	44.3%	22.7%	6.8%	9.1%
	Other Users (N=31)	19.4%	54.8%	25.8%	--	--
FIELDS OF INFORMATION THAT ARE PRINTABLE	Government Users (N=70)	7.1%	27.1%	31.4%	18.6%	15.7%
	Commercial Users (N=80)	7.5%	37.5%	36.3%	12.5%	6.3%
	Educational Users (N=88)	0.5%	36.4%	44.3%	13.1%	5.7%
	Other Users (N=31)	--	9.7%	29.0%	51.6%	9.7%
FIELDS OF INFORMATION THAT ARE SEARCHABLE	Government Users (N=70)	2.8%	32.9%	25.7%	14.3%	24.3%
	Commercial Users (N=80)	2.4%	48.8%	30.0%	12.5%	6.3%
	Educational Users (N=88)	2.5%	39.8%	37.5%	13.6%	6.8%
	Other Users (N=31)	9.7%	51.6%	25.8%	12.9%	--
SUBJECT/ CONTENT COVERAGE	Government Users (N=70)	4.3%	21.4%	44.3%	15.7%	14.3%
	Commercial Users (N=80)	--	21.3%	41.3%	28.8%	8.8%
	Educational Users (N=88)	--	21.6%	37.5%	34.1%	6.8%
	Other Users (N=31)	--	3.2%	38.7%	32.3%	25.8%

Exhibit 123. Report by Multiple-Data-Base Searchers, by Organization
Type, on Degree of Confusion with Selected Potential
Problem Areas

We were somewhat surprised by the relatively low confusion associated with the subject/content coverage of data bases, since this is one of the more frequently expressed concerns that we receive from on-line users. However, we saw similar data in Chapter 7 on the general question of problems that users were having in identifying the appropriate data base(s) for a search.

The unstructured responses provided by searchers to the question on confusion in using multiple data bases included many system-related concerns, such as use of the "command language." Those that are specific to data-base use are summarized below:

Lack of vocabulary or index terms.

Special subject groupings.

Differences in entering terms, such as authors' initials preceded with a comma or without, and plurals vs. singulars.

Duplication of journal coverage.

Determining which data base is most economical.

Various codes used in different data bases.

Changes between older and newer materials.

Search vocabularies.

Lack of standardization.

Overlap of hits across data bases.

One user indicated that the use of multiple data bases was not confusing but that it was boring to repeat searches in different data bases. Another user said that the problem was not really one of confusion but, rather, a lack of familiarity with the files that were used only occasionally.

We have some indication from the unstructured responses on this question, and from several other problem-area questions in the survey, that some searchers were concerned about the overlap of citations across different data bases. In our on-site interviews, we asked how frequently the searchers encountered duplicate citations. Although the question was not applicable for about one-fourth of the interviewees, who generally use only one data base, the remaining interviewees indicated that they encountered duplications only occasionally or hardly at all. We asked this group to indicate the data-base combinations for which multiple citations occurred most frequently. Most of the overlap for this group of searchers was occurring with different combinations of data bases that included Chemical Abstracts Condensates, TOXLINE, and MEDLINE. Another small number reported that duplicates appeared between MEDLINE and Psychological Abstracts, and two interviewees pointed out that overlaps occurred within TOXLINE, which is a composite data base of six different files.

We asked the interviewees whether they or their end-users found duplicate citations bothersome, or whether there were any beneficial aspects to the overlap across files. Most of them indicated that they did not find duplications bothersome. Some indicated that they can sometimes get complete information from two different citations, e.g., one citation may have a better source description, and another may have a better abstract. One interviewee indicated that "we fully expect and want the duplications," and from several responses, we learned that the overlaps give both the searcher and the end-user confidence in the search results.

11. MAJOR AREAS OF IMPACT

The changes that are occurring within the on-line using community can be viewed from several perspectives. In our questionnaires, we examined attitudes, practices, and, where possible, indirect measures of the degree to which on-line services have been affecting the behavior of the individuals involved or the ways in which the service or work environment of these individuals has changed.

Several areas of potential impact are described in the following four sections: 1) Benefits: Expectations versus Real Gains, 2) The Cost-Effectiveness of On-Line Searching, 3) Changes in Modes of Operation and the Service Image, and 4) Impact on Staff and Staffing. We recognize the inherent limitations in our interpretations due to the lack of complete "before" and "after" pictures. Clearly, a longitudinal study of some kind would be preferred for capturing these kinds of data. However, the present data help to provide an initial, useful assessment of the value of on-line services.

BENEFITS: EXPECTATIONS VERSUS REAL GAINS

We asked managers to think back to their startup period with the on-line services and to indicate the main benefits that they had anticipated would accrue from using an on-line system. They were given as choices a number of benefits that are frequently associated with on-line system use. Two additional choices were provided: "We didn't know what to anticipate" was provided for those who had no clear-cut expectations for their on-line experience, and an "Other" category was provided for those who had additional objectives to describe. Responses of the managers to this question are shown in Exhibit 124. Respondents were asked to choose as many of the categories as they felt applied to their situation; thus the percentages add up to more than 100%.

The benefit most often anticipated by managers was better service through faster turnaround time. A second widely hoped-for benefit was better service through access to additional sources of information. (For Commercial users, this benefit was cited by almost 83% of the respondents.) It is interesting to note that fewer than half of the managers cited greater precision in retrieval as an expected benefit of on-line searching. The ability of on-line systems to help users in refining their search strategies to obtain a high proportion of relevant material (and to exclude irrelevant material) has been an acclaimed benefit of computer-based searching, but it appears that the need for precision has not been perceived to be as great as the need for speed and for the ability to access many sources.

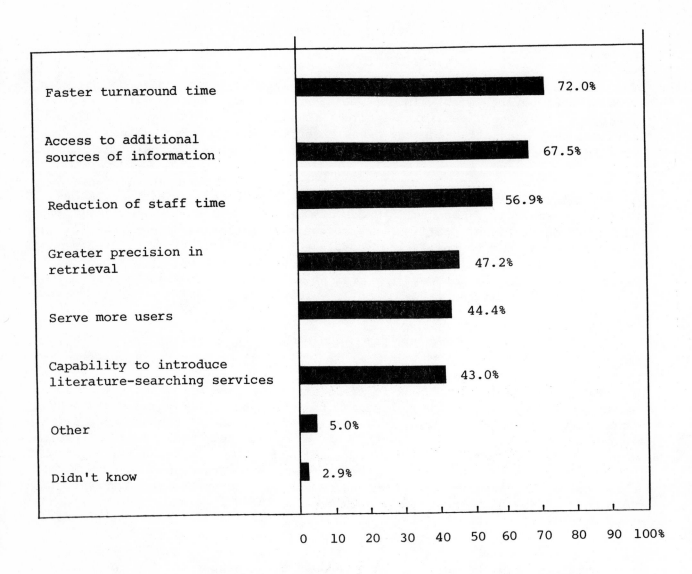

Exhibit 124. Managers' Responses to the Question: What did your
              organization initially anticipate would be the <u>main</u>
              benefit of using on-line systems? (N=472)

One of the most important, and perhaps most socially significant, benefits of
on-line services is that, for 43% of the organizational units participating in
the Manager questionnaire survey, the availability of the on-line systems
permitted them to establish a literature-searching service within their organization. In other words, for these organizations, the on-line systems were not

viewed as a supplementary tool for the support of an already existing service.*
In the organizational-type analysis, the responses to this choice were:

Government Users	(N=101)	38.6%
Commercial Users	(N=152)	34.9%
Educational Users	(N=145)	60.0%
Other Users	(N=74)	32.4%

As can be seen, the establishment of new literature-searching services is
particularly pronounced for educational institutions.

Five percent of the respondents specified benefits other than those listed in
the question. Several managers remarked that a major benefit that they had
expected was reduction of searching costs. Another benefit mentioned frequently
was increased user interest in the library/information center. Closely related
to this latter benefit was the expectation, cited by several respondents, that
on-line capacity would increase the prestige of the library/information center.
Some Managers indicated that they hoped the on-line system could be used for
Interlibrary Loan verification.

The second part of the question on anticipated benefits asked the managers to
indicate whether these benefits had, in general, been realized and to provide a
brief explanation. Nearly 92% of the managers responded that all or most of
the expected benefits had been realized. Only about 4% of the managers replied
that the on-line system had not as yet met their early expectations, and another
4% did not respond to this questionnaire item.

In commenting on their success with on-line searching, managers most often noted
a reduction in search time, the ability to serve more users, and access to
information previously not available. Also mentioned was increased user satisfaction. One manager wrote that in his organization more bibliographies were
being compiled per week than before the on-line system became operational. This

---

*We have a puzzling anomaly in our data relative to this subset of our
study population. On the question of expected benefits, 43% of the respondents reported that they had not previously provided literature-searching services. In one of the final questionnaire items (See Appendix A, question 3,
in the User Satisfaction section), we asked respondents to indicate how their
users were reacting to on-line searching, in comparison with the organizational
unit's previous literature-searching services. In response to this question,
only about 24% noted that users had previously done their own searches and
therefore they had no basis for making a comparison. On the basis of unstructured responses that follow in this section, we believe that the difference
between the 24% and 43% may reflect the difficulty that some managers had in
characterizing their pre-on-line service. Some organizations that did not consider themselves as having provided literature-searching services may, in fact,
have been providing or supporting them to some extent. The 43% figure is
probably a more accurate reflection of the size of the no-previous-service
group, even though some of them may have already been providing some limited
literature-searching services.

organization reportedly now has a highly successful service, with 200-300 searches being performed per month. Formerly only minimal literature-searching services had been available.

Another manager wrote that, in the days when all searching was done manually, literature-searching services were available only to a few select faculty members and administrative personnel. With the use of the on-line system, this organization has been providing literature-searching services to all students and staff, as well as to outside hospital personnel. Other managers reported similar changes.

With respect to increased access to information, one manager indicated that better information was available, because the staff knew what was available and where to look for it. A similar response by another manager was that on-line searching had permitted the organization to perform literature searches of a depth and quality that were not possible with manual searching. This organization has also been able to provide types of searches that were not previously feasible because of cost. In another organization, the on-line system has made available many data bases that, although important, were so infrequently used that it was not possible to justify purchasing the hard-copy reference tools.

One comment regarding user satisfaction came from a manger who wrote that engineers, scientists, and researchers in his organization more readily accepted the results of on-line literature searching than they did the results of manual searches.

Approximately 4% of the managers reported that the benefits that they had anticipated from the on-line system had not yet been forthcoming. In the brief explanations that followed this negative response, there seemed to be one characteristic common to most of these less-than-satisfied organizations: many of these organizations were still in the initial stages of on-line system use and did not feel that they had enough experience as yet with the system to evaluate it. Managers of some of these organizations indicated a belief that as soon as more expertise was developed, the hoped-for benefits of on-line searching would indeed be forthcoming.

The major complaint of the remaining managers--those who were experienced users of on-line systems--was that their initial expectations of accurate and current information were not being met. One comment pertinent to this problem was expressed by a manager who wrote that the quality of the data base being searched determines the quality of the search. He suggested that many supposedly all-inclusive data bases were not as complete as had been expected. Another manager complained that the turnaround time on retrospective on-line searches was no better than it had been when the searches were performed manually. (One presumes that he used off-line printing to obtain most of the search results.) Still another commented that researchers in the organization were disappointed with the system because they expected the system to answer questions for them, rather than just generate bibliographic citations. Such an expectation, however, shows some lack of understanding of the purpose and capabilities of on-line bibliographic systems. Perhaps a more thorough examination of the potential benefits of the on-line system, and better communication with the researchers, was needed in this organization.

COST-EFFECTIVENESS OF ON-LINE SEARCHING

The response choices in the previous section alluded to the cost-effectiveness issue in a relative way, e.g., savings in staff time, and some of the respondents also indicated in their unstructured responses that they were able to reduce costs absolutely with the on-line services. In subsequent sections of the questionnaire we asked managers and searchers directly about the costs of using the services relative to other literature-searching methods. These questions were framed as attitudinal items and did not require detailed cost-comparison analyses--a matter for another study.

As the earlier chapter on costs suggests, there are many ways to view the costs of providing on-line literature-searching services. Some organizations can compare cost elements associated with their already existing literature-searching services. Others, primarily in the 43% group of organizations that had previously provided only minimal services, or none at all, must evaluate the costs of providing on-line literature searches without the cost-comparison context. This second group must, first of all, weigh the value of the new service and then assess the impact on staffing and other budget items. A detailed study would be needed to understand fully the basis for our on-line user population's views, but it is useful to examine their general attitude toward the cost-effectiveness of on-line searching.

Both managers and searchers were asked to compare the cost-effectiveness of on-line searching with that of manual searching and batch-mode processing. Overall, the response data clearly show that a majority of the managers and searchers associated with on-line services have found on-line searching to be either as cost-effective as, or more cost-effective than, manual searching and batch-mode searching. Managers were asked to react to the statement: "On-line searching is more cost-effective than manual searching." Their responses were as follows:

- 74.5% strongly agreed or agreed with the statement

- 6.7% strongly disagreed or disagreed

- 18.6% had no opinion or chose not to respond

The managers' responses were found to be related to the number of regular searchers in their organizations and to the number of on-line searches performed monthly. As might be expected, the more searchers there were in the organization, and the more searches that were conducted, the more likely it was that the manager believed on-line searching to be more cost-effective than manual searching. About 69% of the managers who had only one searcher agreed or strongly agreed with the statement about cost-effectiveness, compared to 83% of the managers with three or more searchers; and 70% of the managers whose organizations performed fewer than 20 on-line searches monthly were in agreement with the statement, compared to 90% of those whose organizations perform more than 56 searches monthly.

Searchers' responses to the statement that "On-line searching is economical compared to manual searching" are shown below:

- 73.2% strongly agreed or agreed with the statement that on-line searching is economical, compared to manual searching

- 5.8% strongly disagreed or disagreed with the statement

- 20.9% had no opinion or chose not to respond

The "no opinions" and "no responses" in each group probably reflect, in most cases, an inability on the part of those managers and searchers to compare costs because the necessary cost data or experience were not available in their organizations.

Managers and searchers were positive in their reactions about the cost-effectiveness of on-line searching, relative to batch-processing, although not as positive as they were in their comparisons of cost-effectiveness between on-line searching and manual searching. Managers were asked to react to the statement that "On-line searching is not as cost-effective as searching in batch processing," and the following responses were obtained:

- 9.4% agreed or strongly agreed with the statement

- 50.6% disagreed or strongly disagreed

- 39.7% either had no opinion or did not respond

The searchers were asked to react to a similar statement: "On-line searching is economical, compared to batch-system processing." (As the reader can see, this statement makes a positive comparison, whereas the statement given to managers was a negative comparison.) The following responses were obtained from searchers:

- 29.3% agreed or strongly agreed

- 10.6% disagreed or strongly disagreed

- 60.0% either had no opinion or did not respond

Roughly the same percentage of managers and searchers--9% of the managers and 11% of the searchers--expressed the belief that batch-processing is more economical than on-line searching. However, over one half of the managers felt that on-line searching is no less economical than batch-processing, compared to

29% of the searchers. It is interesting to note that 60% of the searchers and nearly 40% of the managers were unable to answer the question, probably because they had either had no previous experience with batch-processing, or they did not have access to comparative data on the two methods of searching.

MODE OF OPERATION AND SERVICE IMAGE

As we have already seen, one of the major changes in the service being provided by the libraries or information centers is evidenced in the fact that a considerable number of units have been able to introduce literature-searching services by having access to the on-line systems. Therefore, when we consider the changes in the nature and quality of service, this change must be ranked at the top of the list. However, there are additional questions to ask about the impact of on-line services in other areas of service, particularly for those organizations that had already been providing literature-searching services. We explore several of these potential impact areas in this section: 1) Reliance on On-line Services, 2) Number of End-Users Being Served, 3) Quality of Service, 4) Turnaround Time of Service, and 5) Document Delivery Service.

Reliance On On-Line Services

The managers' report on the proportion of their literature-search requests--both retrospective and current awareness--that were being performed either solely, partly, or not at all on-line, indicate that the on-line services have become a primary resource in these organizations' information services programs.

- 11.9% of the responding organizations have been performing all of their literature searches on-line, and another 54.6% have been doing one-half or more <u>solely</u> on-line

- 16.3% have been performing one-half or more of their searches <u>partly</u> on-line

- 13.0% perform one-half or more of their searches by some other method(s), i.e., <u>not at all on-line</u> (42.6% perform none of their searches by some other method, so at least a part of their searches are performed on-line)

The "100% solely on-line" group (11.9% of the responding organizations) comprises 41.1% Educational users, 26.8% Commercial users, 21.4% Government users, and 10.7% Other users.

The "partly on-line" data suggest that most organizations are complementing on-line searches with either batch or manual searches.

We examined the data on the reliance question from several perspectives--on-line experience, number of systems being used, number of frequent searchers in the organization, and number of searches being done each month. In summary, the data suggest that:

- Organizations with more on-line experience have tended to do a greater proportion of their searches solely on-line. For example, of those with 3 to 6 or more years of on-line experience, 64% were doing between 50 and 100% of their searches solely on-line; of those with 1 to 6 months of on-line experience, a smaller number, about 48%, were doing between 50 and 100% of their literature searches solely on-line.

- The number of systems that were being used by the organizations does not appear to have any relationship to the proportion of searches done solely, partly, or not at all on-line.

- Those organizations with only one searcher have tended to do some-what more of their searches solely on-line than those organizations with three or more searchers. About 61% of those with one searcher, compared to 53% of those with three or more searchers, were doing 50 to 100% of their searches solely on-line.

- Organizations that have been doing more searches have tended to do a greater proportion of their searches solely on-line. Of those organizations doing between 1 and 19 searches per month, about 42% were doing 50 to 100% solely on-line; of those doing between 20 and 55 searches per month, about 57% were doing 50 to 100% solely on-line; and of those doing 56 to 999 or more searches per month, about 67% were doing 50 to 100% solely on-line.

The display in Exhibit 125 suggests an order of reliance on on-line services for each identified organizational type: Educational institution users have been relying most heavily on on-line services; Government users Commercial organization users, third. Because the response choices are per-centages and the respondents are also given in percentages, it is important to understand how this display should be read. In the first line across, for example, the reader sees that 31.7% of the 101 Government organization users in our study were performing from 1 to 49% of their searches solely on-line; that 53.5% of these users were performing from 50 to 100% of their searches solely on-line; and, that 14.8% of the users could not or did not provide us with any data.

The reliability of the data from this question is dependent upon the degree to which the using organization was maintaining records on, or had a general awareness of, the ways in which all literature requests were being satisfied. From the non-responding population data, it would appear that Commercial organizations were better prepared to describe quantitatively the role of on-line searching within their total service. Although not as precise as one would like, the data point to a strong reliance on on-line systems, but also show that on-line services have not completely replaced other searching modes.

	PERCENTAGE OF SEARCHES		
	1-49%	50-100%	No Response
Government Users (N=101)	31.7%	53.5%	14.8%
Commercial Users (N=152)	50.0%	48.0%	2.0%
Educational Users (N=145)	29.7%	55.9%	14.4%
Other Users (N=74)	33.8%	44.6%	21.6%

Exhibit 125. Percentages of Managers, by Organization Type Reporting 1-49% or 50-100% of Retrospective and Current Awareness Searches Performed Solely On-line

For 416 organizations that reported using a combination of methods for searching the literature, we show in Exhibit 126 that about 92% were continuing to use manual searches, and about 35% were continuing to use batch computer searches. About 63% of those who were using batch computer searches had access to an in-house computer facility, and another group of about the same size were using (in some cases, additionally) external information/computer services.

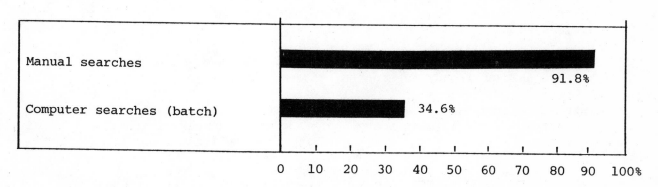

Exhibit 126. Percentage of Respondents Using Manual or Batch Processes to Fulfill Search Requests not Fully Satisfied by On-line Systems (N=416)

In follow-up interviews with searchers, we learned why they believed that it was important to retain the manual-searching capability and tools. Many searchers were using the printed products to obtain copies of the abstracts--which may or may not be available on-line, depending upon the data base and the system--and to search back years that were not available on-line. For example, the machine-readable Chemical Abstracts Condensates that is available on-line dates from 1969 on one system, from 1970 on another system, and from 1972 on a third system. The printed volumes of Chemical Abstracts (CA) date back to 1907.

Other searchers were continuing to use the printed products because they used a structured vocabulary that was not available in the machine-readable version. A data base that illustrates this difference is again Chemical Abstracts Condensates. The machine-readable data base available on-line has indexer-assigned, but non-standardized keywords that reflect concepts represented in the titles, abstracts, and documents and, in addition, automatically indexed title words. On the other hand, the cumulative CA indexes contain controlled subject headings assigned by indexing specialists. Dr. Robert Buntrock, of Standard Oil of Indiana, reports that one method may be preferred over another for some kinds of subject searches: "At the Amoco Research Center, we too have compared search results for CA Condensates and the CA [printed] Indexes, and have found examples for the superiority of CA Condensates, superiority of the Indexes, and virtual equivalence."* In comparing the different retrievals accomplished by searching manually and on-line, Dr. Buntrock offers several illustrations of different searches that are better accomplished by either method. For example, he suggests that the printed indexes are less practical for general searches but more efficient in searches for specific compounds.

Several comments made by the interviewees further illustrate why a combination of methods is used, or the reason that one method may be preferred over another:

> "We continue to use manual searching because of the on-line searching costs. We feel that machine searching augments printed product use."

> "We use manual searching to verify bibliographic data for interlibrary loan."

> "We fall back on the printed products if the system is down or if the terminal is already in use."

Several users indicated that they did not use an on-line system for simple searches, e.g., single-term searching or document number searches.

---

*Buntrock, Robert E., Standard Oil Co. (Indiana), Amoco Research Center, Naperville, Illinois 60540. (From a paper presented at the "Symposium on User Reactions to CAS Data and Bibliographic Services," 169th National Meeting of the American Chemical Society, Philadelphia, Pa., April, 1975.)

Many of our interviewees indicated that they were continuing to subscribe to the printed indexing/abstracting products corresponding to the on-line data bases, and to use them for the purposes described above, as well as for providing continued shelf access (i.e., do-it-yourself service) to their patrons.

Number of End-Users Being Served

The organization that decides to initiate on-line service must be prepared for the possibility that the popularity of the service will promote an increase in the number of end-users of its information services. As shown in Exhibit 127, a majority of managers indicated that the provision of on-line services has had an effect on the number of users they have been serving, particularly within the academic community.

	All Managers (N=472)	Government Users (N=101)	Commercial Users (N=152)	Educational Users (N=145)	Other Users (N=74)
The number of users has increased.	52.3%	44.6%	38.8%	67.6%	60.8%
The number of users has not been affected, but the way we serve them has been.	30.5%	36.6%	42.8%	19.3%	19.7%
The on-line service allows us to serve more users, but it is not the only reason we are serving more users.	16.7%	17.8%	18.4%	16.6%	12.2%
The number of users has not been affected.	14.8%	13.9%	20.4%	9.0%	16.2%

Exhibit 127. Managers' Responses to Question: How has the on-line service affected the number of users of your information services?

Because the managers were asked to indicate all appropriate statements, the percentages in Exhibit 127 total more than 100%. Over half of the respondents indicated that the on-line service has indeed been responsible for an increase in the number of users. Almost 17% of the respondents have seen an increase in the number of users, brought about partly by the on-line service. Thus it would seem that the on-line searches can be a significant drawing force for the service unit as a whole.

An increase in end-users naturally means an increase in the number of search requests that must be processed by the staff. Searchers in one organization saw a ten-fold increase in the number of search requests over a 12-month period after the on-line service was instituted. Although the experience of this organization may not be typical, many managers did claim impressive gains in the number of clients using the information services of the organization.

An increase in search requests may have an important impact on the resources of the organization, both human and physical. Searchers were asked to assess the impact of on-line searching on their workload and their productivity, the data for which are reported in more detail in the next section. Briefly, 49% of the searchers reported that their workload had increased with this new service. We also learned, however, that the increased speed and efficiency of on-line searching over other modes of searching increased the productivity of 76% of the searchers and presumably helped to offset some of the increase in workload. It is not possible to tell from our data the amount of the offset.

Interestingly, the increase in workload to serve more end-users directly has not necessarily meant that new staff had to be added. Only 22% of the managers believed that the introduction of on-line services necessitated adding additional personnel to the staff. As might be expected, managers from organizations that performed a large number of searches on a monthly basis most often reported that a need for additonal personnel existed: only 16% of the organizations that performed fewer than 20 on-line searches each month reported the need for additional personnel, compared to 36% of the organizations that performed 56 searches or more each month.

Quality of The Service

One of the areas of impact that is most difficult to investigate is the effect of on-line retrieval on the quality of literature-searching services. To keep our study within manageable bounds, we had to forego contacting the end-users to help us answer the quality-related questions and, instead, we elected to probe this area by having the managers and searchers report their perceptions of the quality of searches.

Searchers' Comparisons

Searchers were asked to compare the quality of searches obtained from an on-line system to searches performed manually or by batch processing. Regarding manual vs. on-line searches, they were asked to comment on the statement "On-line searching cannot match the quality of a manually performed search." The respondents were given five response options, shown in Exhibit 128 along with the resulting data. Approximately 68% of the searchers disagreed or strongly disagreed with this statement.

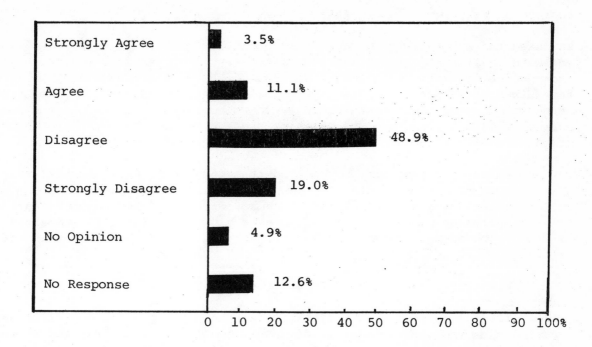

Exhibit 128. Searchers' Responses to Statement: On-line
searching cannot match the quality of a
manually performed search. (N=801)

We must recognize that the nature of an end-user's request is an important
missing ingredient in this question and in the responses. Regardless of the
extent to which the respondents agreed or disagreed with the statement, they
were probably thinking about some kinds of searches that are better performed
manually, or could not even be performed via the on-line system because of the
lack of availability of relevant data bases. Therefore, our conclusion must
be a modest one, with the data showing that, in general, a switch to on-line
searching does not, or at least need not, diminish the quality of searches
performed in an organization.

We next asked the searchers to react to the statement "On-line searching cannot match the quality of a batch-performed search." The searchers who
responded overwhelmingly disagreed with the statement.

- 58.2% strongly disagreed or disagreed with the statement

- 3.6% strongly agreed or agreed

- 38.2% had no opinion or did not respond

As we saw in earlier on-line vs. batch questions, many on-line searchers either
had no experience with batch searching or were not sufficiently familiar with
it to make the requested comparison.

End-Users' Reactions

We asked the managers to compare their end-users' reactions to on-line search-ing with their reactions to the literature-searching services available before the on-line service. Twenty-four percent of the managers said that prior to the introduction of the on-line system no literature searching services had been available in their organizations, so no comparison of the old and new systems was possible. The responses of those managers who were able to make a comparison can be summarized as follows:

- 46.6% of the managers indicated that end-users have generally seemed more favorable in their expressions of satisfaction with the on-line search results. About 75% of these end-users found on-line search-ing to be preferable to manual searching, and about 42% preferred it to batch-mode searching

- 2.3% reported that end-users seemed less favorable in their expres-sions of satisfaction with the on-line search results

- 18.4% indicated that there has not been any discernible difference in users' expressions of satisfaction

- 8.6% of the managers did not respond to the question

These responses indicate that the majority of those organizations that offered manual and/or batch literature-searching services before the on-line service was initiated have found their end-users to be very positive about this new literature-searching tool.

Approximately 68% of the managers reported that the end-users of their litera-ture-searching services have widely different expectations of the on-line search results, as compared to other kinds of search results. The ways in which these managers (a total of 323) characterized the different expectations were as follows:

- 88% reported that their users expected the on-line service to provide <u>faster service</u>

- 69% have found that their users expected <u>more references</u> from the on-line service

- 60% reported that their users expected the on-line service to provide <u>fewer references</u>

- 10% reported that their users expected <u>less relevance</u> or preci-sion from the on-line service (i.e., a larger percentage of irrelevant citations)

- 6% noted that their users expected greater relevance or preci-sion (i.e., a smaller percentage of irrelevant citations)

While almost all of the end-users have been expecting faster service from the on-line service, they have not been so uniformly consistent in their other expectations. Almost equal numbers of managers have found, on the one hand, that end-users expected more references, and on the other, that they expected fewer references. This same dichotomy is apparent with user expectations for relevance or precision from the on-line service. Thus, while most managers reported that their users felt positive toward on-line searching, in general, there were some differences in what they expected the service to provide.

Some 27% of the managers who reported that their individual users did have widely different expectations of the on-line search results, as compared to other kinds of search results, have also found that these expectations carried over into other areas of service provided by their organizations. The most predominant carry-overs, noted by over one-half of this group, were that users expected faster turnaround for all searches, and faster hard-copy, journal, and interlibrary loan backup service. In this vein, one manager wrote that requesters were irritated to learn that manual searches could not be provided as quickly as computer searches. Other representative comments were as follows:

"Users seem to think that we are automated in everything."

"Users are more demanding."

"We are expected to have the latest information available from almost every field or discipline."

Average Turnaround Time on Search Requests

Almost 45% of the using organizations in our study were providing their users with search results within one day, from the time that the request was received until the search results were given to the end-user. Approximately 10% of the organizations reported that their average time was one hour or less, which indicates that some part or all of their search results were being printed directly on-line and that the end-user was located nearby to receive the results in person.

Over 80% of all search requests were being filled within one week of their receipt. As indicated in Exhibit 129, Commercial organizations have been providing the fastest service--most frequently one-day service. Since one-day service requires on-line printing, this fact is consistent with the data we reviewed in Chapter 5, which showed greater average search times for Commercial users.

We have already indicated that faster turnaround time was an expected benefit of the on-line services, and one that has generally been realized. We did not pursue in detail the differences between on-line services and other modes of literature searching, with respect to turnaround time, but we did explore the level of user satisfaction with the reported turnaround times for on-line searches.

	One Day or Less	1.5 Days to One Week	Over One Week	No Response
Government Users (N=101)	37.6%	39.6%	9.9%	12.9%
Commercial Users (N=152)	47.4%	40.8%	5.9%	5.9%
Educational Users (N=145)	41.4%	39.3%	2.8%	16.5%

Exhibit 129.   Average Turnaround Time for Search Requests, from Point of Receiving Request to Giving End-User Search Results, Reported by Managers, by Organizational Type

About 86% of the managers indicated that their end-users were satisfied with the on-line turnaround time that they were providing. Only about 7% said that end-users were not satisfied with their turnaround time, and this group was asked to indicate what would be necessary for them to decrease the lag time. The responses dealt primarily with off-line printing and postal delays, and were not limited to one country; as one non-U.S. manager said: "Better turn-around time would mean getting a new Mussolini to run Italy's PTT...." Some of these respondents suggested decentralized off-line printing capabilities, higher baud rates for on-line printing options, and faster off-line service from some of the suppliers. Other managers who believe that a search is not complete until the full-text documents can also be delivered indicated that the sources for obtaining these documents would need to be re-evaluated and their services be improved, or that their own journal holdings would need to be increased.

Only two or three managers indicated that more staff would be required. One manager took exception to the idea that faster turnaround was needed, saying: "There is too much emphasis on turnaround time to justify on-line searching... 95% of our users don't need instant turnaround....real impact has been on being able to retrieve relevant information from 'dirty' files." The remaining few responses referred to more and better access, and to less down-time with the suppliers' computers.

Document-Delivery Service

Many managers indicated that the on-line service has caused an increase in the use of other than staff resources. The following data show the responses of the managers to a question asking specifically whether the number of requests for full-text copies of documents had changed since on-line service was insti-tuted.

- 56% of the total manager population reported that the number of requests for full-text copies of documents had grown in their organization. This growth is split between a "significant" increase, in one half of the organizations, and a "moderate" one, in the other half.

- For 2%, the number of requests has decreased; this decrease has been "significant" for 25% of these organizations, and "somewhat" of a decrease for the other 75%.

- For 20% the number of requests has stayed about the same as before.

- 15% found the question inapplicable to their operations.

- 7% did not respond.

The impact of the increase in requests for full-text copies of documents on the acquisitions or collection program of the affected organizations has varied, as can be seen in Exhibit 130. (It should be noted here that, although this question was to be answered only by those managers who indicated above that their organizations had experienced an increase in the number of requests for full-text documents since the initiation of on-line services, more than that number responded. Thus the percentages for Exhibit 130 have been computed from this new total of responding managers.)

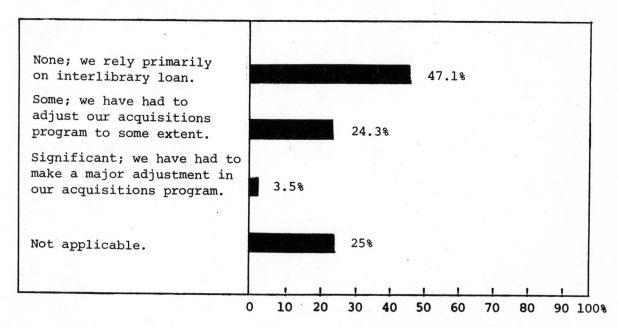

Exhibit 130.   Managers' Responses to Question: What impact has an increase in full-text copies of documents had on your collection or acquisitions program? (N=346)

Almost one half of the organizations that have experienced an increase in demand for full-text copies have been relying primarily on interlibrary loan for obtaining materials that they did not have; thus there has been no impact on their acquisitions program. The question that we were not able to pursue in detail was how the increased number of requests was impacting on the interlibrary loan systems being used by these various organizations. We believe that this is one of the most important questions that need to be studied over the next year or so.

For those 28% of the organizations that had to adjust their acquisitions, either some or significantly, most of them reported that they had to increase their journal subscriptions. A much smaller number reported the need for adjustments in their monographic collections.

About 25% of the respondents found the question to be inapplicable to their mode of operation. We are assuming that, for the most part, there were at least two components in this group, the first of which consisted of individuals who were themselves end-users and who did not maintain collections. We are speculating that they answered this question because they have seen their own requests for full-text copies of documents increase with their use of on-line services. We believe the second component consisted of those organizations that were performing literature searches for end-users but were not also providing the full-text copies of documents. An example of this situation would be the small, private literature-searching organization that supplies bibliographies but is not involved in obtaining the full-text documents for clients.

STAFF AND STAFFING

We believe that it is very important to understand the impact of the on-line services on the staff of a using organization. We gathered data on the impact of on-line services on staff productivity, partly as an extension of the cost-related considerations associated with the use of the services but, in addition, we felt it was important to couple this aspect with data on staff attitudes and morale. The achievement of goals in the areas of efficiency and cost-savings will have only a limited long-term impact on a service if the people who work with the innovation are not willing, or able, to work with the new tool. As we pointed out in an earlier chapter, a key to the successful use of the on-line systems is the level and quality of intellectual participation by the staff members who are doing the searching.

It is in this context that we have reviewed the study results from several questionnaire items in both the Searcher and Manager questionnaires about staffing requirements associated with the provision of on-line literature-searching services and about staff attitudes and morale.

Staff Productivity

We asked both managers and searchers about staff productivity in relation to on-line searching. Managers were asked to respond to the statement that "The productivity of staff is greatly increased by the use of on-line services." Five response options were given, as shown in Exhibit 131. In summary:

- 75.6% of the managers agreed or strongly agreed with the statement

- 11.4% disagreed or strongly disagreed

Thus an overwhelming majority of the managers believed that the overall impact of on-line searching has been to increase staff productivity in the organization.

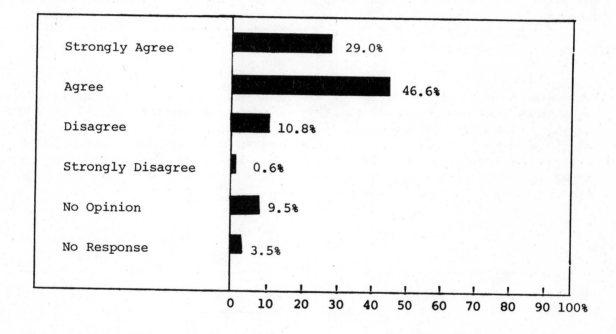

Exhibit 131. Managers' Responses to Statement: The productivity of staff is greatly increased by the use of on-line services. (N=472)

It is interesting to note that the managers' perceptions of productivity were correlated with the number of searchers in the organization and with the number of searches performed on a monthly basis. In organizations with larger searching staffs and more searches to conduct, managers were more likely to report that staff productivity had increased by the use of on-line services. Some 79% of the managers with only one searcher indicated that staff productivity had increased, compared to 95% of the managers with 3 or more searchers; and 68% of the managers whose organizations were performing between 1 and 19 on-line searches on a monthly basis believed that staff productivity had increased, as compared to 88% of the managers whose organizations were processing over 56 on-line searches monthly.

The searchers were asked to respond to a slightly different statement: "On-line searching allows the information specialist or librarian to spend his/her time more productively." Again the response was overwhelmingly positive:

- 76.6% of the searchers agreed or strongly agreed with the statement

- 6.7% of the searchers disagreed or strongly disagreed with the statement

The responses from both survey groups to these statements further corroborate the data shown in the first section, on anticipated benefits, where several key outcomes from increased staff productivity were viewed as expected (and realized) benefits: better service through faster turnaround time; reduction of staff time needed for literature searching; and capability to serve more users.

Associated with staff productivity, and with several other impact areas, is the question of whether additional staff are needed to support on-line literature-searching services. On the basis of their experience in seeing on-line services integrated into an ongoing operation, managers were asked to respond to the following statement: "The introduction of on-line services demands that additional personnel be added to the staff." As shown in Exhibit 132, the majority of respondents disagreed with this statement.

	Strongly Agree	Agree	Disagree	Strongly Disagree	No Opinion	No Response
All Managers (N=472)	8.4%	13.9%	52.9%	12.5%	8.0%	4.0%
Government Users (N=101)	9.9%	10.9%	58.4%	9.9%	5.9%	5.0%
Commercial Users (N=152)	2.0%	5.9%	63.8%	15.8%	7.9%	4.6%
Educational Users (N=145)	13.8%	24.1%	42.1%	8.3%	8.3%	3.4%
Other Users (N=74)	6.8%	14.9%	44.6%	17.6%	9.5%	6.8%

Exhibit 132. Responses of Managers to Statement: The introduction of on-line services demands that additional personnel be added to the staff.

In Chapter 5, we noted that most searchers in our study population were spending only about 10% of their workweek with the on-line systems. However, we
have also noted that the number of users being served is increasing, and,
according to searchers, workloads are also increasing. With the divided opinion
among Educational users that is shown in Exhibit 132, we should probably reserve
judgment on whether on-line services will eventually demand increased staff
resources.

Staff Attitudes and Morale

We asked managers whether any significant changes in staff attitudes or morale
had occurred as a result of the introduction of on-line searching.   Their
responses were as follows:

- 48.7% found that there had been a significant change

- 42.3% reported no significant change

- 8.6% were either uncertain or did not respond to the question

Those managers who indicated that significant changes had occurred were asked
to describe these changes.

A majority of the 48.7% group of respondents reported that the changes in
attitudes they had observed were positive ones. The most often cited change
was what the managers perceived as an increased sense of professionalism and
accomplishment for the staff. Their newly developed expertise with on-line
searching was making it possible for them to provide better service to their
end-users, and they were finding that their jobs were more rewarding.

Some managers reported that the change in attitude stemmed from increased
interest in, and enthusiasm toward, literature searching because the on-line
system had taken much of the drudgery and tedium out of searching. In this
vein, one manager wrote that on-line searching had brought about a greater willingness on the part of the library staff to see what the literature had to
offer.

A few managers (approximately 15 out of 200) who responded to the question on
staff attitudes indicated that the change in staff attitudes and morale had
been negative. The most often stated complaint--and one that, interestingly
enough, actually attests to the success of on-line searching--was that the on-
line system had proved so popular with the clientele that the staff had been
deluged with requests for on-line searches. These same managers indicated that
the size of the staff had not grown to offset the increase in the use of the
facility, and their present staff was faced with much more work. Another
reason for the decrease in morale, voiced by a few managers, was that the staff
had less confidence in the completeness of a search performed on-line; these
staff members were afraid that they had not obtained all of the references
pertinent to the requester's search problem.

Staff Attitudes Toward On-Line Searching

As we have already indicated, staff attitudes can play an important role in determining the overall success or failure of any innovation in an organization. If the staff has preconceived prejudices against the new tool, it is very likely to be used only grudgingly, and perhaps not well. Regardless of the level of management support for the innovation, in the long run it is the staff members who actually work with the new tool who determine its success.

In an effort to understand the staff attitudes toward on-line searching, both before and after the service was instituted in the organization, searchers were asked to compare their initial feelings about using the on-line system with the way they felt about the on-line system at the time they were completing the questionnaire. Several alternatives were posed, and the searchers were instructed to choose any of those that applied. Exhibits 133 and 134 show the results of their responses. (Because of the multiple responses, the percentages do not add up to 100%.)

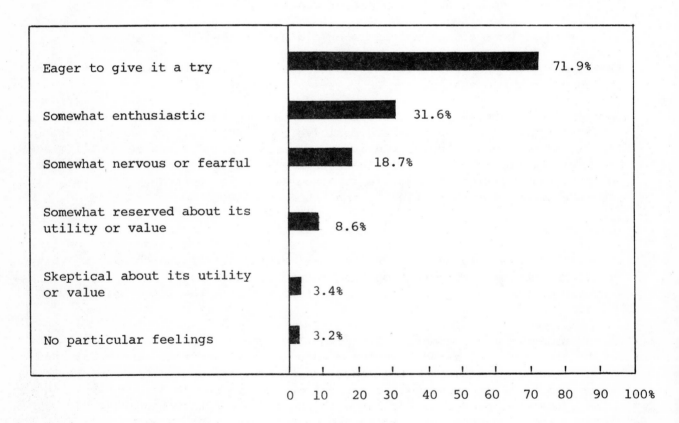

Exhibit 133. Searchers' Responses to Question: What were your initial feelings about using the on-line system? (N=801)

As the reader can see, the vast majority of searchers were either eager or at least somewhat enthusiastic about trying out the on-line system. Only 19% were nervous or fearful about using this new tool. Another 3% expressed initial doubt about the utility or value of the system.

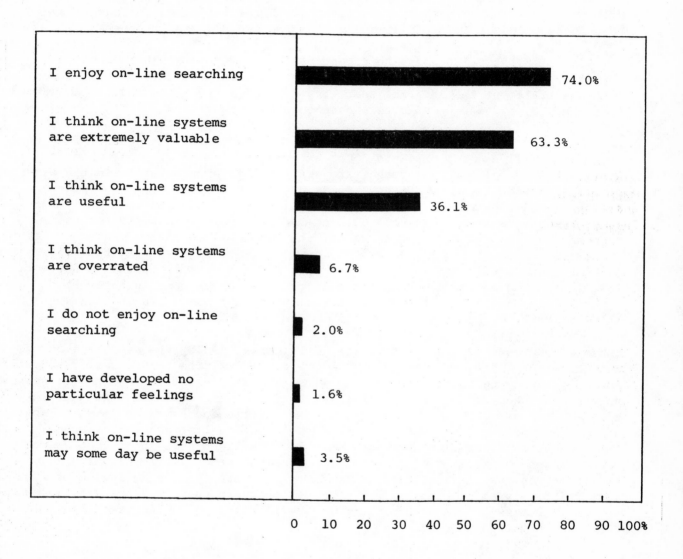

Exhibit 134. Searchers' Responses to Question: How do you feel now about using the on-line system? (N=801)

From Exhibit 134, it is also apparent that the vast majority of searchers did not lose their initial enthusiasm once the on-line systems were being used. Nearly three fourths of the searchers reported that they enjoyed on-line searching, while 63% believed that the systems were extremely valuable. Some searchers were not convinced that on-line searching was as valuable as its advocates claimed, but these individuals constituted a small minority of the survey population.

To explore further the searchers' attitudes toward the services, we confronted them with several attitudinal statements about on-line searching and asked about the extent to which they agreed or disagreed with them. Exhibit 134 shows their responses to these statements. The allowable responses included the following: Strongly Agree, Agree, Disagree, Strongly Disagree, and No Opinion. For display purposes, the Strongly Agree and Agree responses have been aggregated, as have the Strongly Disagree and Disagree responses.

A review of Exhibit 135 shows that most of the searchers who have come into contact with on-line searching value it highly. Approximately 86% disagreed with the statement that on-line searching is only a fad, thus indicating also that they believe it is definitely here to stay.

Automation projects are often said to intimidate workers, making them fear that their jobs will be made obsolete. The experience with on-line searching appears to have allayed all such fears--if they had ever existed--in the minds of most individuals in our study population. On the contrary, 70% of the searchers believe that on-line services will not diminish the need for reference personnel and the on-line searching capability is seen by 49% of the searchers as <u>increasing</u> the workload of the library-information center staff. Presumably, these searchers foresee that more users will be attracted to a facility that offers on-line searching as a reference tool. Although the workload is seen as being on the increase in many organizations, an interesting corollary is that 77% of the searchers believed that on-line searching was allowing them to spend their time more productively.

These responses also show that on-line service is seen by the searchers as one method for expanding and improving library or information center services. Some 79% agreed that on-line services were making it possible for them to serve more users. Another 87% agreed that services have improved with the institution of this new service. There seems to be little doubt in the minds of most of the respondents that, whenever it can be used, on-line searching is an improvement over manual searching. Only 14.6% believe that an on-line search cannot match the quality of a manually performed search; while 68% have no such reservations. Given the fact that on-line retrieval technology is still in a relatively early stage of development, there is every reason to believe the the benefits of using this technology will continue to increase and to become even more apparent.

	Strongly Agree/ Agree	Strongly Disagree/ Disagree	No Opinion	No Response
On-line searching:				
. . . will reduce the need for reference personnel.	15.7%	70.1%	4.2%	10.0%
. . . makes it possible to serve more users.	79.0%	8.6%	2.7%	9.6%
. . . cannot match the quality of a manually performed search.	14.6%	67.9%	4.9%	12.6%
. . . cannot match the quality of a batch-performed search.	3.6%	58.2%	24.2%	14.0%
. . . is economical compared to batch-system processing.	29.3%	10.6%	44.9%	15.1%
. . . allows the information specialist to spend his/her time more productively.	76.6%	6.7%	5.7%	11.0%
. . . is only a passing fad.	0.6%	86.1%	2.9%	10.4%
. . . increases the workload of the library-information center staff.	49.1%	33.6%	6.5%	10.9%
. . . improves services in libraries or information centers.	86.5%	1.4%	1.2%	10.7%
. . . is economical compared to manual searching.	73.2%	5.8%	9.8%	11.1%

Exhibit 135.   Responses of Searchers to Several Attitudinal Questions Related to On-Line Use (N=801)

12. FINAL DISCUSSION

It is unlikely that another major questionnaire survey effort will be conducted on the broad scale in which this study was done, for some time. A considerable amount of baseline data has been derived from this effort and we hope that they will serve as an impetus to, and provide support for, further planning, study, and development in the design and use of on-line retrieval services.

In addition to providing new knowledge about on-line systems, the study data help to corroborate certain opinions and individual experiences that have evolved over the past several years and that are being heard at professional meetings and becoming a part of the professional literature. At the time we initiated this study, there was very little literature on user experience with on-line systems. Within the past year, we have seen the beginnings of a comprehensive body of literature developing from the users' point of view, extending and complementing the literature that has predominated in the past, on the design and evaluation of on-line systems (not services) and on tape- and SDI-oriented processing centers. We hope that the present study will provide a useful framework for individuals and groups to build upon the study data with additional, more precise comparisons and more in-depth descriptions of their own experiences and practices.

The study data also help us to identify trends upon which both suppliers and users can project future needs and begin planning for some of the eventualities that our data portend. In yet other areas, the study data help to identify needs for further study and research.

The discussion in the following sections highlights some of the major findings of our study and some of the issues and questions that require further attention.

On-Line System Users. On-line bibliographic retrieval services are being used primarily by libraries and information service centers in commercial organizations, universities, and federal government agencies. Searchers for these organizations are primarily information intermediaries--librarians and information specialists. About half of these searchers have subject expertise; most of the others have general reference experience. The scientists, technicians, businesspersons and others who do their own searching are currently a small minority, but their numbers are growing steadily.

Whether on-line systems should be used by information intermediaries or by end-users is certain to remain a topic for debate over the coming years. The new interface arrangement, with the end-user sitting "side-saddle" at the terminal with the searcher, is probably the most promising alternative to a short-term resolution of the either/or argument but, for the long term, it is not particularly productive to continue posing the alternatives in mutually exclusive terms. It is important to differentiate among end-users and among organizational working environments, and to recognize that even today there is no "right" or "wrong" approach. Some end-users--those who are willing to invest

in the learning that is required and who perceive the terminal use as a part
of their role--are, and will continue to be, able to conduct their own searches
successfully. We should be learning from these individuals in preparation for
better serving the larger population of end-users in the years to come.

The continuing improvements in computer and communications technology, and the
decreasing costs of using that technology, will help to facilitate the extension of on-line use beyond the library and technical information center and
into the research area, the business office, the classroom and--eventually--
the home. This extension to users other than information professionals will
require improved training methods and user aids and, of course, more easily
usable retrieval systems. It will also require the interest and support of
information professionals, some of whom will need to shift their role from
that of information searcher to that of teacher and consultant, as more end-
users develop the interest and ability to do their own searching. It is clear
that the on-line and data base suppliers alone will not be able to handle the
broad-based training requirements of the end-user population and that the
information intermediary must become a central resource in this training effort.

Growth of On-Line System Use. During the past five years, the on-line retrieval services have developed a solid foundation for continued acceptance and
growth. They are now regarded by most information professionals as very cost-
effective tools for searching the literature. This acceptance is evident in
the increasing numbers of using organizations, in the increasing amount of use,
and in the increasing reliance on on-line services by the present users. A
subtle trend within this pattern is the growth of a cadre of highly experienced
users. Many individuals appear to be "staying with" their searching positions,
and a considerable number have now amassed several years of experience in on-
line searching.

There are several implications for on-line suppliers in these two trends. On-
line suppliers will need to be able to accommodate many more simultaneous users
and to provide even greater service reliability through backup computer, telecommunications, and data base storage systems. The growing experience of the
present user population--together with the entry of new, and perhaps less frequent users--suggests that the next generation of on-line systems design must
be geared for a wider spectrum of experience levels. The more experienced
users will need minimal interaction with the system and will require maximum
flexibility in directing it; in effect, the system will need to be so transpar-
ent as to be "barely there." On the other hand, the more infrequent users who
obtain access to the system will require more tutorials and more guidance
throughout the searching process so that they do not need to re-learn the system every time they use it. In additon to these system design considerations,
perhaps the biggest challenge of all will be the development, by the on-line
suppliers and data base developers, of ways to reduce the real or apparent dis-
parities among data bases and to create the most efficient and least confusing
format for handling subject-vocabulary differences.

Introduction and Management of On-Line Services. The components of a body of
knowledge embracing the management of on-line literature-searching services
within an organization are only now beginning to be identified and discussed

in special workshops and professional meetings. Some of these areas were addressed in our study:

- budgeting and accounting

- selection and training of staff

- acquisition and placement of terminals

- management of staff time

- philosophies relative to cost-recovery practices

- procedures for interacting with end-users and scheduling times for on-line searches

- promotion and evaluation of services

There are not yet any clear "rights" and "wrongs" associated with most of these various areas, but there is a need for the considerations in each area to be defined in a systematic way. The new manager and the manager of presently growing systems have many questions that need answering. For example, should an organization establish guidelines for the amount of time that will be spent, per search, on the terminal? How many citations are to be printed on-line? Off-line? What kind of internal staff communication and review of searches, if any, should be established? Should staff members become specialists in particular data bases or on one on-line system? Even after such questions are answered, the answers or the resulting guidelines will require periodic review. Probably the primary candidates for the development and continuing review of guidelines are the areas of budgeting and internal education and promotion.

Staff Training. One of our major candidates for immediate attention is the area of training. We hope that some studies will be done, in a relatively controlled environment, to determine how to space the learning of multiple data bases and multiple systems, so as to maximize the positive learning effects, and how best to teach users about data bases and systems.

Even minimal growth in the number of on-line users over the next several years will force some changes in current training methods. The suppliers of on-line services have trained most of the current user population, but we foresee a need, in the near future, for others to play an important role in training users. Formal, supervised training should remain the preferred training method, but it will need to be provided more and more by other groups, including library schools, data base developers, and professional associations. In addition, self-teaching units, through programmed-learning and multimedia products, will need to be developed and made available at a nominal price.

Search Times. We believe that such things as the elements of cost and typical search costs are now widely known and that the cost-effectiveness of on-line searching has been clearly established. We hope that new studies in these areas go beyond simple per-search time comparisons and move toward the clarification of more complex issues and the solution of more complex problems. For example, a careful look at pre-terminal planning activities, relative to different kinds of data bases and different kinds of vocabulary aids, would be very useful for both data base developers and on-line suppliers, as well as for searchers. Post-search evaluation and user-searcher interaction after the search has been completed are also worthy of much more attention. And, for those studies dealing with search times, we hope that all the elements of cost identified in this study will be duly considered and that "search" will be clearly defined, particularly where more than one data base is searched in response to a given user request.

Cost-Recovery. On-line services are having a profound impact on the philosophy of library/information reference service. Many institutions that have begun using on-line services have had to modify or compromise a free-service philosophy to cope with the unexpectedly high demand for on-line service, a demand that has strained or overwhelmed existing budgets and required either the curtailment of service or the imposition of user charges. Adoption of a cost-recovery philosophy has not been universally welcomed, but many information professionals feel that it can help to foster the development of a more active information-service role that libraries and information centers seek and that the on-line services can support. Several questions remain to be debated and resolved, e.g., what cost elements should be included in the fees, should there be a disparity between the charges for an on-line search and those for other reference services, and should fee schedules be the same for all classes of end-users.

The public library community is only now beginning to face the for-fee question that the universities (and others) have been facing for several years. On-line services can obviously be useful in reducing the disparity between the "haves" and the "have-nots" in terms of information access, but the fee for service may introduce a new kind of disparity, in terms of ability to afford service.

System and Data Base Use. Searchers favor some systems over others because the data bases that they offer best meet their end-users' needs, because they learned one system first and feel more comfortable with it, and for other reasons, such as system capabilities, costs, and nationalistic feelings about supporting their country's service. The system-preference issue is highly complex. From the using organizations' point of view, data base availability and cost are among the most important factors determining a searcher's choice of a system for a given search. However, if searchers are unable to shift between systems, because of the preemptive "learned-first" effect, organizations may need to divide staff responsibilities by systems, and even to share search requests among several staff members, each of whom conducts searches on the data bases available on their respective systems. This approach would not be available, of course, to the many organizations that have one-person libraries or information centers. We believe that the use of multiple systems will be increasingly important and that most searchers should develop the skills necessary to perform comprehensive searches involving several systems and data bases.

The study confirms that on-line services are a highly effective tool for dis-
seminating the secondary information developed by the world's abstracting and
indexing services. However, the study data also show that the on-line services
are effectively shifting the bottleneck in information services from the locating of references to the locating and provision of full-text copies of the
information identified. Further study of the mechanisms for full-text copy
delivery deserves national-level attention so that the ripple-effect from
increased use of secondary sources does not generate an unmanageable problem
in completing the bibliographic chain.

*   *   *   *   *   *   *   *

On-line bibliographic retrieval systems have been in existence for nearly 15
years, but only in the past 5 years has their full potential begun to be
realized. The SDC study has shown that these systems are highly regarded by
those who have used them and that, in spite of growing pains from as-yet-
imperfect technology, on-line searching is here to stay and the best is yet to
come.

The study has also shown that, with the speed, comprehensiveness, and precision
of on-line searching has come a concomitant improvement in the image and morale
of the information professionals involved, stemming from the end-users' appreciation of both the more responsive reference service and the special skills of
the searchers. Some of the data developed by the study and presented in this
report should help these information professionals to take a more active and
meaningful role in the development and expansion of information service to
their present users and to the broader public that is not yet well served with
information.

The study has also provided data that should help the data base developers and
the suppliers of on-line services to simplify the job of mastering the new
multiplicity of information resources and to provide ever more responsive
services to their clients. For information science researchers, the study
raises, and, in some areas, explores, a number of questions and problems that
warrant further examination, through controlled experiments, field studies, and
even careful anecdotal reports. The importance of on-line technology has been
clearly established; responsibility for furthering its development and for
achieving its full potential rests with all of these groups.

APPENDIX

The following two appendices contain frequency data from each of the two questionnaires, the Manager questionnaire (Appendix A) and the Searcher questionnaire (Appendix B). We have reformatted the actual questionnaire items to permit the respondent data to be included, and we have eliminated most of the open-ended, unstructured questionnaire items and the various typographical aids that were used to clarify and emphasize the instructions to respondents. However, all of the original items and the structured response choices are represented in these two appendices.

MANAGER QUESTIONNAIRE

A. BACKGROUND QUESTIONS

1. Which one of the following best describes your organization? (N=472)

7 (1.5%) City or County Government Agency	0 (-) Public Library
152 (32.2%) Commercial or Industrial Organization	6 (1.3%) School District (local, intermediate, county)
84 (17.8%) Federal Government Agency	10 (2.1%) State/Provincial Government Agency
2 (0.4%) Junior/Community College	137 (29.0%) University or College
42 (8.9%) Non-Profit or Not-for-Profit Organization	32 (6.8%) Other

2. Please indicate the organizational unit in which you work, and in which the on-line systems are actually used. (Check only one.) (N=472)

2 (0.4%) Acquisitions or Cataloging Unit	1 (0.2%) Personnel or Industrial Relations
8 (1.7%) Computer Services Division or Group	3 (0.6%) Public Relations
87 (18.4%) Department or Subject-Area Library	205 (43.4%) Special Library or Information Services Group
22 (4.7%) Information Analysis Center	53 (11.2%) Technical Program, Research or R & D Unit (e.g., program branch, academic department)
61 (12.9%) Main Reference Library	17 (3.6%) Other
6 (1.3%) Marketing or Corporate Planning	7 (1.5%) No Response

3. How many **different** on-line literature-searching systems (excluding any internal systems) do you currently subscribe to, or have access to?

(N = 471)
Range = 1.0 - 12.0
Mean = 1.96
Median = 1.00
Mode = 1.00

(N = 472)	
0 = 3 (0.6%)	3 = 67 (14.2%)
1 = 233 (49.4%)	4 = 28 (5.9%)
2 = 119 (25.2%)	5 - 12 = 21 (4.4%)
No Response = 1 (0.2%)	

4. How long has your organization had access to these on-line systems?

	SYSTEMS			
Length of Time Used	SYSTEM 1 (N=472)	SYSTEM 2 (N=472)	SYSTEM 3 (N=472)	SYSTEM 4 (N=472)
1 - 3 months	18 (3.8%)	45 (9.5%)	27 (5.7%)	15 (3.1%)
3 - 6 months	71 (15.0%)	47 (9.9%)	35 (7.4%)	4 (2.9%)
6 - 12 months	118 (25.0%)	80 (16.9%)	33 (6.9%)	6 (1.2%)
1 - 3 years	209 (44.2%)	60 (12.7%)	22 (4.6%)	10 (2.1%)
3 - 6 years	45 (9.5%)	5 (1.1%)	0 (-)	0 (-)
Over 6 years	5 (1.0%)	0 (-)	0 (-)	0 (-)
No Response	6 (1.2%)	235 (49.8%)	355 (75.2%)	427 (90.4%)

5. Please indicate below the clienteles for whom you do any kind of literature searches--on-line, batch, manual, etc. First, check the USER CATEGORIES at the left that describe your present users and add any other groups you presently serve that are not listed. Leave blank any groups that are not now served, even though you may consider them potential users. Second, for each group you checked, indicate how frequently they use your literature-searching services.

USER CATEGORIES (Check as many as apply.)	DEGREE OF USE (N=472)			
	Rare or Infrequent Users of Service	Occasional Users of Service	Frequent Users of Service	No Response
A. Group Users				
( ) Departments or other Organizational units, as a group	65 (13.7%)	73 (15.4%)	53 (11.2%)	281 (59.5%)
( ) Project or Research Teams, as a group	61 (12.9%)	113 (23.9%)	75 (15.8%)	223 (47.2%)
B. Individual Users				
( ) Administrative or Managerial Personnel	104 (22.0%)	169 (35.8%)	32 (6.7%)	167 (35.3%)
( ) Editors/Writers	59 (12.5%)	43 (9.1%)	17 (3.6%)	353 (74.7%)
( ) Engineers	48 (10.1%)	70 (14.8%)	96 (20.3%)	258 (54.6%)
( ) Faculty or Teachers	26 (5.5%)	49 (10.3%)	136 (28.8%)	261 (55.3%)
( ) Graduate Students	34 (7.2%)	55 (11.6%)	124 (26.2%)	259 (54.8%)
( ) Legal Staff	58 (12.2%)	28 (5.9%)	13 (2.7%)	373 (79.0%)
( ) Marketing/Sales Personnel	48 (10.1%)	44 (9.3%)	28 (5.9%)	352 (74.5%)
( ) Physicians and Other Health Practitioners	32 (6.7%)	49 (10.3%)	149 (31.5%)	242 (51.2%)
( ) Policy Planning Personnel	48 (10.1%)	58 (12.2%)	21 (4.4%)	345 (73.0%)
( ) Program Specialists (Civil Service)	30 (6.3%)	15 (3.1%)	16 (3.3%)	411 (87.0%)
( ) Researchers or Scientists	22 (4.6%)	81 (17.1%)	278 (58.9%)	91 (19.2%)
( ) Undergraduate Students	69 (14.6%)	52 (11.0%)	27 (5.7%)	324 (68.6%)
( ) Other	3 (0.6%)	15 (3.1%)	16 (3.3%)	438 (92.8%)

6. Approximately how many staff members of your unit, or individuals in your organization, are currently performing on-line searches, both regularly and on an infrequent basis?

Number of "regular" searchers (using the system at least once every week or two) is:

Number of "infrequent" searchers (using the system only once every month or so) is:

(N=425)		(N=276)	
Range = 1.0 - 50	1 = 125 (26.4%)	Range = 1.0 - 50.0	1 = 95 (20.1%)
Mean = 3.4	2 = 114 (24.1%)	Mean = 5.9	2 = 74 (15.6%)
Median = 2.3	3 = 76 (16.1%)	Median = 2.1	3 = 29 (6.1%)
Mode = 1.0	4 = 27 (5.7%)	Mode = 1.0	4 = 19 (4.0%)
	5 - 50 = 83 (19.5%)		5 - 200 = 59 (12.5%)
No Response = 47 (9.9%)		No Response = 276 (41.5%)	

(N=472) at top right of left box; (N=472) at top right of right box.

7. What are the positions of the "regular" and the "infrequent" searchers?

	(N=425) "Regular" Searchers	(N=276) "Infrequent" Searchers
Librarians (general reference experience)	163 (38.3%)	69 (25.0%)
Librarians or information specialists with specific subject expertise	269 (63.2%)	92 (33.3%)
Other professionals or technical personnel (e.g., educators, scientists, program specialists, researchers)	110 (25.8%)	115 (41.6%)
Graduate Students	14 (3.2%)	23 (8.3%)
Undergraduate students	2 (0.4%)	10 (3.6%)
Clerical personnel or paraprofessionals	53 (12.4%)	48 (17.3%)
Others	8 (1.8%)	11 (3.9%)

8. Indicate the communications method(s) used to access the system(s). (If you are using more than one system, remember to use the same number assignments you used in Question 4.)

	SYSTEMS			
	SYSTEM 1 (N=472)	SYSTEM 2 (N=472)	SYSTEM 3 (N=472)	SYSTEM 4 (N=472)
Through Direct Dial to the Supplier's Computer:				
Local Call	64 (13.5%)	24 (5.0%)	14 (2.9%)	6 (1.2%)
Long Distance (commercial)	45 (9.5%)	28 (5.9%)	15 (3.1%)	7 (1.4%)
Leased Line	67 (14.1%)	17 (3.6%)	11 (2.3%)	5 (1.0%)
WATS	43 (9.1%)	18 (3.8%)	9 (1.9%)	3 (0.6%)
FTS	22 (4.6%)	9 (1.9%)	4 (0.8%)	3 (0.6%)
Through a Network to the Supplier's Computer:				
ARPANET	3 (0.6%)	2 (0.4%)	1 (0.2%)	0 (-)
DATAROUTE and/or INFODAT	8 (1.6%)	2 (0.4%)	2 (0.4%)	1 (0.2%)
TYMSHARE	298 (63.4%)	159 (33.6%)	69 (14.6%)	26 (5.5%)

9. If you reach the system through a network, indicate below how you make connections with the network.

	SYSTEMS			
	SYSTEM 1 (N=309)	SYSTEM 2 (N=163)	SYSTEM 3 (N=72)	SYSTEM 4 (N=27)
Local Call	214 (69.2%)	110 (67.4%)	49 (68.0%)	20 (74.0%)
Long Distance	69 (22.3%)	45 (27.6%)	18 (25.0%)	7 (25.9%)
WATS	51 (16.5%)	19 (11.6%)	12 (16.6%)	5 (18.5%)

B. INTEGRATION OF ON-LINE SERVICES INTO THE USING ORGANIZATION

Goals and Objectives

1. What did your organization initially anticipate would be the main benefit of using on-line systems? (Check as many as apply.) (N=472)

		No Response
319 (67.5%)	Better service through access to additional sources of information	153 (32.4%)
340 (72.0%)	Better service through faster turnaround time	132 (27.9%)
269 (56.9%)	Reduction of staff time needed for literature searching	203 (43.0%)
223 (47.2%)	Better service through greater precision in retrieval	249 (52.7%)
210 (44.4%)	Capability to serve more users	262 (55.5%)
203 (43.0%)	Capability to introduce literature-searching services	269 (56.9%)
14 (2.9%)	We didn't know what to anticipate	458 (97.0%)
24 (5.0%)	Other	448 (94.9%)

2. Do you believe that these benefits have, in general, been realized? (N=472)

434 (91.9%) = Yes   18 (3.8%) = No   2 (0.4%) = Some   18 (3.8%) = No Response

Budgeting and Accounting

1. Did you have any significant problems in justifying using the on-line services or getting formal approval to start using them? (N=472)

85 (18.0%) =Yes   376 (79.6%) = No   11 (2.3%) =   No Response

2. Do you maintain a separate budget and accounting system for on-line services? (N=472)

    297 (62.9%)   Yes, for all systems we use.

     23 (4.8%)   Yes, for some systems we use.

    146 (30.9%)   No

      6 (1.2%)   No Response

(If you answered NO, please skip to section titled "Staff," page 9.)

3. What was your cost-recovery goal when you first introduced on-line services? (N=320)

     51 (15.9%)   To recover all costs from users or their organizations/units.

    102 (31.8%)   To recover a portion of some of the costs.

      4 (1.2%)   To make a profit.

    160 (50.0%)   There was no cost-recovery goal; we planned to absorb the full cost in our unit's budget.

      3 (0.9%)   No Response

4. Has this original goal regarding cost-recovery changed since you first introduced the service? (N=320)

    80 (25.0%) = Yes   226 (70.6%) = No   2 (0.6%) = Maybe   12 (3.7%) = No Response

5. Do your accounting or charging procedures for on-line services differ in any important ways from accounting or charging procedures for your other literature-searching services? (N=320)

    62 (19.3%) = Yes   121 (37.8%) = No   134 (41.8%) = Not Applicable   3 (0.9%) = No Response

6. Please estimate the average cost per search (across all data bases and systems for which you maintain records) to your organization or unit.

Average cost per search:

(N=286)
Range = $1.00 - $99.00
Mean = $23.83
Median = $17.16
Modes = $20.00 and $25.00

7. Please indicate below which cost elements are included in this estimate.

COST ELEMENT (N=286)	Included in Your Costs?		
	Yes	No	No Response
1. Staff Time (at the terminal)	126 (44.0%)	123 (43.0%)	37 (12.9%)
2. Staff Time (pre-terminal)	108 (37.7%)	136 (47.5%)	42 (14.6%)
3. Staff Time (post-terminal)	95 (33.2%)	145 (50.6%)	46 (16.0%)
4. Terminal Rental or Purchase	134 (46.8%)	114 (39.8%)	38 (13.2%)
5. Computer-related Costs	231 (80.7%)	32 (11.1%)	23 (8.0%)
6. Communications and Communications Equipment	203 (70.9%)	52 (18.1%)	31 (10.8%)
7. Off-Line Printing	233 (81.4%)	36 (12.5%)	17 (5.9%)
8. Organization Overhead or Share of Facilities	43 (15.0%)	165 (57.6%)	78 (27.2%)
9. Share of Subscription or Minimum to On-Line Supplier	93 (32.5%)	118 (41.2%)	75 (26.2%)
10. Other	18 (6.2%)	2 (0.6%)	266 (93.0%)

8. Please indicate the average minutes that your staff spends per search:

STAFF TIME

Minutes per search at the terminal

```
(N=303)

Range = 2.0 - 99.0

Mean   = 19.1
Median = 15.3
Mode   = 15.0
```

Minutes per search in pre-terminal work

```
(N=290)

Range = 2.0 - 99.0

Mean   = 20.7
Median = 15.1
Mode   = 15.0
```

Minutes per search in post-terminal work

```
(N=274)

Range = 1.0 - 99.0

Mean   = 17.7
Median = 10.1
Mode   = 10.0
```

9. Please indicate below the average number of citations or pages, per search, that are printed off-line:

OFF-LINE PRINTING

Citations per search

(N=224)
Range = 2.0 - 301.0
Mean   = 74.8
Median = 50.5
Mode   = 50.0

OR

Pages per search

(N=68)
Range = 1.0 - 200.0
Mean   = 17.4
Median = 9.9
Mode   = 10.0

10. Do you now charge users or their organizations/units for on-line searches? (N=320)

    180 (56.2%) = Yes   131 (40.9%) = No   9 (2.8%) = No Response

If YES, please check the applicable statement(s) below. (N=180)

 49 (27.2%)   The charge per search is fixed.

134 (74.4%)   The charge is variable, depending on the search, the data base, or the user.

 8 (4.4%)   There are no per-search charges; we use a subscription type arrangement that provides for a certain number of searches for a total subscription fee.

23 (12.7%)   Other

11. If you indicated above that you charge users, per search, please indicate below the cost elements on which you compute the charges.

COST ELEMENT (N=180)	Included in Your Costs?		
	Yes	No	No Response
1. Staff Time (at the terminal)	65 (36.1%)	75 (41.6%)	40 (22.2%)
2. Staff Time (pre-terminal)	56 (31.1%)	80 (44.4%)	44 (24.4%)
3. Staff Time (post-terminal)	44 (24.4%)	90 (50.0%)	46 (25.5%)
4. Terminal Rental or Purchase	58 (32.2%)	80 (44.4%)	42 (23.3%)
5. Computer-related Costs	145 (80.5%)	14 (7.7%)	21 (11.6%)
6. Communications and Communications Equipment	122 (67.7%)	26 (14.4%)	32 (17.7%)
7. Off-Line Printing	149 (82.7%)	15 (8.3%)	16 (8.8%)
8. Organization Overhead or Share of Facilities	30 (16.6%)	91 (50.5%)	59 (32.7%)
9. Share of Subscription or Minimum to On-Line Supplier	47 (26.1%)	75 (41.6%)	58 (32.2%)
10. Other	18 (10.0%)	1 (0.5%)	161 (89.4%)

Staff

1. How many individual(s) did you initially select to be on-line system searchers? (Consider only the period of up to 30 days from the time your organization first began on-line searching.)

If you were not involved in this initial startup period, please check this box -- 54 (11%) -- and answer the question only on the basis of the time when you first became involved.

a. Initial Number of Searchers:

(N=449)
Range = 1.0 - 40.0
Mean = 2.8
Median = 1.5
Mode = 1.0

(N=472)	
1 = 179 (37.9%)	4 = 23 (4.8%)
2 = 119 (25.2%)	5 - 40 = 60 (12.7%)
3 = 68 (14.4%)	No Response = 23 (4.8%)

b. Were you included in this number, at that time? (N=472)

277 (58.6%) = Yes   176 (37.2%) = No   19 (4.0%)= No Response

c. Does this number include professionals that were outside your own organizational unit? (N=472)

55 (11.6%) = Yes   390 (82.6%) = No   27 (5.7%) = No Response

If YES, how many?

(N=50)
Range = 1.0 - 22.0
Mean = 3.2
Median = 1.6
Mode = 1.0

1 = 23 (41.8%)
2 = 13 (23.6%)
3 - 22 = 14 (25.4%)
No Response = 5 (9.0%)

2. What was the basis for selecting these individuals: (N=472)

		No Response
357 (75.6%)	They were trained librarians or information specialists.	115 (24.3%)
137 (29.0%)	They were familiar with computers or automation.	335 (70.9%)
194 (41.1%)	They were familiar with one or more of the data bases (through coding for batch searches or manual searches of the printed products.)	278 (58.9%)
37 (7.8%)	They had previously used the system(s) we were subscribing to.	435 (92.1%)
119 (25.2%)	They seemed to have the "right" personality or had expressed an interest in using the terminals.	353 (74.7%)
84 (17.8%)	They were the only staff available at the time.	388 (82.2%)
5 (1.0%)	I do not know.	467 (98.9%)
33 (6.9%)	Other	439 (93.0%)

3. Have you found that some individuals are much better suited to be on-line searchers than others? (N=472)

   295 (62.5%) = Yes   106 (22.4%) = No   16 (3.3%) = Maybe   55 (11.6%) = No Response

4. Did you meet any resistance by, or sense any apprehension among, the original staff members assigned to searching? (N=472)

   100 (21.1%) = Yes   326 (69.0%) = No   29 (6.1%) = Do not know   17 (3.5%) = No Response

5. Do you believe any significant changes in staff attitudes or morale have occurred due to the introduction of on-line searching? (N=472)

   231 (48.9%) = Yes   200 (42.3%) = No   3 (0.6%) = Maybe   38 (8.0%) = No Response

6. On the basis of your experiences in seeing on-line services integrated into an on-going operation, indicate the way that you feel about each of the statements below. (N=472)

Statement	Strongly Agree	Agree	Disagree	Strongly Disagree	No Opinion	No Response
The introduction of on-line services into an organization requires special planning and supervision.	159 (33.6%)	240 (50.8%)	31 (6.5%)	2 (0.4%)	24 (5.0%)	16 (3.3%)
The productivity of staff is greatly increased by the use of on-line services.	137 (29.0%)	220 (46.6%)	51 (10.8%)	3 (0.6%)	45 (9.5%)	16 (3.3%)
The introduction of on-line services demands that additional personnel be added to the staff.	40 (8.4%)	66 (13.9%)	250 (52.9%)	59 (12.5%)	38 (8.0%)	19 (4.0%)
On-line services should "pay their own way" in an organization.	46 (9.7%)	152 (32.2%)	151 (31.9%)	24 (5.0%)	81 (17.1%)	18 (3.8%)
On-line searching is not as cost-effective as searching in batch processing.	7 (1.4%)	38 (8.0%)	155 (32.8%)	84 (17.8%)	168 (35.5%)	20 (4.2%)
On-line searching is more cost-effective than manual searching.	152 (32.2%)	200 (42.3%)	30 (6.3%)	2 (0.4%)	69 (14.6%)	19 (4.0%)

Getting Started: Equipment and Facilities

1. Was the purchase or rental of a terminal a major barrier in your obtaining approval or getting started? (N=472)

       47 (9.9%) = Yes   272 (57.6%)= No   141 (29.8%) = Not Applicable   12 (2.5%) = No Response

2. Did you receive consultation from any source in deciding on the particular terminal(s) you use? (N=472)

      295 (62.5%) = Yes   147 (31.1%) = No   30 (6.3%) = No Response

    a. If YES, please check the source: (N=295)

       126 (42.7%) On-line service supplier

       148 (50.1%) Our own computer or data processing staff

        97 (32.8%) Other on-line system users

        78 (26.4%) Terminal suppliers

        16 (5.4%) Other

    b. Was this consultation adequate?

      279 = Yes   20 = No   2 = Maybe

3. Where is/are the terminal(s) located? (Check as many as apply.) (N=472)

		No Response
211 (44.7%)	In a separate "terminal" room within the library or information center area	261 (55.3%)
98 (20.7%)	In an open area, e.g., reference or reading room	374 (79.2%)
140 (29.6%)	In an office or offices throughout the building	332 (70.3%)
55 (11.6%)	In no special place; we use it/them on a shared basis with others in the organization	417 (99.3%)
26 (5.5%)	In a special security area	446 (94.4%)

a. Were there special considerations or problems involved in deciding on this arrangement? (N=472)

183 (38.7%) = Yes   258 (54.6%) = No   31 (6.5%) = No Response

b. Is the location of the terminal important?

344 (72.8%) = Yes   100 (21.1%) = No   28 (5.9%) = No Response

Promotion of On-Line Services

1. Did you formally announce or otherwise promote the use of on-line searches in your organization? (N=472)

393 (83.2%) = Yes   68 (14.4%) = No   11 (2.3%) = No Response

a. If YES, please check as appropriate: (N=393)

326 (82.9%) Sent around newsletters, flyers, and/or announcements to different users/groups

259 (65.9%) Conducted special group meetings, presentations, and/or demonstrations

252 (64.1%) Performed sample searches for key individuals throughout the company or organization

46 (11.7%) Other

2. Have you developed special materials to "tell the story" of on-line searching for users? (N=472)

141 (29.8%) = Yes   311 (65.8%) = No   20 (4.2%) = No Response

3. Do you believe a special "marketing" program is needed to promote your on-line search services?   (N=472)

    115 (24.3%)   Yes, a full internal marketing program is essential

    168 (35.5%)   Yes, but only on a limited scale

    53 (11.2%)   No, "word-of-mouth" is sufficient

    97 (20.5%)   No, our normal program of announcing services is sufficient for promoting on-line searches, as well

    19 (4.0%)   No, we do not promote on-line searches in any way

    20 (4.2%)   No Response

C. IMPACT OF ON-LINE SEARCHING ON THE INFORMATION CONSUMER

Background: Service Operations

1. What is the average number of on-line literature searches performed in your organization/institution each month?

(N=432)
Range = 1.0 - 999.9
Mean   = 69.2
Median = 29.9
Mode   = 25.0

2. Please indicate below the way(s) in which your information consumers (i.e., users) interact with the on-line system. Read over all five alternatives. Then, for each of them, check the appropriate response in the right-hand columns to show the degree to which the alternative is used.

ALTERNATIVE SEARCHER/ USER INTERACTIONS	DEGREE OF USE (N=472)			
	Most Searches	Many Searches	Few Searches or None	No Response
The user discusses search problem with the searcher, or provides a written description of the problem for the searcher, but does not participate in the actual performance of his/her search at the terminal.	298 (63.1%)	74 (15.6%)	80 (16.9%)	20 (4.4%)
The user works with the searcher at the terminal, providing guidance and feedback to the searcher while he/she actually operates the terminal.	87 (18.4%)	125 (26.4%)	226 (47.8%)	34 (7.4%)
The user is in contact with the searcher while the search is being performed, but he is not physically located at the searcher's terminal.	8 (1.7%)	30 (6.4%)	378 (80.1%)	56 (11.9%)
The user performs the search himself in a centrally located terminal area, where assistance is available, on request, from an expert searcher-resource person.	20 (4.2%)	25 (5.3%)	370 (78.4%)	57 (12.1%)
The user performs the search and operates independently in his/her own office or laboratory area.	14 (3.0%)	12 (2.5%)	380 (80.5%)	66 (14.0%)

3. If you indicated above that the user is not physically located at the searcher's terminal, but is in contact with him/her while the search is being performed, please indicate below what contact arrangements are used.

<u>69</u> The user is in his/her own office or laboratory, talking with the searcher over a telephone.

<u>1</u> The user is at a slaved terminal in a different location.

<u>12</u> Other arrangement.

4. What percentage (approximate) of all literature-search requests—both retrospective and current awareness—that you received are performed:

Solely on-line	<u>49.02%</u> = Mean (N=472)
Partly on-line	<u>19.34%</u> = Mean (N-472)
Not at all on-line	<u>17.02%</u> = Mean (N=472)
Partial Response/No Response	<u>14.62%</u>
TOTAL	100%

5. For those retrospective searches or current awareness searches that are not fully satisfied by the on-line system(s), please indicate what other procedures are used to fulfill the search request. (N=472)

<u>382 (80.9%)</u> Manual search   <u>90 (19.0%)</u> No Response

<u>144 (30.5%)</u> Computer search,   <u>328 (69.4%)</u> No Response
            using batch techniques

Is the computer searching done: (N=144)

<u>91 (63.1%)</u> in-house?   <u>92 (63.8%)</u> with outside information
                                                    or computer services?

User Practices and User Preferences

1. How has your provision of on-line services affected the number of users of your information services? (Check as many statements as are appropriate.) (N=472)

<u>No Response</u>

<u>247 (52.3%)</u>   The on-line service seems to have increased the number of users.   225 (47.6%)

<u>70 (14.8%)</u>   The on-line service has not affected the number of users we serve.   402 (85.1%)

<u>144 (30.5%)</u>   The on-line service has not directly affected the number of users we serve, but it has affected the way in which we serve them.   328 (69.4%)

<u>79 (16.7%)</u>   The on-line service has allowed us to serve more users, but, by itself, it is not the reason we are serving more users.   393 (83.2%)

2. Do your users know when a search is likely to be performed on-line? (N-472)

<u>274 (58.0%)</u> Most do   <u>25 (5.3%)</u> Don't know

<u>140 (29.6%)</u> Some do   <u>22 (4.6%)</u> No Response

<u>11 (2.3%)</u> None do

3. Do your users ask for searches to be performed by one process or another, i.e., do they ask specifically for either a computerized search or a manual search?

<u>246</u> = Yes   <u>200</u> = No   <u>26</u> = No Response

If YES, do they generally express a preference for one particular process?

<u>252</u>   Yes

<u>8</u>   No, they do not

4. Have the ways in which users phrase their search requests changed with the implementation of the on-line service or over the period since on-line services were introduced? (Check the appropriate columns for each statement that you believe applies.)

STATEMENT OF REQUEST FROM USERS	DEGREE OF APPLICABILITY (N=472)				
	Most Users	Some Users	Few Users	No Users	No Response
Users now state their requests more broadly than they previously did.	12 (2.5%)	78 (16.5%)	133 (28.1%)	119 (25.2%)	130 (27.5%)
Users now state their questions more specifically than they previously did.	138 (29.2%)	136 (28.8%)	50 (10.5%)	53 (11.2%)	95 (20.1%)
Users now ask specifically that a serach be run on a certain on-line system.	71 (15.0%)	117 (24.7%)	54 (11.4%)	127 (26.9%)	103 (21.8%)
Users now ask specifically that a search be run on a certain data base or group of data bases.	61 (12.9%)	118 (25.0%)	95 (20.1%)	90 (19.0%)	108 (22.8%)
Users now request that the search results be screened before they get them.	21 (4.4%)	45 (9.5%)	100 (21.1%)	194 (41.1%)	112 (23.7%)
Users now request that the search results not be screened by the searcher.	27 (5.7%)	32 (6.7%)	62 (13.1%)	231 (48.9%)	120 (25.4%)
Other	16 (3.3%)	2 (0.4%)	0 (-)	0 (-)	454 (96.1%)

5. Has the number of requests for full-text copies of documents changed since on-line service was instituted? (N=472)

    264 (55.9%) Yes, the number of requests has grown: (N=264)

    132 (50.0%) Significantly
    132 (50.0%) Somewhat } (N=264)

    8 (1.6%) Yes, the number of requests has decreased: (N=8)

    2 (25.0%) Significantly
    6 (75.0%) Somewhat } (N=8)

    94 (19.9%) No, the number of requests has stayed about the same as before.

    69 (14.6%) Not applicable.

    37 (7.8%) No Response

6. If the number of requests for full-text copies has increased, what impact has this had on your collection or acquisition program?

    163 None; we rely primarily on interlibrary loan for obtaining materials that we do not have.

    84 Some; we have had to adjust our acquisitions program to some extent. (Check applicable categories.)

        72 in journal subscriptions

        34 in microfiche collections

        27 in monograph orders

    12 Significant; we have had to make a major adjustment in our acquisitions program. (Check applicable categories.)

        9 in journal subscriptions

        5 in microfiche collections

        3 in monograph orders

    87 Not applicable.

7. Do individual users have widely different expectations of the on-line search results, as compared with other kinds of search results? (N=472)

323 (68.4%) = Yes   110 (23.3%) = No   5 (1.0%) = Maybe   34 (7.2%) = No Response

a. If YES, please check those expectations that users have expressed. They expect the on-line service to provide: (N=323)

284 (87.9%) faster service

222 (68.7%) more references

193 (59.7%) fewer references

18 (5.5%) greater relevance or precision (i.e., a smaller percentage of irrelevant citations)

32 (9.9%) less relevance or precision (i.e., a larger percentage of irrelevant citations)

b. If YES, do you also find that these expectations related to on-line searching carry over into other areas of service you provide? (N=323)

88 (27.2%)= Yes   225 (69.6%)= No   3 (0.9%)= Maybe   7 (2.1%)= No Response

8. a. Do the end users of the search results generally regard the layout and format of computer printouts of bibliographical information as satisfactory? (N=472)

287 (60.8%)= Yes   21 (4.4%)= No   141 (29.8%)= No real basis   23 (4.8%)= No Response
                                                      for judging

b. Do users have any difficulties in identifying the different parts or elements of the citation? (N=472)

151 (31.9%) = Yes   283 (59.9%) = No   38 (8.0%) = No Response

c. Does someone in your organization add any explanatory notes or comments to the final search product? (N=472)

266 (56.3%) = Yes   178 (37.7%) = No   28 (5.9%) = No Response

9. Have you encountered any reluctance on the part of some users to allow their search requests to be performed on-line? (N=472)

49 (10.3%) = Yes   401 (84.9%) = No   22 (4.6%) = No Response

If YES, please answer the following questions. (If NO, skip to question 10.)

a. What reasons are given for this reluctance? (N=49)

14 (28.5%) Concern about security, when their search is related to a new and proprietary idea or project they are working on.

20 (40.8%) A mistrust of machine-retrieval, either in terms of precision or recall.

16 (32.6%) Other

b. Is the number of security-conscious users significantly large?

60 No, only a few users express concern about security.

6 Yes, a number of users express concern.

10. Do you believe that on-line access to some of the major bibliographic files is exerting any observable changes on the traditional information-seeking habits of your users? (N=472)

299 (63.3%) = Yes   131 (27.7%) = No   9 (1.9%) = Maybe   33 (6.9%) = No Response

User Satisfaction

1. For searches that are performed on-line, how long does it take to handle the average request from the point of receiving the request to the time the user has the citations or abstracts that result from the search? (N=472)

Mean = 2.1 Hour(s)   or   Mean = 2.0 Day(s)   or   Mean = 1.4 Week(s)
   (N=90)   (N=242)   (N=86)

2. Are users generally satisfied with this turnaround time? (N=472)

408 (86.4%) = Yes   32 (6.7%) = No   32 (6.7%) = No Response

3. How do users react to on-line searching, in comparison with your previous literature-searching services? (Check a or b or c or d.) (N=472)

a. 114 (24.1%) Users used to do their own searches, so we have no basis for comparison.

b. <u>220 (46.6%)</u> Users generally seem more favorable in their expressions of
satisfaction with the on-line search results.

     <u>93</u> (42.2%) More favorable than with batch-mode search results. ⎫
                                                                                          ⎬ (N=220)
    <u>166</u> (75.4%) More favorable than with manual-search results. ⎭

c. <u>11 (2.3%)</u> Users generally seem less favorable in their expressions of
satisfaction with the on-line search results.

      <u>0</u> (-) Less favorable than with batch-mode search results. ⎫
                                                                                        ⎬ (N=11)
    <u>11</u> (100%) Less favorable than with manual-search results. ⎭

d. <u>87 (18.4%)</u> There does not appear to be any discernible difference in users'
expressions of satisfaction with the on-line search results.

    <u>10</u>   There is no difference between on-line and batch-
mode search results.

    <u>38</u>   There is no difference between on-line and manual
search results.

SEARCHER QUESTIONNAIRE

A. BACKGROUND QUESTIONS

1. Which one of the following <u>best</u> describes your parent organization? (N=801)

10 (1.2%) City or County Government Agency	0 (-) Public Library
247 (30.8%) Commercial or Industrial Organization	12 (1.5%) School District (local, intermediate, county)
163 (20.3%) Federal Government Agency	19 (2.4%) State/Provincial Government Agency
0 (-) Junior/Community College	252 (31.5%) University or College
62 (7.7%) Non-Profit or Not-For-Profit Organization	36 (4.5%) Other

2. Please indicate the organizational unit in which you work. (N=801)

9 (1.1%) Acquisitions or Cataloging	1 (0.1%) Personnel or Industrial Relations
14 (1.7%) Computer Services Division or Group	0 (-) Public Relations
192 (24.0%) Department or Subject-Area Library	364 (45.4%) Special Library or Information Services
15 (1.9%) Information Analysis Center	94 (11.7%) Technical Program, Research, or R & D Unit (e.g., program branch, academic department)
86 (10.7%) Main Reference Library	
8 (1.0%) Marketing or Corporate Planning	18 (2.2%) Other

3. Which of the following best describes your current position? (N=801)

39 (4.9%) Administrator	98 (12.2%) Professional/Technical person (e.g., scientist, educator, physician)
9 (1.1%) Clerk or Secretary	
9 (1.1%) Data Processing Specialist	18 (2.2%) Research Assistant
6 (1.0%) Graduate Student	0 (-) Undergraduate Student
615 (76.8%) Librarian/Information Specialist	7 (1.0%) Other

4. How long have you been performing on-line literature searches? (N=801)

    13 (1.6%) Less than one month   343 (42.8%) 1 - 3 years

    50 (6.2%) 1 - 3 months   54 (6.7%) 3 - 6 years

   108 (13.5%) 3 - 6 months   4 (0.5%) Over 6 years

   223 (27.8%) 6 - 12 months   6 (0.7%) No Response

5. Prior to your beginning to use an on-line system for literature searching, had you used an interactive system for some other purpose? (N=801)

   152 (19.0%) = Yes   635 (79.3%) = No   14 (1.7%) = No Response

6. How many different on-line literature searching systems (excluding any internal, private systems) do you use? (N=801)

Mean   = 1.7
Median = 1.0
Mode   = 1.0

Range = 1 - 10 (N=801)	
1 = 462 (57.7%)	3 = 105 (13.1%)
2 = 203 (25.3%)	4 or more = 31 (3.9%)

7. How many different _bibliographic_ data bases do you access?

(N=783)
Mean   = 6.6
Median = 4.9
Mode   = 1.0

Range = 1 - 34 (N=801)			
1 = 144 (18.0%)	4 = 78 (9.7%)	7 = 42 (5.2%)	10 = 34 (4.2%)
2 = 74 (9.2%)	5 = 80 (10.0%)	8 = 32 (4.0%)	over 10 = 151 (18.8%)
3 = 60 (7.5%)	6 = 68 (8.5%)	9 = 20 (2.5%)	
	No Response = 18 (2.5%)		

B. GENERAL QUESTIONS

Training and Learning

1. Did you receive formal training from the system supplier? (N=801)

<u>340 (42.4%)</u> = Yes   <u>356 (44.4%)</u> = No   <u>102 (12.7%)</u> = Some   <u>3 (0.3%)</u> = No Response

   a. If YES, please indicate the extent of this training by checking the appropriate column or columns.

I received formal training for:							
SYSTEM 1 (N=801)		SYSTEM 2 (N=339)		SYSTEM 3 (N=136)		SYSTEM 4 (N-31)	
On One Data Base	On Several Data Bases	On One Data Base	On Several Data Bases	On One Data Base	On Several Data Bases	On One Data Base	On Several Data Bases
169 (21.1%)	247 (30.8%)	46 (13.6%)	80 (23.6%)	25 (18.4%)	22 (16.2%)	5 (16.1%)	4 (12.9%)
No Response 385 (48.1%)		213 (62.9%)		89 (65.4%)		22 (71.0%)	

b. If NO, please indicate the way(s) in which you first learned to use each of the systems.

	SYSTEM 1 (N=801)	SYSTEM 2 (N=339)	SYSTEM 3 (N=136)	SYSTEM 4 (N=31)
I applied my previous experience with on-line systems on non-bibliographic files.	42 (5.2%)	25 (7.4%)	7 (5.1%)	2 (6.5%)
I applied my previous experience with another on-line literature searching system.	27 (3.4%)	97 (28.6%)	41 (30.1%)	14 (45.2%)
I received instruction from another staff member who had been trained by the on-line service supplier.	239 (29.8%)	83 (24.5%)	27 (19.9%)	8 (25.8%)
I read the user's manuals and documentation provided by the on-line service supplier.	299 (37.3%)	150 (44.2%)	57 (41.9%)	19 (61.3%)
I learned through programmed instruction on the computer.	23 (2.9%)	7 (2.0%)	2 (1.5%)	1 (3.2%)
I taught myself without having any previous experience or reading any documentation.	13 (1.6%)	7 (2.0%)	3 (2.2%)	0 (-)
Other	44 (5.5%)	8 (2.4%)	2 (1.5%)	1 (3.2%)

3. We recognize that "efficiency" at the terminal is not easily quantifiable. However, we would like you to estimate the length of time that you believe it took before you became "comfortable and fairly efficient" at conducting searches on the system.

   a. For formally trained searchers (those trained either by on-line suppliers or by highly experienced instructors):

Length of Time to Become Efficient	SYSTEM 1 (N=801)	SYSTEM 2 (N=339)	SYSTEM 3 (N=136)	SYSTEM 4 (N=31)
1 to 5 Days	85 (10.6%)	50 (14.7%)	16 (11.8%)	2 (6.5%)
1 to 4 Weeks	146 (18.2%)	33 (9.7%)	14 (10.3%)	4 (12.9%)
1 to 2 Months	74 (9.2%)	11 (3.2%)	8 (5.9%)	2 (6.5%)
2 to 4 Months	36 (4.5%)	4 (1.2%)	4 (2.9%)	0 (-)
Over 4 Months	23 (2.9%)	3 (0.9%)	0 (-)	0 (-)
I do not yet feel "comfortable and fairly efficient"	5 (0.6%)	19 (5.6%)	5 (3.7%)	1 (3.2%)
No Response	432 (53.9%)	219 (64.6%)	89 (65.4%)	22 (71.0%)

   b. For searchers not formally trained:

Length of Time to Become Efficient	SYSTEM 1 (N=801)	SYSTEM 2 (N=339)	SYSTEM 3 (N=136)	SYSTEM 4 (N=31)
1 to 5 Days	54 (16.7%)	32 (9.4%)	18 (13.2%)	3 (9.7%)
1 to 4 Weeks	106 (13.2%)	44 (13.0%)	11 (8.1%)	6 (19.4%)
1 to 2 Months	46 (5.7%)	21 (6.2%)	4 (2.9%)	1 (3.2%)
2 to 4 Months	31 (3.9%)	8 (2.4%)	5 (3.7%)	3 (9.7%)
Over 4 Months	10 (1.2%)	1 (0.3%)	0 (-)	0 (-)
I do not yet feel "comfortable and fairly efficient"	10 (1.2%)	20 (5.9%)	9 (6.6%)	3 (9.7%)
No Response	544 (68.0%)	213 (62.0%)	89 (65.4%)	15 (48.3%)

4. For infrequent system users only:

   a. If you consider yourself an infrequent user, i.e., if weeks or months pass between times that you use the system, then please check below the statements that apply to your general feeling of being "comfortable and fairly efficient" with the system. (N=174)

   <u>98 (56.3%)</u>   I am fairly comfortable and efficient at the terminal.

   <u>51 (29.3%)</u>   I am barely comfortable and probably not very efficient.

   <u>25 (14.4%)</u>   I feel that I have to re-learn the system every time I use it.

b. If you feel fairly comfortable at the terminal, how soon did you become comfortable (understanding that some sessions may have been spaced over a period of time)?

<u>9</u> At my first terminal session.

<u>95</u> After several terminal sessions (about how many sessions? <u>4.6</u> = Mean).

5. Have you participated in any advanced-training or refresher sessions? (N=801)

Yes = <u>308 (38.5%)</u>　　　No = <u>479 (59.8%)</u>　　　No Response = <u>14 (1.7%)</u>

If YES, do you believe they are useful?

Yes = <u>294 (95.5%)</u>　　　No = <u>11 (3.6%)</u>　　　No Response = <u>3 (0.9%)</u>

If NO, do you believe they could be useful?

Yes = <u>389 (81.2%)</u>　　　No = <u>45 (9.4%)</u>　　　No Response = <u>45 (9.4%)</u>

6. When you first began searching, how long did the average retrospective literature search take you to perform at the terminal? (N=722)

Minutes

Range = 3.0 - 180
Mean   = 29.0
Median = 24.7
Mode   = 30.0

How long do your average searches take now? (N=728)

Minutes

Range = 1.0 - 150
Mean   = 17.3
Median = 13.7
Mode   = 10.0

7. How many iterations (different terminal sessions for a given search) are typically required to satisfy a search request in an on-line search?   (N-758)

Iterations

Range = 1.0 - 7.5
Mean   = 1.4
Median = 1.0
Mode   = 1.0

Is this number comparable to your previous mode of searching?

235 (31.0%) Number of iterations is about the same as for our batch/manual searches.

                        Batch = 55

                        Manual = 174

                        Both   = 6

 43 (5.7%) Number of iterations is now greater; it used to be 1.4 (Mean) iterations for our batch/manual searches.

                        Batch = 6

                        Manual = 37

 99 (13.1%) Number of iterations is now fewer; it used to be 3.3 (Mean) iterations for our batch/manual searches.

                        Batch = 19

                        Manual = 78

                        Both   = 2

237 (31.3%) No basis for comparison; we did not perform literature searches before.

143 (18.9%) No Response

8. Indicate below whether you believe there is any difference in quality between the search results you get now compared to the results you obtained as a "beginner." (N=801)

207 (25.8%) The difference is great

387 (48.3%) The difference is moderate

123 (15.4%) There is little difference

 73 (9.1%) No basis yet for comparing

 11 (1.4%) No Response

9. If you are an information intermediary, indicate whether the expressions of satisfaction with search results from your clients or users have changed from when you were a beginner. (N=801)

   113 (14.1%) Noticeable change

   274 (34.2%) Little change

   139 (17.4%) No change

   166 (20.7%) No basis yet for judging reactions

   109 (13.6%) No Response

System Features

1. Listed below are a number of features offered by one or more on-line retrieval systems for entering searches. For each feature with which you are familiar, please check its level of importance to you from one of the choices in columns 1, 2, or 3. Second, indicate your level of usage by checking one of the choices in columns 4, 5, or 6. (If you are not familiar with a feature, please indicate its potential value to you by responding in the "Importance" columns only. Leave "Level of Use" columns blank.)

No Response		FEATURES	IMPORTANCE (N=801)			LEVEL OF USE			
			Very Useful	Useful	Not at all Useful	Heavily Used	Some-times Used	Rarely or Never Used	N=
		The system allows a user to:							
35 (4.4%)	1.	Truncate or enter word-stems to retrieve on all possible suffixes.	447 (55.8%)	303 (37.8%)	16 (2.0%)	273 (35.6%)	339 (44.3%)	65 (8.5%)	766
47 (5.9%)	2.	Specify the data element, (i.e., field or category) from which the term is to be searched.	352 (43.9%)	361 (45.1%)	41 (5.1%)	238 (31.6%)	363 (48.1%)	81 (10.7%)	754
134 (16.7%)	3.	Use relational operators (greater than, less than, between).	103 (12.9%)	334 (41.7%)	230 (28.7%)	30 (4.5%)	136 (20.4%)	214 (32.1%)	667
156 (19.5%)	4.	Use word-proximity operators.	181 (22.6%)	379 (47.3%)	85 (10.6%)	104 (16.1%)	223 (34.6%)	124 (19.2%)	645
16 (2.0%)	5.	Use all Boolean operators (AND, OR, AND NOT).	749 (93.5%)	36 (4.5%)	0 (-)	737 (93.9%)	28 (3.6%)	3 (0.3%)	785
41 (5.1%)	6.	Combine terms with one or more operators in one instruction to the system.	598 (74.7%)	149 (18.6%)	13 (1.6%)	523 (68.8%)	142 (18.7%)	29 (3.8%)	760
59 (7.4%)	7.	Incorporate previous searches, by number, in new search statements or entries.	472 (58.9%)	217 (27.1%)	53 (6.6%)	358 (48.2%)	100 (13.5%)	107 (14.4%)	742
72 (9.0%)	8.	Store a search that can be run again at a later time.	320 (40.0%)	307 (38.3%)	102 (12.7%)	47 (6.4%)	101 (13.9%)	241 (33.1%)	729
118 (14.7%)	9.	Search character strings sequentially or serially in fields or categories that are not directly searchable.	322 (40.2%)	300 (37.5%)	61 (7.6%)	141 (20.6%)	267 (39.1%)	91 (13.3%)	683
729 (91.0%)	10.	Other(s)	64 (7.9%)	8 (0.9%)	0 (-)	43 (59.7%)	14 (19.4%)	1 (0.1%)	72

2. Listed below are a number of features offered by one or more on-line retrieval systems for the search output. Please indicate both the importance and level of use of each feature with which you are familiar by checking the appropriate columns. (If you are unfamiliar with a feature, please indicate its potential value to you by responding in the "Importance" columns only. Leave "Level of Use" columns blank.)

No Response		FEATURES	IMPORTANCE (N-801)			LEVEL OF USE			N=
			Very Useful	Useful	Not at all Useful	Heavily Used	Some-times Used	Rarely or Nev-er Used	
		The system allows a user to:							
35 (4.4%)	1.	Request standard or pre-defined print formats.	472 (58.9%)	244 (30.5%)	50 (6.2%)	513 (67.0%)	109 (14.2%)	44 (5.7%)	766
69 (8.6%)	2.	Tailor or specify his or her own print formats.	338 (42.2%)	300 (37.5%)	94 (11.7%)	232 (31.7%)	168 (23.0%)	117 (16.0%)	732
62 (7.7%)	3.	Specify the sorting of output by designated categories (e.g., author, year).	285 (35.6%)	411 (51.3%)	43 (5.4%)	112 (15.2%)	211 (28.6%)	174 (23.6%)	739
114 (14.2%)	4.	Specify the sorting of output by number of hits.	166 (20.7%)	372 (46.4%)	149 (18.6%)	76 (11.1%)	146 (21.3%)	219 (31.9%)	687
35 (4.4%)	5.	Specify off-line printing of search results to be run by the supplier.	625 (78.0%)	132 (16.5%)	9 (1.1%)	531 (69.3%)	158 (20.6%)	31 (4.0%)	766
156 (19.5%)	6.	Have a search strategy that is entered on-line run in batch mode by the supplier.	150 (18.7%)	279 (34.8%)	216 (27.0%)	42 (6.5%)	57 (8.8%)	139 (21.6%)	645
100 (12.5%)	7.	Receive citation displays in upper and lower case.	77 (9.6%)	202 (25.2%)	423 (52.8%)	57 (8.1%)	28 (4.0%)	138 (19.7%)	701
771 (96.3%)	8.	Other(s)	22 (2.7%)	8 (0.9%)	0 (-)	12 (40.0%)	8 (26.7%)	10 (33.3%)	30

3. Listed below are a number of features offered by one or more on-line retrieval systems that are aids in the on-line interaction. Please indicate both the importance and usefulness of each feature with which you are familiar by checking the appropriate columns. (If you are unfamiliar with a feature, please indicate its potential value to you by responding in the "Importance" columns only. Leave "Level of Use" columns blank.)

No Response		FEATURES	IMPORTANCE (N-801)			LEVEL OF USE			N=
			Very Useful	Useful	Not at all Useful	Heavily Used	Some-times Used	Rarely or Nev-er Used	
		The system allows a user to:							
39 (4.9%)	1.	Display on-line the alpha-betical index or dictionary.	442 (55.2%)	274 (34.2%)	47 (5.9%)	276 (36.2%)	263 (34.5%)	88 (11.5%)	762
46 (5.7%)	2.	Display on-line the list of related terms or hierarch-ical thesaurus.	429 (53.6%)	298 (37.2%)	28 (3.5%)	193 (25.6%)	282 (37.4%)	99 (13.1%)	755
32 (4.0%)	3.	Obtain explanations of sys-tem features on-line.	236 (29.5%)	464 (57.9%)	69 (8.6%)	45 (5.9%)	335 (43.6%)	302 (39.3%)	769
98 (12.2%)	4.	Enter comments on-line to other terminals.	83 (10.4%)	329 (41.1%)	291 (36.3%)	19 (2.7%)	99 (14.1%)	254 (36.1%)	703
58 (7.2%)	5.	Enter comments on-line to the supplier.	175 (21.8%)	467 (58.3%)	100 (12.5%)	48 (6.5%)	219 (29.5%)	313 (42.1%)	743
132 (16.5%)	6.	Control the length or form of system messages.	206 (25.7%)	336 (41.9%)	127 (15.9%)	179 (26.8%)	121 (18.1%)	90 (13.5%)	669
27 (3.4%)	7.	Receive announcements on-line from the supplier about important system-related information.	487 (60.8%)	269 (33.6%)	18 (2.2%)	315 (40.7%)	279 (36.0%)	56 (7.2%)	774
63 (7.9%)	8.	Monitor elapsed time or CPU usage on-line.	445 (55.6%)	234 (29.2%)	59 (7.4%)	420 (56.9%)	128 (17.3%)	49 (6.6%)	738
38 (4.7%)	9.	Display history of search strategy.	391 (48.8%)	331 (41.3%)	41 (5.1%)	224 (29.4%)	266 (34.9%)	161 (21.1%)	763
66 (8.2%)	10.	Enter several instructions to the system at one time.	375 (46.8%)	324 (40.4%)	37 (4.6%)	234 (31.8%)	187 (25.4%)	71 (9.7%)	735
775 (96.8%)	11.	Other(s)	24 (3.0%)	2 (0.2%)	0 (-)	15 (57.7%)	4 (15.4%)	1 (3.8%)	26

4. Do variations in response time from the system generally bother you? (N=801)

       638 (79.7%) = Yes   153 (19.1%) = No   10 (1.2%) = No Response

If YES, please describe how you react to variations in system response time.

REACTION	FREQUENCY OF REACTION (N=638)			
	Usually	Sometimes	Rarely or Never	No Response
I terminate my terminal session and try again later.	125 (19.6%)	365 (57.2%)	145 (22.7%)	3 (0.5%)
I terminate my terminal session and complete the search in some other way.	8 (1.3%)	115 (18.0%)	512 (80.3%)	3 (0.5%)
I put up with it.	311 (48.7%)	217 (34.0%)	107 (16.8%)	3 (0.5%)
I call the supplier to ask what's happening before I make a decision.	70 (11.0%)	231 (36.2%)	333 (52.2%)	4 (0.6%)

Support Services

Off-Line Printing

1. Is off-line printing (done by the on-line service supplier) available to you through the system(s) you use?

    40 (0.5%)   Yes, but only on some of the systems we use

   745 (93.0%)   Yes, on all systems

     2 (0.2%)   No

    54 (6.7%)   No Response

2. How do you obtain the **final** list of references from your on-line search? With what frequency?

PRINTING OPTIONS	FREQUENCY OF USE				
	Most of the Time	Much of the Time	Only Occasionally	Never	No Response
On-line, at the terminal	318 (39.7%)	230 (28.7%)	188 (23.5%)	8 (0.9%)	57 (7.1%)
Off-line, from the on-line service supplier	275 (34.3%)	262 (32.7%)	204 (25.5%)	16 (2.0%)	44 (5.5%)

3. If you do both on-line and off-line printing, how do you decide which to use? Please be specific as possible, and state any applicable principles that have been established in your organization:

4. Do you currently experience any significant or frequent problems with off-line printing?

    111 (13.9%) = Yes   644 (80.4%) = No   46 (5.7%) = No Response

If YES, please describe:

Schedules and Access Time

1. How many hours a week do you generally spend at the terminal? (N=801)

Hours

Range = .10 - 50
Mean   = 3.9
Median = 2.1
Mode   = 1.0

a. What is the average length of time you spend at any one terminal session? (N=801)

Minutes

Range = 1 - 270
Mean   = 33.0
Median = 30.2
Mode   = 30.0

b. How many searches do you generally perform in one week? (N=801)

Searches

Range = .5 - 322
Mean = 9.6
Median = 5.2
Mode = 1.0

2. Please describe the way in which you schedule your time at the terminal by checking the applicable level of frequency for each choice. (N=801)

SCHEDULE APPROACH	FREQUENCY OF USE				
	Most of the Time	Sometimes	Rarely	Never	No Response
I go to the terminal whenever a request is processed to the point of being ready for the computer search.	423 (52.8%)	151 (18.9%)	73 (9.1%)	30 (3.7%)	124 (15.5%)
I go to the terminal whenever I need to.	414 (51.7%)	188 (23.5%)	61 (7.6%)	23 (2.9%)	115 (14.4%)
I have to coordinate my scheduling of time at the terminal with other staff members or colleagues in other areas of my organization.	181 (22.6%)	209 (26.1%)	177 (22.1%)	129 (16.1%)	105 (13.1%)
I schedule, in advance, the time that I will spend at the terminal on a given day.	89 (11.1%)	102 (12.7%)	166 (20.7%)	298 (37.2%)	146 (18.2%)
I make appointments with a client or colleage for a specific time.	78 (9.7%)	175 (21.8%)	181 (22.6%)	230 (28.7%)	137 (17.1%)

3. On the basis of your scheduling approach and level of system usage, what amount of access from the supplier(s) for most data bases--is generally required or adequate to meet your needs? (Complete both a and b.)

FREQUENCY	SYSTEMS			
	SYSTEM 1 (N=801)	SYSTEM 2 (N-339)	SYSTEM 3 (N=136)	SYSTEM 4 (N=31)
a. Days per week				
7 days	14 (1.7%)	2 (0.5%)	3 (2.2%)	0 (-)
6 days	43 (5.4%)	11 (3.2%)	5 (3.7%)	4 (12.9%)
5 days	611 (76.3%)	243 (71.7%)	79 (58.1%)	21 (67.7%)
4 days	12 (1.5%)	7 (2.1%)	6 (4.4%)	1 (3.2%)
3 days	32 (11.0%)	16 (4.7%)	8 (5.9%)	2 (6.5%)
2 days	10 (1.2%)	10 (2.9%)	6 (4.4%)	0 (-)
1 day	45 (5.6%)	18 (5.3%)	9 (6.6%)	1 (3.2%)
No Response	34 (4.2%)	32 (9.4%)	20 (14.7%)	2 (6.5%)
b. Hours per day				
1 or 2 hours	145 (18.1%)	51 (15.0%)	25 (18.4%)	10 (32.3%)
3 or 4 hours	112 (14.0%)	67 (19.8%)	24 (17.6%)	7 (22.6%)
5 to 8 hours	368 (45.9%)	145 (42.8%)	46 (33.8%)	10 (32.3%)
Over 8 hours	128 (16.0%)	35 (10.3%)	13 (9.6%)	2 (6.5%)
No Response	48 (6.0%)	41 (12.1%)	28 (20.6%)	2 (6.5%)

Communications with Suppliers

1. Indicate below the level of importance you place on the availability of telephone or interactive, terminal-to-terminal consultation (e.g., regarding questions about system usage or problems) with staff members of the on-line service suppliers.

   a. By Telephone:

   551 (68.8%)   Essential

   201 (25.1%)   Important, but not essential

    24 (3.0%)   Not needed

    25 (3.1%)   No Response

b. By Terminal:

168 (21.0%) Essential

421 (52.6%) Important, but not essential

143 (17.9%) Not needed

69 (8.6%) No Response

2. Indicate the amount of contact you have, by telephone or terminal-to-terminal, with suppliers.

452 (56.4%) Some

262 (32.7%) Very little

73 (9.1%) None, thus far

14 (1.7%) No Response

3. Do you receive newsletters and other regular notices from suppliers?

635 (79.3%) Yes, from all of them

109 (13.6%) Yes, from some of them

45 (5.6%) No

12 (1.5%) No Response

If YES, how useful to you are they?

585 (73.0%) Very useful

155 (19.4%) Somewhat useful

1 (0.1%) Not at all useful

60 (7.5%) No Response

4. Have you purchased or received any system usage documentation. e.g., user's manuals, from your supplier(s)?

689 (86.0%) Yes, from all of them

60 (7.5%) Yes, from some of them

34 (4.2%) No

18 (2.2%) No Response

Searching: Problems and Solutions

1. Indicate the degree to which any of the following areas are problems for you.

PROBLEM AREAS	FREQUENCY OF PROBLEMS				
	In most searches or terminal sessions	In some searches or terminal sessions	In very few searches or terminal sessions	Never	No Response
1. Identifying the appropriateness of a data base or data bases for a given search.	12 (1.5%)	137 (17.1%)	405 (50.6%)	240 (30.0%)	7 (0.8%)
2. Preparing a search strategy (including selecting terms and deciding how they should be combined).	60 (7.5%)	381 (47.4%)	303 (37.8%)	49 (6.1%)	8 (0.9%)
3. Assessing the relevance of the search results at the terminal and deciding when the search is actually done.	58 (7.2%)	290 (36.2%)	378 (47.2%)	67 (8.4%)	8 (0.9%)
4. Diagnosing what appear to be system-related problems.	34 (4.2%)	303 (37.8%)	383 (47.8%)	73 (9.1%)	8 (0.9%)
5. Diagnosing what appear to be my own errors.	27 (3.4%)	226 (28.2%)	450 (56.2%)	89 (11.1%)	9 (1.1%)
6. Other	11 (1.4%)	15 (1.9%)	2 (0.2%)	0 (-)	773 (96.5%)

2. Please describe the kinds of total-system-related problems that you experience and the frequency with which they are experienced. (If you are not familiar with a system component, or if the component is not applicable, please leave the response blank.) (N=801)

KIND OF PROBLEM	FREQUENCY OF OCCURRENCE					
	About once during a terminal session	About once every 2 or 3 terminal sessions	Occasionally (About once every 6 or so terminal sessions	Rarely	Never	No Response
Establishing Connections						
1. Can't get a telephone line out of my own organization.	11 (1.4%)	34 (4.2%)	49 (6.1%)	220 (27.0%)	367 (45.8%)	120 (15.0%)
2. Have trouble in logging into the communications network.	25 (3.1%)	93 (11.6%)	246 (30.7%)	290 (36.2%)	61 (7.6%)	86 (10.7%)
3. Have trouble in logging into the host computer.	23 (2.9%)	102 (12.7%)	334 (41.7%)	227 (28.3%)	40 (5.0%)	75 (9.4%)
4. Get disconnected by our own switchboard.	2 (0.2%)	5 (0.6%)	27 (3.4%)	137 (17.1%)	487 (60.8%)	143 (17.9%)
Equipment Problems						
1. Terminal.	8 (1.0%)	26 (3.2%)	71 (8.9%)	432 (53.9%)	179 (22.3%)	85 (10.6%)
2. Dataphone.	4 (0.4%)	6 (0.7%)	15 (1.9%)	169 (21.1%)	255 (31.8%)	352 (43.9%)
3. Telephone Coupler.	5 (0.6%)	12 (1.5%)	34 (4.2%)	207 (25.8%)	309 (38.6%)	234 (29.2%)
4. Lines or computers of the communication network.	26 (3.2%)	74 (9.2%)	233 (29.1%)	267 (33.3%)	62 (7.7%)	139 (17.4%)
5. Supplier's computer system.	26 (3.2%)	79 (9.9%)	303 (37.8%)	256 (32.0%)	39 (4.9%)	98 (12.2%)
Problems During System Use						
1. Disconnection from the host computer.	14 (1.7%)	72 (9.0%)	292 (36.5%)	314 (39.2%)	53 (6.6%)	56 (7.0%)
2. Apparent loss of control of the program (i.e., nothing seems to work right).	10 (1.2%)	29 (3.6%)	115 (14.4%)	367 (45.8%)	200 (25.0%)	80 (10.0%)
3. Intermittent transmission of "garbage" characters.	42 (5.2%)	55 (6.9%)	169 (21.1%)	386 (48.2%)	98 (12.2%)	51 (6.4%)
4. Totally unintelligible transmissions.	19 (2.4%)	14 (1.7%)	57 (7.1%)	375 (46.8%)	253 (31.6%)	83 (10.4%)
5. Loss of data (i.e., incomplete transmission).	20 (2.5%)	29 (3.6%)	108 (13.5%)	411 (51.3%)	173 (21.6%)	60 (7.5%)
Undiagnosed Difficulties	17 (2.1%)	26 (3.2%)	79 (9.9%)	209 (26.1%)	87 (10.9%)	383 (47.8%)

4. How seriously do these problems interfere with your work pattern? (N=801)

  52 (6.5%)   Very Seriously

262 (32.7%)   Somewhat seriously

341 (42.6%)   Not very seriously

  80 (10.0%)   Hardly at all

  66 (8.2%)   No Response

5. Indicate below how you have learned to diagnose problems that occur. (N=801)

397 (50.0%)   By calling the on-line service supplier.

  43 (5.4%)   By learning how the on-line service supplier interprets the printout(s) that we send to illustrate a problem(s).

341 (42.6%)   By trying to eliminate, one at a time, each of several possibilities.

134 (16.7%)   By referring to a checklist provided by the on-line service supplier.

114 (14.2%)   I don't feel that I have yet learned to diagnose most problems.

  98 (12.2%)   Other.

General Attitudes

1. What were your initial feelings about using the on-line system? (Check as many as apply.) (N=801)

  27 (3.4%)   Skeptical about its utility or value

150 (18.7%)   Somewhat nervous or fearful

  69 (8.6%)   Somewhat reserved about its utility or value

  26 (3.2%)   No particular feelings

253 (31.6%)   Somewhat enthusiastic

576 (71.9%)   Eager to give it a try

2. How do you feel <u>now</u> about using the on-line information systems?   (Check as many as apply.) (N=801)

<u>593 (74.0%)</u>   I enjoy on-line searching.

<u>13 (1.6%)</u>   I have developed no particular feelings.

<u>16 (2.0%)</u>   I do not enjoy on-line searching.

<u>507 (63.3%)</u>   I think on-line systems are extremely valuable.

<u>289 (36.1%)</u>   I think on-line systems are useful.

<u>54 (6.7%)</u>   I think on-line systems are over-rated.

<u>28 (3.5%)</u>   I think on-line systems may someday be useful.

3. Many statements have been made relative to the impact of on-line searching. If you are an information intermediary (e.g., librarian or information specialist), please indicate the degree to which you agree with the statements in section "a" only. If you an "end user" performing searches only for yourself or a project team, please answer section "b" instead, on the following pages.

a. Information-Intermediary Searchers Only:

STATEMENT	DEGREE OF AGREEMENT (N=801)					
	Strongly Agree	Agree	Disagree	Strongly Disagree	No Opinion	No Response
1. On-line searching will reduce the need for reference personnel.	33 (4.1%)	93 (11.6%)	337 (42.1%)	224 (28.0%)	34 (4.2%)	80 (10.0%)
2. On-line searching makes it possible to serve more users.	225 (28.1%)	408 (50.9%)	52 (6.5%)	17 (2.1%)	22 (2.7%)	77 (9.6%)
3. On-line searching cannot match the quality of a manually performed search.	28 (3.5%)	89 (11.1%)	392 (48.9%)	152 (19.0%)	39 (4.9%)	101 (12.6%)
4. On-line searching cannot match the quality of a batch-performed search.	9 (1.1%)	20 (2.5%)	282 (35.2%)	184 (23.0%)	194 (24.2%)	112 (14.0%)
5. On-line searching is economical, compared to batch-system processing.	57 (7.1%)	178 (22.2%)	71 (8.9%)	14 (1.7%)	360 (44.9%)	121 (15.1%)
6. On-line searching allows the information specialist or librarian to spend his/her time more productively.	184 (22.0%)	429 (53.6%)	44 (5.5%)	10 (1.2%)	46 (5.7%)	88 (11.0%)
7. On-line searching is only a passing fad.	5 (0.6%)	0 (-)	223 (27.8%)	467 (58.3%)	23 (2.9%)	83 (10.4%)
8. On-line searching increases the work load of the library/information center staff.	96 (12.0%)	297 (37.1%)	208 (26.0%)	61 (7.6%)	52 (6.5%)	87 (10.9%)
9. On-line searching improves services in libraries or information centers.	358 (44.7%)	335 (41.8%)	10 (1.2%)	2 (0.2%)	10 (1.2%)	86 (10.7%)
10. On-line searching is economical compared to manual searching.	269 (33.6%)	317 (39.6%)	42 (5.2%)	5 (0.6%)	79 (9.8%)	89 (11.1%)

b. For End-User Searchers Only:

	DEGREE OF AGREEMENT (N=801)					
	Strongly Agree	Agree	Disagree	Strongly Disagree	No Opinion	No Response
1. On-line systems cannot be used in a cost-effective way by end users.	4 (0.5%)	14 (1.7%)	72 (9.0%)	39 (4.9%)	21 (2.6%)	651 (81.3%)
2. On-line searches performed by the end user produce better quality results than those performed by an information intermediary.	10 (1.2%)	52 (6.5%)	48 (6.0%)	15 (1.9%)	20 (2.5%)	656 (81.9%)
3. On-line system used by end users will decrease after the novelty has worn off.	2 (0.2%)	31 (3.9%)	76 (9.5%)	25 (3.1%)	18 (2.2%)	649 (81.0%)
4. Manual searches by the end user produce better results than those performed on the on-line systems.	2 (0.2%)	17 (2.1%)	82 (10.2%)	27 (3.4%)	19 (2.4%)	654 (81.6%)
5. Manual searches performed by the information intermediary produce better results than those performed by them on on-line systems.	2 (0.2%)	15 (1.9%)	72 (9.0%)	19 (2.4%)	38 (4.7%)	655 (81.8%)

C. MULTIPLE DATA BASE USAGE

(N=639)

1. In general, how did you learn enough about the contents and coverage of the data bases so that you could decide when to use a particular data base for a particular search question?

METHOD OF LEARNING ABOUT THE DATA BASE	FREQUENCY OF USE (N=639)			No Response
	Used for Most Data Bases	Used for Some Data Bases	Used for Only One Data Base	
From information (tools or training) provided by the on-line supplier.	369 (57.7%)	126 (19.7%)	25 (3.9%)	119 (18.6%)
From information (descriptions, authority lists, training) provided by the data base supplier (if a different organization than the on-line service supplier).	148 (23.2%)	159 (24.9%)	40 (6.3%)	292 (45.7%)
From previous experience with the file through manual searches of their corresponding printed indexes.	224 (35.1%)	195 (30.5%)	44 (6.9%)	176 (27.5%)
From previous experience with the file through coding searches for batch-processing.	38 (5.9%)	54 (8.5%)	54 (8.5%)	493 (77.2%)
From my colleagues.	141 (22.1%)	147 (23.0%)	22 (3.4%)	329 (51.5%)
From trial and error, or actual experience.	207 (32.4%)	183 (28.6%)	24 (3.8%)	225 (35.2%)
Am still learning by experience, with each search I perform.	233 (36.5%)	151 (23.6%)	12 (1.9%)	243 (38.0%)
Other	10 (1.6%)	2 (0.3%)	1 (0.2%)	626 (98.0%)

2. Describe below the way in which you apply the availability of multiple files to a single search, and the frequency with which you use this approach.

SEARCH APPROACH	FREQUENCY OF USE (N=639)				
	For Most Searches	For Some Searches	For Few Searches	Never	No Response
I use one data base for one search.	308 (48.2%)	143 (22.4%)	100 (15.6%)	42 (6.6%)	46 (7.2%)
I use a second data base when I have had no success in the first data base.	77 (12.1%)	219 (34.2%)	19 (29.9%)	99 (15.5%)	53 (8.3%)
I select the different data bases that are relevant to the search and try the search on each one.	277 (43.3%)	167 (26.1%)	99 (15.5%)	58 (0.9%)	38 (6.0%)
When the number of hits in the search on one file is not as great as I expected -- or what the user expected -- I try the search on another file.	101 (15.8%)	201 (31.5%)	196 (30.7%)	92 (14.4%)	49 (7.7%)
Regardless of the results from the search on the first data base, I try the search on another file just to confirm my understanding of its contents or to gamble on finding something relevant.	56 (8.8%)	88 (13.8%)	217 (34.0%)	230 (36.0%)	48 (7.5%)

3. Many of the files available today vary considerably in the degree to which the subject access terms are derived from a controlled vocabulary.

For each statement below, indicate the impact of different vocabulary structures on your searching behavior by checking the column or columns for different vocabularies that apply.

STATEMENTS	SUBJECT VOCABULARIES (N=639)				
	Controlled Terms Only	Controlled, Plus Free Language Terms	Free Terms Only	It Makes No Difference	No Response
I have the most success with searches performed on data bases with ...	148 (23.2%)	310 (48.5%)	51 (8.0%)	52 (8.1%)	78 (12.2%)
I have learned most quickly about the coverage and scope of data bases with ...	256 (40.1%)	148 (23.2%)	44 (6.9%)	100 (15.6%)	91 (14.2%)
I am most efficient (time-wise) when performing searches on data bases with ...	255 (39.9%)	194 (30.4%)	47 (7.4%)	50 (7.8%)	93 (14.6%)
When performing searches in subject areas in which I am most comfortable or knowledgeable, I prefer data bases with ...	108 (16.9%)	311 (48.7%)	85 (13.3%)	47 (7.4%)	88 (13.4%)
When performing searches in subject areas in which I am not particularly comfortable or knowledgeable, I prefer data bases with ...	217 (34.0%)	251 (39.3%)	48 (7.5%)	36 (5.6%)	87 (13.6%)
When performing searches on data bases with which I have had prior experience (e.g., through coding for batch-system searches), I prefer data bases with ...	100 (15.6%)	213 (33.3%)	46 (7.2%)	74 (11.6%)	206 (32.2%)
I prepare more for searches on data bases with ...	210 (32.9%)	130 (20.3%)	127 (19.9%)	75 (11.7%)	97 (15.2%)

4. It is generally believed that using more than one--and particularly several--data bases can be confusing to searchers. Please indicate below the statement that best reflects your general reaction to using several data bases. (N=639)

  11 (1.7%)   Searching on more than one data base is a major problem and one that seriously affects my efficiency.

249 (39.0%)   Searching on more than one data base is sometimes confusing, but the problems are not insurmountable, nor do they generally affect my searching efficiency.

329 (51.5%)   Searching on more than one data base has not been a source of confusion for me.

  50 (7.8%)   No Response

DESCRIPTION OF DATA BASES IN AREAS OF:	DEGREE OF CONFUSION (N=260)				No Response
	Great	Moderate	Low	None	
Subject or Content Coverage	4 (1.5%)	63 (24.2%)	107 (41.2%)	74 (28.5%)	12 (4.1%)
Time (period of years) Coverage	12 (4.6%)	43 (16.5%)	103 (39.6%)	91 (35.0%)	11 (4.2%)
Form of subject term entry (single terms, precoordinated terms, inverted index terms, subheadings)	39 (15.0%)	136 (52.3%)	56 (21.5%)	16 (6.2%)	13 (5.0%)
Fields of information that are printable	14 (5.4%)	90 (34.6%)	107 (41.2%)	38 (14.6%)	11 (4.2%)
Fields of information made searchable by the on-line services supplier	9 (3.5%)	113 (43.5%)	84 (32.3%)	36 (13.8%)	18 (6.9%)
Vocabulary aids or resources	19 (7.3%)	71 (27.3%)	104 (40.0%)	44 (16.9%)	22 (8.5%)
Other	8 (3.1%)	7 (2.7%)	3 (1.2%)	1 (0.3%)	241 (92.7%)

5. During your first three months of experience with on-line systems, how many different data bases
    did you begin learning?   (Circle one.) (N=639)

    1 = 208 (32.6%)   5 = 44 (6.9%)

    2 = 125 (19.6%)   6 = 26 (4.1%)

    3 = 87 (13.6%)   7 and over = 53 (8.3%)

    4 = 54 (8.4%)   No Response = 45 (7.0%)

    a. If you learned only one, do you think that you could have learned more at that time?   (N=208)

        149 (71.6%) = Yes   59 (28.4%) = No

    b. If you learned more than one, do you believe it would have been easier or better to have
        become thoroughly familiar with one data base before learning others?

        87 (22.6%) = Yes   296(76.7%) = No   3 (0.7%) = Maybe

D. MULTIPLE SYSTEM USAGE

(N=339)

1. Do you use each system a more or less equal amount of time?

   <u>38 (11.2%)</u> = Yes   <u>259 (76.4%)</u> = No   <u>42 (12.4%)</u> = No Response

2. If you use one system more than others, please indicate the reasons for this greater use by checking all applicable statements. (N=259)

   A. <u>121 (46.7%)</u> I learned to use the system first and feel most comfortable with it.
   B. <u>202 (78.0%)</u> It offers access to more of the data bases I need.
   C. <u>78 (30.1%)</u> It has a greater range of capabilities.
   D. <u>70 (27.0%)</u> It has better response times.
   E. <u>54 (20.8%)</u> The supplier offers better customer support.
   F. <u>76 (29.3%)</u> It uses an interactive language that is easier to understand and remember.
   G. <u>70 (27.0%)</u> The supplier's reference materials (e.g., user's manuals) helped more in understanding system features.
   H. <u>71 (27.4%)</u> It is available on a schedule that is more convenient to me.
   I. <u>34 (13.1%)</u> It has better reliability (i.e., the least down time).
   J. <u>61 (23.6%)</u> The supplier has done a better job of structuring the data bases for on-line use.
   K. <u>59 (22.8%)</u> The supplier has included a greater number of years in its data base(s).
   L. <u>66 (25.4%)</u> Other

   Now, go back and please circle the one most important reason for this greater use. (N=259)

B = 124 (47.9%)	J = 9 (3.5%)
L = 33 (12.7%)	D = 7 (2.7%)
A = 23 (8.9%)	H = 7 (2.7%)
F = 13 (5.0%)	G = 4 (1.5%)
K = 13 (5.0%)	E = 2 (0.8%)
C = 10 (3.9%)	I = 0 (-)

   No Response = 14 (5.4%)

3. It is generally believed that using more than one system can be confusing. Please indicate below your general reaction to using more than one system.

   <u>13 (3.8%)</u> Using more than one system is a major problem and seriously affects my efficiency.

   <u>162 (47.8%)</u> Using more than one system is sometimes confusing but the problems are not insurmountable nor do they generally affect my efficiency.

   <u>106 (31.3%)</u> Using more than one system has not been a source of confusion for me.

If you responded to either of the first two choices above, please indicate the degree of confusion, if any, that you experience in each of the specific areas given below. (N=175)

POTENTIAL AREAS OF CONFUSION	DEGREE OF CONFUSION				No Response
	Great	Moderate	Low	None	
1. Procedures for logging in	10 (5.7%)	38 (21.7%)	74 (42.3%)	48 (27.4%)	5 (2.9%)
2. Relating capabilities or features with the correct system	18 (9.1%)	79 (45.1%)	63 (36.0%)	12 (6.9%)	5 (2.9%)
3. Procedures for expressing Boolean combinations	9 (5.1%)	41 (23.4%)	67 (38.3%)	53 (30.3%)	5 (2.9%)
4. Understanding messages from the system	7 (4.0%)	36 (20.6%)	72 (41.1%)	52 (29.7%)	8 (4.6%)
5. Procedures for entering searches	19 (10.9%)	58 (33.1%)	71 (40.6%)	20 (11.4%)	7 (4.0%)
6. Procedures for issuing printing instructions	17 (9.7%)	65 (37.1%)	63 (36.0%)	24 (13.7%)	6 (3.4%)
7. Relating schedules for access time to the correct system	6 (3.4%)	32 (18.3%)	61 (34.9%)	68 (38.9%)	8 (4.6%)
8. Other	5 (2.9%)	9 (5.1%)	2 (1.1%)	0 (-)	159 (90.9%)

4. Do you believe that your use of several systems reduces your efficiency, i.e., increases the time it takes to perform a search? (N=339)

  14 (4.1%)   Yes, on all of the systems I use.

  90 (26.6%)   Yes, on some of the systems I use.

177 (52.2%)   No, it does not affect my efficiency.

  58 (17.1%)   No Response

6. During your first three months of experience with on-line systems, how many different systems did you begin learning? (Circle one) (N=339)

$$1 = \underline{166} \ (49.0\%)$$

$$2 = \underline{99} \ (29.2\%)$$

$$3 = \underline{11} \ (\ 3.2\%)$$

No Response = $\underline{10}$ (2.9%)

a. If you learned only one, do you think that you could have learned at least one more within the same "beginner's" period? (N=166)

104 (62.7%) = Yes   58 (34.9%) = No   4 (2.4%) = No Response

b. If you learned more than one, do you believe it would have been easier or better to have become thoroughly familiar with one system before beginning to learn others? (N=120)

47 (39.2%) = Yes   68 (56.7%) = No   5 (4.2%) = No Response